TRAVELS AND ADVENTURES

IN EASTERN AFRICA.

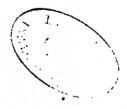

A ZOOLU WARRIOR & HIS DAUGHTER.

London, Published by E.Churton, 26, Holles St.

12 — 79

1278

TRAVELS AND ADVENTURES

IN

EASTERN AFRICA,

DESCRIPTIVE OF THE ZOOLUS, THEIR MANNERS, CUSTOMS, ETC. ETC.

WITH

A Sketch of Natal.

BY NATHANIEL ISAACS.

IN TWO VOLUMES.

VOL. I.

LONDON:
EDWARD CHURTON, 26, HOLLES STREET.
1836.

LONDON :
BRADBURY AND EVANS, PRINTERS,
WHITEFRIARS.

PREFACE.

It is not without inconceivable apprehension and diffidence, that I submit these volumes for the consideration of the public; nor should I have presumed to appear as a narrator of my own adventures, but from the influence and persuasion of friends, whose kind solicitude I have never experienced but with feelings of the deepest gratitude. I have submitted to their earnest injunctions, it is true; but I have not done so, without duly estimating the responsibility attached to the labours of an author. I have acquiesced somewhat reluctantly, from the fear of the reproaches which my temerity may excite; and I am not without those unhappy forebodings which the dread of censure (for my want of discretion) usually generates.

It is some consolation to me, however, to feel, that, in these my humble labours, I have not been actuated by any vain hope of acquiring fame, nor by any anticipations of advantage accruing from the diffusion of my details.   Impelled by the warm importunities of individuals, who had cursorily glanced over my notes, and thought that some information might be gleaned from them, useful to commerce and interesting to the general reader, I have yielded to their suggestions, and humbly send forth my journal with all the imperfections which inexperience produces, and without that order and arrangement which is held to be essential towards attaining for it any small share of public commendation.

I am led, rather sanguinely I confess, to hope that my readers will find occasionally some of my narratives not altogether destitute of amusing materials, nor void of matter to awaken their interest, and to excite their surprise and sympathy.

My adventures have taken place in a country where civilisation has not yet made any strides;— where rational man has not yet trodden to shed the light of truth among the ignorant, nor to inculcate a knowledge of religion; for the natives of those districts of Africa to which my travels have been particularly confined are yet strangers to such blessings.   I am aware that many circumstances I have detailed may seem, to those who have no know ledge of the customs and manners of the savage and uncivilised tribes of the African Continent, to be somewhat incredible, if not highly exaggerated; but I trust in the candid and liberal feelings of the public for confidence in that which I submit, until it can be fairly assumed, that I have exceeded the limits of probability and truth.

It will be found, it is thought, throughout the whole of my pages, that I have submitted nothing from hearsay; all my details are indisputably from my own observation, and from incidents occurring within my own knowledge. I have offered nothing from the communication of others; neither have I presumed to solicit the attention of my readers to aught but that of which I have had ocular demonstration, or in which I have been actually engaged.

It is not my wish to offer any lengthened apology for having, perhaps injudiciously, prepared my journal for publication; and as vanity had no share in the design, I hope I may claim the indulgence of the reader and appeal to him for the same candid and liberal sentiment, as is to be found in the Quarterly Review of October, 1816,—namely: "When we find Englishmen exposing themselves with their eyes open to all the inconveniences and hardships of painful and perilous journeys, to the effects of bad climates and pestilential diseases, not merely out of idle curi-

osity, but for the sake of seeing with their own eyes,
hearing with their own ears, and of obtaining that
information and receiving those impressions which
books alone can never give, we ought to be proud of
this national trait, peculiarly characteristic, we believe,
of British youth; and so far from witnessing their
literary omissions with critical severity, we should
consider their communications entitled to every indulgence."

I could not hope for a more liberal feeling towards
me than that which the highly gifted conductors of
that distinguished review usually shew to an inexperienced writer; particularly when they are sensible
that he has no other motive for submitting his observations, than purely to contribute his mite towards
the public stock of information.

N. ISAACS.

INTRODUCTION.

IT is, I believe, generally admitted, that the discoveries in Africa have extended to nearly three fourths of that vast continent, and that not only have the Northern and Western divisions been pretty accurately described and satisfactorily delineated, but that the Southern quarter has, of late years, been visited by travellers of great scientific attainments, and of comprehensive and diversified talents, who with laudable zeal have traversed a large portion of its interior and inhospitable regions, extensively and minutely investigated its general features, and ascertained, with considerable precision, its capabilities, either for the purposes of agricultural experiments or commercial speculation.

For a well-grounded knowledge in the natural history and geographical outlines of the Northern and Western divisions we are indebted mainly to those able and indefatigable, yet unfortunate travellers, Park, Denham, and Clapperton, who in the eager and sanguine pursuit of their object, the source of the long-sought Niger, fell a sacrifice in the cause of discovery, either by the hand of the savage and barbarous tribes with whom they had intercourse, or to the baneful and pernicious effects of a noxious and destructive climate. Their journals, although cut off on the eve of accomplishing the aim of their most ardent solicitude, have afforded considerable information on subjects entertaining to Englishmen, and enriched the stores of science by contributions of no ordinary interest and value.

The brothers Lander have furnished us with descriptive details of their journey to Bornon, where the lamented Captain Clapperton met his premature end. Of their progress thither, and their subsequent descent of the Niger, their account is not only highly gratifying—inasmuch, as it developes a very large proportion of the interior of Western Africa—but it furnishes us with a conclusive testimony of the advantages to be derived from an intercourse with the natives located in the immediate vicinity of that great river. Their diary is read with increased interest; it depicts in a clear and comprehensive manner the difficulties which they encountered, their privations, and their occasional conflicts with the tribes through whose districts they had to pass; and innumerable other incidents, which at times arrested their progress, and have given to their undertaking the character of a bold and an intrepid effort;—it has, moreover, added much to the stock of information before acquired in this part of the African continent.

Southern Africa has likewise had its almost trackless forests, impenetrable jungles, and extensive wastes, partially explored, and minutely described by Barrow, Burchell, and others, and subsequently by Thompson. Their excursions have been elaborately and clearly laid down, and they furnish us with luminous information, and exhibit no inconsiderable acquaintance with a country before but little known, either as it regarded its geographical position or its statistical history. To obtain a correct knowledge, therefore, of its general features much anxiety had been manifested, and much solicitude evinced, by scientific and enterprising persons, who sought to add to the attainments of science, and to discover unknown resources, and a new field for the display of genius, and for the diffusion of knowledge.

Part of Eastern Africa, the Zoola or Fumos country, on the other hand, is but little known; it has scarcely been trodden by the foot of a European. Its interior regions and features have not been described, nor the outlines of its vast boundaries satisfactorily ascertained. Some instances have been related of individuals having, by fortuitous circumstances, been thrown on its savage and unknown shores, where many perished, while others were more fortunate in reaching some European settlements, after encountering all the hardships incident to wandering on a wild and uninhabited coast. It is evident that this portion of the Eastern division of the African continent, therefore, has not been penetrated by any European, either for the purpose of description, or for delineating its outlines, and that the little knowledge we have collected respecting its position and its capabilities, has arisen from accidental visits and from adventitious circumstances. A mere superficial sketch of an occasional approach to its coasts may be extant, and in all probability may have been satisfactorily received, and have contained matter not only valuable, but amusing and attractive to the reader; but its descriptions are, doubtless, of the country contiguous to the sea, and not of that general and comprehensive nature which aims at a clear and expanded view of any district within those dominions. Such an account can only have been conjectural, and could not have conveyed any evidence of intercourse, or have afforded us more than a faint idea of what the interior actually presents.

Africa, notwithstanding the laborious efforts that have been made to explore her almost measureless tracts, and to define those particular positions which have exclusively attracted travellers, yet may offer many extraordinary objects, which may be held highly deserving of our wonder and admiration. The naturalist, the mineralogist, and the botanist may yet discover many productions of nature, that will amply compensate them for the labour of research; and those splendid collections which now adorn our own country may be greatly enriched by many additional specimens from the animal, mineral, and vegetable creation with which Africa abounds.

In Eastern Africa a wide field is still unexplored, and left open for the enterprising and ardent discoverer; and an immense range of territory remains to be surveyed by those who seek to gather fame in the fields of science, or wish to accumulate materials from which a complete geographical and statistical work may be digested for the edification of the public.

Towards filling up this chasm, which the discoveries in Africa have left to be supplied in its south-eastern quarter, I design to contribute in the following volumes. I am fully aware of the importance of such an undertaking, and sensible that it is a desideratum which requires the aid of a more competent and able delineator than myself to supply, without apprehending the censure which my imperfections may merit, and my very limited education unavoidably occasion. But I am not to be deterred from my purpose, nor to be induced to depart from my primary intention, of submitting a diary of my residence in Natal, by any considerations of a personal nature. I do not aspire to the distinction of an accurate delineator of objects, that have come under my immediate notice; nor do I anticipate an unqualified approbation of my details; but I trust I may be permitted to hope that their arrangement and the imperfections of the execution will not meet with too heavy a condemnation, when it is known that they emanate from a young and inexperienced individual.

Before adverting any further to the design of these volumes, I may be permitted, it is hoped, without incurring the reproof of my readers, or subjecting myself to the imputation of vanity, to submit a few observations explanatory of myself, and of the motives by which I was irresistibly impelled to leave my native home, and subsequently to engage in an exploratory expedition, when neither education nor experience had qualified me for such an enterprise. I am willing to concede, that my conduct has savoured somewhat of temerity; and especially when I reflect that it is highly expedient that an individual, who contemplates such an undertaking and seeks to acquire fame and advantages from its execution, should possess a moderate share of attainments, and no inconsiderable degree of cool and practical experience.

I left England in the year 1822, at the age of fourteen, when it will be seen I could not have acquired any great advancement or eminence in scholastic knowledge, nor had I made that progress which my sanguine relatives fondly anticipated. It was deetermined, several years before I quitted England, that my destination should be Saint Helena, in which

island Mr. S. Solomons, my maternal uncle, resided,
a merchant of unquestionable reputation, and highly
esteemed for the warmth of his friendship and hospitality, as well as for the integrity of his character—
distinctions which have been conferred on him by all
who have had an intercourse with that island, and
which have eminently tended towards the attainment
of the confidential and the responsible appointments
of Consul, with which he has been honoured by their
majesties the King of the Netherlands and the King
of the French. My departure for that island was,
however, in the first instance delayed, owing to the
great difficulty which at that time existed in obtaining
the East India Company's permission to proceed
thither, in consequence of its being the place of exile
of the late Emperor Napoleon.   Not until some time
had elapsed after his decease, could the obstacles to
my going out be removed; but, when permission
was given, my anxious and affectionate mother reluctantly prepared me for the voyage, and I sailed in
the brig Margaret, Captain Johnson, elated with the
prospect of an auspicious passage, and with the
sanguine anticipations of a cordial reception by a
worthy and an estimable friend ; not reflecting in the
least upon the obstacles and vicissitudes with which,
in my progress, I might often have to combat.   Our
passage was one of no ordinary duration; it was a
monotonous one; nothing incidentally occurred to
remove the gloom which calms and contrary winds

had generated. Our Captain, too, contributed not a little to the dejection which our tedious progress excited; for, in a state of almost constant inebriety, he usually forgot the civilities of a gentleman, and, instead of enlivening the scene, increased its weariness. I was too young to attempt to expostulate with a man of his propensities; and, as I was too weak to contend, I thought it discreet to succumb. Without any variation, without a single day of reviving and soul-stirring enjoyment, through a voyage of four months, was I unfortunately doomed to endure the caprice and submit to the offensive behaviour of an individual, whom, from his station, I should have been pleased to have respected, and from whom I ought to have received courtesy and attention.

On the 6th of October, 1822, we made the island; nothing could have exceeded the manifestions of joy which followed the announcement of " land a-head." Every eye beamed with delight, and every face evinced the happiness that occupied the heart at the thought of entering our destined port. I participated largely in that pleasure which seemed to be generally depicted in the countenances of all; and I could not restrain the impulse which induced me, notwithstanding his equivocal conduct during the passage, to shake the captain by the hand, and congratulate him on our safe arrival, as he let go the anchor in the roadstead of St. Helena. I hastened ashore, and was received with great kindness by my uncle, with whom I continued engaged in mercantile operations for upwards of two years, felicitously situated and greatly indulged. The insipidity and monotony of the counting-house, however, at last became insupportable, and having imbibed a strong predilection for the sea, those pursuits and avocations which in the outset were engaging, in the sequel became too burdensome to be endured. The generous feelings of my relative permitted me, though somewhat reluctantly, to follow the course which a mind, strongly inclined for an adventurous life, had prescribed as the one most likely to be suitable to my somewhat sanguine and no less fickle and inconstant bias.

My first essay was an unfortunate one, a voyage as supercargo of a small vessel destined for the neighbouring islands of St. Thomas, Princes, and Anna Bona, for the purpose of trading with the natives, which ended unpropitiously; for our little bark, not being very staunch, and in all probability not having been very circumspectly examined previously to our departure, before we had made much progress, and were out of sight of land, sprang a leak, and made four feet water, which compelled us to put back; on our re-anchorage the hold was found to be nearly filled with water, and our cargo much damaged. The voyage was consequently abandoned; and I returned, greatly chagrined, to resume those irksome labours of which I had before had enough to give me a distaste for any further participation in the sweets they afforded.

In 1825, however, the brig Mary, commanded by Lieutenant King of the royal navy, arrived from England laden with goods consigned to my uncle: with this officer I soon formed an intimacy; this intimacy in the sequel ripened into friendship, and we became, as it were, almost inseparable companions, till death prematurely overtook him while on the coast of Natal. My gallant friend, after landing his cargo, projected a voyage of a speculative nature, in which he made me an offer to accompany him. I readily embraced his proposition, particularly as he designed proceeding to the Cape of Good Hope, and from thence to the east coast of Africa to open an intercourse with the natives. My uncle immediately assented to my accompanying him, and I repaired on board his vessel. On the 28th of June we weighed anchor, and after a pleasant passage arrived at Table Bay on the 1st of August, where I landed and remained some time.

It will be perceived from the preceding remarks, that my education has been exclusively commercial; that the counting-house has been my school, and my principal preceptor, an indulgent uncle. Taught, therefore, nothing beyond that which might qualify me for mercantile pursuits, I can lay no claim to the acquirements of literature, or the attainments of science; and as the motives by which I was induced to become the companion of Lieutenant King emanated from the impulse of curiosity, and the attractions of commercial speculation, I sought nothing but to sate the one and to promote the other. I never contemplated becoming an author, for I never designed to engage in any exploratory expedition. My engaging in the latter was the effect of accident, and not altogether of choice; and my becoming the former does not arise from any vain desire to be thought competent to submit my own details for the perusal of the public, but from a conviction, that nothing more will be required by my intelligent readers, than a plain and distinct diary of my proceedings in that part of the country to which they particularly refer. I do not presume to aim at any ornamental or figurative descriptions, either of the country, its inhabitants, or its resources, conceiving it will be more acceptable to those who may be anxious to obtain information, that it should be conveyed with brevity and distinctness, and without ornament or prolixity. My hope of commanding any degree of attention will rest solely on the facts which I shall submit; I anticipate nothing in the way of approbation, but such as the truth and accuracy of my details may elicit.

As there were many incidents, during our residence in Eastern Africa, of which Lieutenant King was an observer, and whose journal, after the death of that estimable young officer, came into my possession, I shall occasionally refer to it, and submit extracts in illustration of the facts which I offer, because I have the gratification to find that many parts of my narrative will receive the recorded testimony of that officer, whose perception was correct, and his discrimination minute and perfect.

His motive for proceeding to the coast of Natal did him infinite honour; the rescue or recovery of a friend, who had gone thither on a speculative trip, and had been absent beyond the ordinary period of such voyages, was an impulse too irresistible for him to delay undertaking it, and that too with inconceivable promptness. I will state his motives as he has recorded them. " On my arrival at the Cape, I found that circumstances prevented me carrying my projected voyage into effect, owing to the lateness of the season; I therefore resolved on passing a few months in any trade that might advantageously offer. This determination, however, was changed when I heard that an old friend of mine, a Mr. Farewell, an East India merchant, had been absent for more than sixteen months on a very hazardous speculation to the eastward, amongst the natives, who, it appeared when on my former voyage on that coast, had never seen a white person. The last accounts received from him was by a vessel called the York, fitted expressly by the government to ascertain whether the party were still in existence. After great difficulty, this vessel reached the port, and returned with the following account—namely, that Mr. Farewell and party had been very much distressed, and would willingly have returned; but, from a part of them being absent in the interior, they remained, in the hope that they might be relieved by some vessel from Delagoa, Madagascar, or other neighbouring port; for, unless one be bound direct, an individual might remain for years before he would be enabled to escape. Under all these circumstances, and, as I have before observed, having visited that quarter, knowing the unpleasant as well as dangerous situation of these enterprising adventurers, and feeling it my duty to render every assistance to them in their unfortunate dilemma, I resolved on personally ascertaining their condition; and having discharged my vessel's cargo, I prepared for the voyage with my companion, Mr. Isaacs, and sailed from the Cape on the 26th of August, with strong anticipations that I should effect the recovery of my long absent friend."

The preceding extract, from the journal of Lieutenant King, will at once confirm what I have before asserted, that our voyage was one of accident, and not of design.

My journal will embrace a space of nearly seven years, being the period of my peregrination in the Zoola and Fumos countries, besides a short visit to the Comoro Islands; and it will, I think, be admitted, that so protracted a residence must have afforded me opportunities of ascertaining a few interesting facts, that may be of moment to the commercial part of the community; and that many incidental circumstances

must have occurred, of which I was a personal
observer, a recital of which may not only be entertaining to the general reader, and afford amusement
in the moments of seclusion, but likewise essentially
tend to serve individuals whose pursuits are speculative, and suggest an inducement to search for information relative to those countries with which they
have had no personal intercourse, and of the resources and capabilities of which they are unable
to form even a feeble estimate.

An historical account of either Zoola or Fumos, will
not be attempted, beyond what I have been able to
collect from the tradition of some of the natives,
there not being any records that I could discover
from which historical facts and circumstances might
be deduced. A topographical view of the interior of
the countries will be submitted, with an account of
the manners and customs of the natives; and such
occasional cursory observations on their natural productions as may not be unacceptable.

For the annexed chart, which will present to my
reader a very correct view of the bay of Natal, I am
indebted to my lamented friend Lieutenant King, as
well as for his able assistance in the drawings
which will be found in this work: and I shall find it
often advisable to refer to the journal of that enterprising young officer, to refresh my memory of many
incidents which occurred during our united tour in
Africa, and which his discriminating mind has left

recorded; designing, had he survived, to have given the public the benefit of his personal observations on that unfrequented coast.

To conclude. I am somewhat sanguine, that when the humble diary of my adventures shall have obtained a little publicity, the South-eastern coast of Africa, and the bay of Natal in particular, will occupy some share of the consideration of mercantile men; and that the time is not far distant, when the government of Great Britain may view the advantages which the port of Natal offers for the extension of commercial enterprize; and that she may, on adverting to her Indian possessions, perceive how valuable an acquisition to her colonial dependencies such a position must be, from its being within the general course of her vessels bound to the eastern portion of her empire.

NATHANIEL ISAACS.

DIRECTIONS TO THE BINDER.

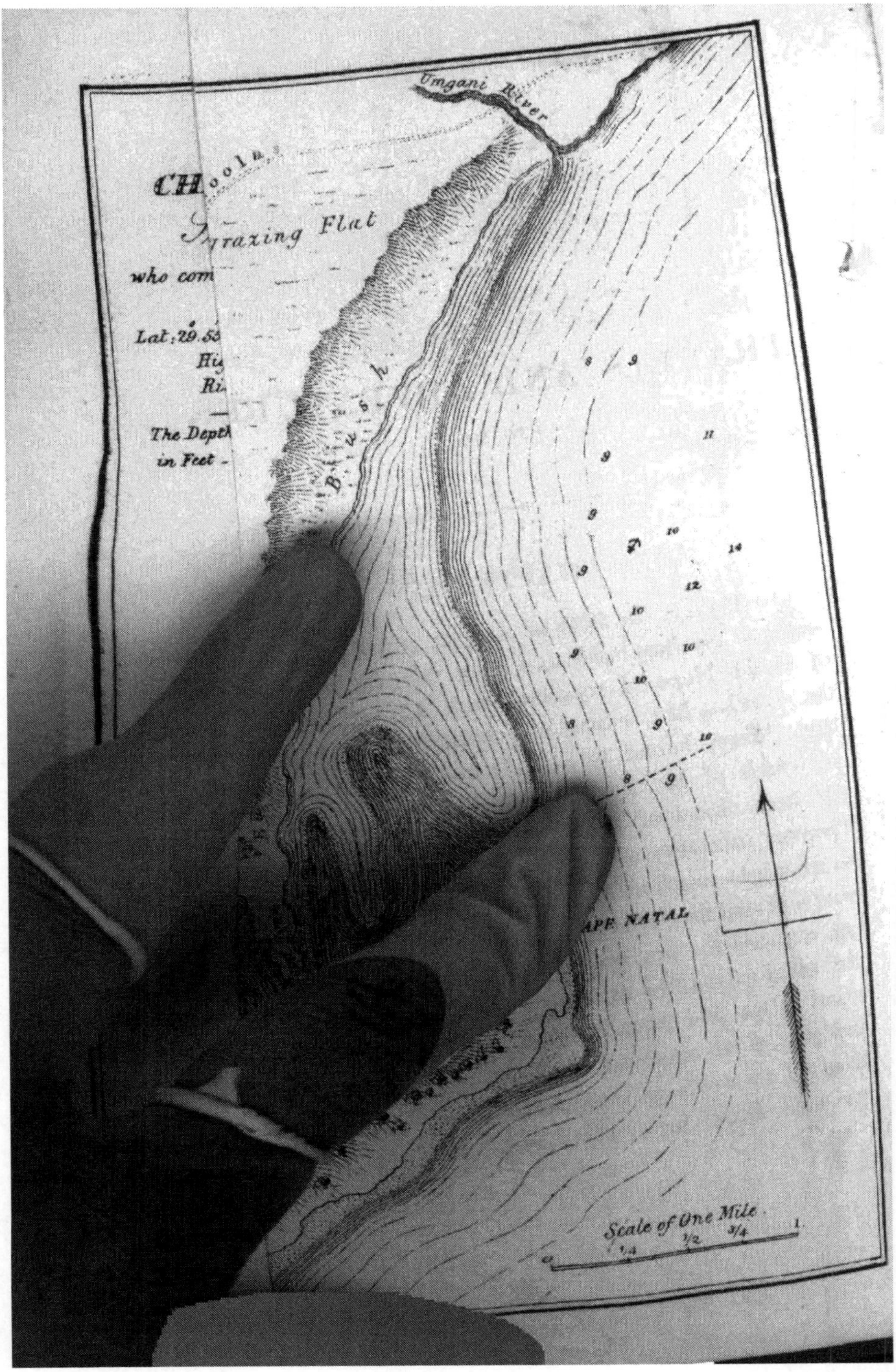
Umgani River
CH
Grazing Flat
who com
Lat: 29.5
Hi
Ri
The Depth
in Feet
Bush
CAPE NATAL
Scale of One Mile
1/4
1/2
3/4
1.

TRAVELS AND ADVENTURES,

ETC. ETC.

CHAPTER I.

On Friday, the 26th of August 1825, after taking leave of my hospitable and kind friends at the Cape of Good Hope, I repaired, with Lieut. King, and the Rev. — M'Clelland and his lady, on board the brig Mary, bound for the eastern coast of Africa in search of Mr. Farewell and his party. This was the first object of our voyage; the second was to open an intercourse with the natives at such points as we might touch at, where it could be accomplished with a probability of success. Nothing worth recording occurred the first few days of our passage, except the usual casualties attending a sea trip, of occasional calms and squalls, and a few other trifling incidents of no moment. Nausea and sea-sickness, those sad torments of inexperienced voyagers, gave me some little inconvenience, but I eventually

overcame them, and enjoyed with renewed gratification, the various scenes as they were presented
to my view, until the 12th, when we arrived,
about 2 P. M., with a light and favourable breeze, and
came to anchor in Algoa Bay, immediately abreast
of the town. We landed the following day, and I
was introduced to Doctor Gill, a traveller in Africa
of some eminence.

14th.—The day being fine, the Rev Mr. M'Clelland
and myself went to see the pyramid erected to the
memory of Lady Elizabeth Donkin, by her husband,
who had been formerly acting governor of the Cape
of Good Hope. Here we passed two days, engaged
in bartering for provisions and preparing for the
prosecution of our travels, which we contemplated
would occupy twelve months. Port Elizabeth in
this Bay, named after the above lady, is a small
but improving settlement. The soil in its vicinity is
sandy, and not at all adapted for agricultural purposes:
nor do the people engage in agriculture, but confine
themselves exclusively to trading with the interior.
Their principal commerce is with the Boors*, who
bring down the produce of their farms, which they
exchange for the manufactures of England. Their
commodities consist chiefly of butter, beans, fruit,
tallow, hides, cheese, potatoes, onions, &c., which are
mostly exported to the Cape, except those consumed

* Dutch farmers.

by themselves. The place is governed by a Commandant appointed by the Commander-in-chief at the Cape.

17th.—At noon we sailed again with a strong breeze from the N.N.W., and in the evening passed the Bird Islands, the Doddington Rock bearing by the compass N. ½ E., being about three-quarters of a league from us. The breeze continuing favourable, we took the advantage of pursuing our course for Natal as near the coast as possible, for the purpose of observation. The next morning at daylight we perceived the River Keiskamma. It does not appear navigable, and at its entrance there is a bar, over which the sea breaks with a moderate swell. The country contiguous to this part seemed productive; and its surface somewhat irregular and of moderate altitude. The pasturage was verdant and flourishing; and we could perceive large herds of cattle indulging in its exuberance. We saw no regular kraals, but several straggling huts studded the coast as far as we could discover with the aid of our glass. On the 19th we were abreast of the Cove Rock. At a short distance from the land this rock looks like an island. We passed it at a distance of about two leagues.

20th.—This morning we had light and baffling winds, attended with a heavy swell, which compelled us to tack and stand off from the shore. At 1 P.M. the breeze freshened, and towards the evening increased to a moderate gale. We occasionally tacked, and stood on and off the coast, but to no purpose, as the current was so strong that it drifted us to westward at the rate of four miles an hour.

21st.—At day-break we found ourselves abreast of the Great Fish River. At 8 A.M. by the compass Cape Padron bore N. by W—distance about four leagues. At 10 A.M. the wind shifted to W.N.W., which enabled us to shape our course as before. We sailed as near the coast as possible, in order to have the advantage of seeing any object that might be worth the traveller's notice. For several successive days we had variable winds, from moderate breezes to strong gales, but perceived little on shore that immediately commanded our attention. We could distinctly perceive that the population of the country was numerous; fires were visible in different parts; and there was an abundance of cattle grazing with playful indifference, heedless alike of the "pitiless gale" and the herdsman's care.

October 1st.—During the last night we were in a state of extreme anxiety, knowing ourselves to be near Natal, and apprehending that the current, somewhat adverse, might make our reckoning imperfect. We advanced under easy sail, and at break of day saw land a-head, which we discovered with no little pleasure to be our port of destination. We crowded all sail, hoping to reach it while the tide was flowing. Passing the entrance to the Bay, we anchored under the bluff point named Cape Natal. Lieut.

King sent the whale-boat, under charge of a seaman (who had before visited the place) and four of his shipmates, to sound on the Bar. After making several ineffectual attempts, they returned, but the surf breaking violently across the mouth of the harbour, they reached the vessel again with considerable difficulty. At this time it was blowing a moderate gale, yet an increase of wind was threatened from the S. E.; and as the vessel was perceived to be drifting towards the land, we slipped our chain cable, and made an effort to beat off a lee shore. Our vessel was a dull sailer, and made so little progress that, when the tide began to ebb, our situation became evidently perilous. We had only one course to pursue, and that was promptly determined on by our commander. He immediately assembled his officers and crew, consulted with them, and pointed out the danger we had to encounter. They unanimously gave their opinion that there was water enough to carry our vessel over the Bar, if she were lightened. She had, previously to this, been prepared for the worst, every article that could be dispensed with in our exigencies having been thrown overboard, not excepting the water. The crew were unanimous for making the port. Our commander, with great coolness and intrepidity, for which he was remarkable, gave the command to put the vessel about. Every man promptly obeyed, and took his station with alacrity. Our little bark soon faced the Bar, which had an awful and even terrific aspect. The surf beat over it with a prodigiously overwhelming force; the foaming of the sea gave it an appearance that would have unnerved any but an experienced seaman; the wind whistling through the rigging, seemed as the knell of our approaching destruction. Every eye could perceive that our case was alarming, nevertheless all were calm, watchful and silent. Not a voice could be heard but that of our commander, who had stationed himself in the companion way, with his eyes intently fixed on the helmsman, giving from time to time the word, "steady." I grasped a rope and lashed myself to the side of the vessel, lest the sea, then breaking over us, should sweep me from the deck. As we approached the high land, every tree was seen to bend to the awful force of the storm. Every rock seemed to threaten peril, and every billow as it yawned before her prow appeared as if it would engulf the ship. At this moment, though my mind was fluctuating between hope and apprehension, my admiration was alike excited at the calm confidence of Lieut. King, and the firm, steady, and watchful conduct of his crew. It is impossible by words to do justice to the collected firmness of that gallant young officer at so appalling a crisis; and I fear I should fall as far short in the attempt to give a faithful representation of the incomparable steadiness and resolution of his men. There appeared to me so evident a proof of skilful seamanship in our commander, and such a desire to do their duty on the part of the crew, that my confidence in ultimate safety was never shaken. But the worst was still to come. We began rapidly to approach the rocks, and every moment was one of immediate peril. I never contemplated witnessing such a scene. On one side, a beautiful and picturesque country presented itself, on the other, the agitated sea bubbling like a cauldron overspread with sparkling foam, from the dashing of its billows on the rugged rocks. It was a scene for the pencil of the painter and the pen of the poet. The ship rolled frightfully; our commander, with an unfaltering voice, "ever and anon" gave the words, "steady," "hard a port," "starboard;" "meet her, meet her," "keep her steady," then by way of encouragement to his men he would occasionally cry "all's right, my lads;" but a terrific sea came foaming and rushing on our quarter with irresistible force; the vessel gave a heavy lurch, and sank into the hollow of the sea, then rose again buoyantly on the foaming wave,—the sailors vociferating, "she is going," "she is going!"—and struck on the bank eastward of the Bar. Lieutenant King, commanding silence and cheering the men, ordered all sail to be set. His voice was heard above the storm—"press her over, my hearties," "now she goes," "all's right;" but at this moment another sea struck her, and brought her broadside to the waves, when all efforts to save her became ineffectual. All had been done that skill,

courage, and seamanship could devise, and unshaken
firmness and resolution accomplish. The next sea,
which made a fair breach over us and unshipped our
rudder, left us no alternative but to repair to the
boats for our personal safety. The whale-boat, however, had been dashed against the vessel's side, and
several of her planks were stove in; the only hope
that remained, therefore, was to get out the long-boat,
which we apprehended might meet the same fate as
the whale-boat. Our only alternative was at length
embraced, the long-boat was lowered from the brig,
and without any delay hauled under her bowsprit
where she could lie in safety. As the tide ebbed,
the sea abated, leaving our vessel upright and high
out of water, which gave us some faint hope of getting her off the bank at the next flood tide, but
subsequently this was found impracticable, and we
abandoned all further idea of attempting it. We
were lowered into the boat by means of a rope
suspended from the bowsprit of the vessel, which
each person held until he could take advantage of
a moment when the waves, by raising the boat,
enabled him to drop from his position with safety.
One of the sailors nearly lost his life, from having
incautiously relinquished his hold of the rope as the
wave receded, and drew the boat from under him;
he in consequence fell into the sea. A Newfoundland dog, however, belonging to the ship, which
the man had been in the habit of caressing, and

making a sort of pet companion of, seeing the poor fellow precipitated into the water, sprang from the deck, seized the drowning sailor by his red shirt, and kept his head above water until a rope was thrown to him from the leeward side of the vessel, when the poor fellow and his canine preserver were safely got on board.

The captain and the crew, although they saw that any further effort to recover the brig was impracticable, sought to save as much of her and of her stores as they could with safety. For this purpose, the kedge anchor was got into the boat, with which some of the men pulled off for the rocks, where they planted the kedge, and, after considerable difficulty, reached the vessel with the end of the line. Every thing that ingenuity and skill could devise, was resorted to for the purpose of recovering the vessel, but without effect.

While our commander and his men were occupied in this duty, my attention was directed to the shore, in the hope of discovering if there were any human habitations near the coast, which, from the rigging, whither I had ascended, I could distinctly survey to a considerable distance; but, although I kept my eye steadily fixed in a direction where it was most probable I should see some inhabitants, if there were any, the whole day had nearly passed without my having descried a living creature. In the evening, however, I perceived one of the natives, whom I surveyed with an apprehensive scrutiny. He was as naked as a negro on the banks of the Niger, but though he manifested no signs of hostility, I did not feel satisfied that his intentions were amicable.

I can scarcely describe my feelings at this crisis; they were not enviable. Wrecked on a desolate and savage coast, and cast in the days of my youth amidst a people whom I imagined not humanised, emotions were awakened within which nothing but my trust and confidence in the protection " of the Giver of all life" could have made endurable. It was the hour of reflection; and the thoughts of an anxious parent, of whose fostering care in my boyhood I had received so many endearing proofs, rushed irresistibly on my mind, and in the poignancy of my grief I became insensible to the dangers by which I was surrounded. But the approach of other natives revived in me some hope which, in the moment of despair, and in the anguish of despondency, I might have forgotten, that I was not bereft of the chance of yet escaping those perils which my bewildered fancy had imagined to be insurmountable, and that there yet remained something to arm my spirit with resolution to meet, and contend with the usual obstacles which accompany the progress of a traveller into unexplored lands.

> " Auspicious hope ! in thy sweet garden grow
> Wreaths for each toil, a charm for every woe."

This distich of the poet suddenly recurring to my mind, revived me from the extreme depression which my late fears and present apprehensions naturally generated. I turned towards my gallant friend, who had been laboriously engaged in taking measures to extricate us from the horrors with which shipwreck is generally accompanied, and observing him in the act of elating his men into a confidence of eventual safety, I at once forgot the sufferings which the past had occasioned, and exulted in the sanguine anticipation that the future might be more productive of gratifying events.

As the journal of Lieut. King abounds with more minute and explicit details of our escape, and illustrates more professionally the causes that led to our disaster, the following extract may not be unacceptable to the reader :—" We experienced this day (the 30th of September) light baffling winds, but, with the assistance of the current, we were the next morning in a good position, Natal head bearing S.W. by W. three leagues distance. On my former voyage, I ascertained the depth and nature of the bar—the time of high water, and other necessary points. Having, however, no wish to enter the harbour with the vessel, we lowered the whale-boat, which I had prepared with a few days' provisions, for myself and those whom I designed to take with me. Being ready, I gave instructions for the vessel to lie off and on shore, until we heard something of those of whom we had come in pursuit. The bar proved too heavy to make an attempt in the boat, and, previously to her return, the vessel was anchored in a good position to enable her to stand out of the bay if required. Unhappily for us, she drove with the increasing gale. The object was now to get the boat on board, which was with difficulty accomplished; but she reached the vessel, which had brought up with nearly a whole cable. We veered the boat astern, and employed all hands in getting clear to make sail, and to stand out until a more favourable opportunity offered; but alas! our attempts were, by this time, evidently fruitless; the vessel sending forward in a most turbulent sea, and the rocks off the point extending too far to weather. On the opposite tack we could do nothing. One opportunity only presented itself, to which it was imperative that we should promptly resort, otherwise I knew that the tide would not admit of success. The harbour was now my object, although, if we were defeated in our attempt to get over the bar, the chances were that every soul on board might perish, or be left destitute, and at the mercy of a horde of savages. To increase the horror of our peculiarly unfortunate situation, not a living soul was to be seen on this desolate coast. Had the natives come out from the jungle and recesses, with which the shore abounds, we should not have been assailed with the apprehension which we foreboded, namely, that when we landed, they would rush down upon us, and make

us a prey to sate their savage propensities. The
fatigue which invariably attends the shipwrecked
mariner, however, in some measure, was borne without murmuring: our time and minds being preoccu-
pied, little was left for reflection; all were engaged
in the great object of effecting some means of escape.
I consulted with my officers and people, as their lives
and the safety of the vessel entitled them to this consideration; and they readily agreed to my proposition as being the best and only method to ensure
success. We now turned to with one heart, got a
spring on our cable from the larboard quarter, and
the head sails, fore-top sail, and fore-sail ready for
casting and setting. We cut our cable, and in less
than three minutes, after getting before the wind, with
all anxiety, she settled between two seas on the bar,
and struck fore and aft with a most awful crash. The
next sea almost overwhelmed us, when she again
repeatedly struck with the same violence, knocking
off her rudder, and starting her floors: at this time
she made a considerable quantity of water. The
ebb tide making out strong, caught her on the larboard bow (which was in deep water) and directed
her head to starboard, out of the proper channel. All
our attempts to obviate this, by bracing the head-sails
to, and setting after-sails, proved ineffectual. The
tide had now left her considerably, with her head
setting into deep water, and rolling desperately. The
sea being too heavy to risk a boat, the only chance that

now remained, was to get a hawser to the beach, and
have it conveyed to the rocks on our larboard beam,
which on a flowing tide might assist the vessel's head
to port, to get her into a better position (although at
this time almost a perfect wreck), where we might be
able to save such necessaries as should afterwards prove
useful; for, in her present situation, the sea would, in
a short time, break her to pieces.

" The whale-boat had been previously stove and
sunk, our jolly-boat was too small, and on examining
our long-boat, we found, from unshipping her from
the chocks, a plank in her bottom had been broken in;
this, however, was soon repaired. In the interim, and
at intervals, we succeeded in cutting the sails from the
yards and in lightening the vessel as much as possible
by taking out everything which it was practicable to
get to the shore, having already observed many parts of
the wreck washing up. In the execution of this duty
the conduct of my men was unexceptionable. Our
boat being ready, we succeeded in launching her, but
almost immediately she filled alongside from the heavy
surges, which continued throughout, making a fair
sweep over us. We veered her under the bows of the
vessel and baled her out for the purpose of carrying
off a hawser to the rocks, in which we could not succeed, the boat having swamped several times. Our
small bower anchor was conveyed aft to the larboard
quarter with the cable, and a purchase on the main
boom end to carry it clear of the vessel, and let go,

which had a trifling good effect, but the scope was
too short. The object in doing this was, to prevent
the vessel forcing on a bank directly ahead, between
which and our present situation was a deep channel.
We succeeded at length in coiling a quantity of new
small line in the boat for the purpose of conveying a
hawser to the shore. Myself and four of the crew
lowered ourselves from the bowsprit into the boat, and
accomplished this part so far as to reach the beach,
but, owing to the strong current, and the line entangling itself with the rocks, it produced no good effect.
We were not only discouraged by this untoward circumstance, but we had our dismal wreck and shipmates
before us. To reach them again appeared almost
impossible, nevertheless we determined on attempting it, and, after much difficulty, having shipped several heavy seas on her way, we providentially effected
our purpose. Previously to our arrival on board
again, I found every thing had been done to lighten
the vessel by throwing overboard such things as would
have reduced our chances of getting on shore. Our
wishes in this particular having been complied with,
we were stimulated to make further efforts.

" The tide was now half flood, and every article
moving about in the hold, when a fortunate sea forced
the vessel from the bar to the inner bank;—I say fortunate, because all our attempts to remove her to a
more eligible position had proved fruitless, and by
having the wreck on this bank, it appeared we should

have a prospect of saving some articles, particularly the pieces from the wreck, in which hope, thank God, we were not disappointed.

" At the time of the vessel being thrown over, almost every moveable article was washed overboard, among which were many things of consequence, but none more so than the carpenter's tools, which had been previously put away. All that could now be found were a few that had been previously secured, which had been used by the carpenter, and afterwards proved to be invaluable to us.

" Some of the crew succeeded in recovering part of their clothes, while others lost their whole stock. Our time was too much occupied with the wreck to enable us to give the least attention to anything of a personal consideration, and I remarked with no little satisfaction, the willing sacrifice which my crew made of those things that might have been useful to them.

" I have much pleasure in acknowledging my entire gratitude to Mr. Hatton, my chief officer, whose indefatigable exertions in the moment of inconceivable danger, called for my most unequivocal demonstrations of praise; and I cannot abstain from remarking of my crew, that I never witnessed men more collected, nor more willing to obey, even at the imminent risk of their lives, than they manifested during our melancholy situation with the wreck; they were but few, but they were faithful, willing, and obedient, and their conduct generally was above all commendation. During eighteen years in the service, I never before met such a disaster, and I trust that a similar one will never again overtake me.

" To the wonderful interposition of Providence can our preservation alone be attributed; to His all-seeing eye we were indebted for firmness in the hour of trial, and for resolution to combat with danger. That God whose attributes are mercy and care, who ' sits in the whirlwind and directs the storm,' shielded us from its wrath, and gave us fortitude to contend with its terrific elements—' to *Him* be all praise.'"

I respond to the pious ejaculations of my gallant companion. My escape from the peril by which I was surrounded, affords me another instance of the power and providence of the Deity; and in the language of the inimitable author of the Shipwreck, let me say,

" With thee, great God, whatever is is just."

The fort and bay of Natal, lies in lat. 29° 55' S. and in long. 30° 41' E; and the coast of Natal extends from point Natal on the southern extremity, to Delagoa Bay on the north. It is said to have been purchased of the natives by the Dutch East India Company, in the year 1690; and afterwards to have become frequented as a harbour for slave ships, as was also Delagoa Bay, where the Dutch had a factory established in 1721. Natal, about that period, is reported

to have commenced at Great Fish River, and was
considered to have been a point of some attraction, as
being "one of the most fertile regions upon earth*."
There is no doubt of the slave trade having been
carried on between this port and the Isle of France
as early as 1719, as mentioned by Captain Drury, who
was engaged in it †.

The country in the interior, however, does not appear to have been visited by Europeans at that time;
it seems not to have been frequented either for the
purposes of exploration or traffic; the boundaries
of the Caffres on the south, and Delagoa Bay on
the north-east, were no doubt the limits to which
travellers have gone or missionaries penetrated. Something, though quite conjectural, has been submitted;
but its character has not been developed by any individual who has acquired a knowledge of it from actual
personal intercourse.

Its climate is not only congenial but salubrious, as
it rarely has the extremes of excessive heat, or intense
cold, but a mean temperature between 50° and 80°. The
soil is rich and fertile, and capable of being rendered
exceedingly productive. It is, at intervals, and of no
long duration, refreshed by gentle showers, no heavy
rains visiting it until the periodical seasons, which
commence with the year and end in April. During
this period the rains are heavy, and fall in torrents,

* Purry's " Mémoire sur le Pays de Cafres, et la Terre de Nuyts."
† Drury's Narrative, p. 441.

accompanied with thunder and lightning of an appalling description. The seasons, however, notwithstanding their being so very heavy and attended too by occasional tempestuous weather, are beneficial to the soil, as tending to destroy those insects which are so baneful to vegetation. The rivers are large; and there are innumerable smaller streams intersecting the whole country; these are highly favourable, not only for the purposes of the natives, but as being conducive to the propagation of herds, and to the growth of all vegetable matter.

The country has an eternal verdure; the dews, which are exceedingly heavy in the absence of rain, are productive of vegetation, and occasion the herbage to shoot to a prodigious height. When this becomes rank and loses its richness, it is burnt off by the natives who set fire to it, as in civilised tropical countries ; after the first rains that fall, it shoots again with extreme luxuriance.

The Portuguese of the Mozambique, from the circumstance of burning this superabundant vegetation, have given this region the name of " Fumo," or the country of smoke.

CHAPTER II.

HAVING somewhat recovered from the gloom which our calamitous situation had created, I resumed my view of the coast opposite to our position, and sought to discover if any more of the natives had made their appearance. Every thing indicated a wild and uncivilised country, where nature had been lavish of her bounty, but where the art and industry of man had been little applied in improving her works. The scenery had an appearance of grandeur—there were verdure, and spontaneous vegetation, but cultivation was confined to occasional patches, and did not extend over regular spaces or extensive plots. There was, however, a savage wildness that could only impress us with forebodings respecting Mr. Farewell and his party, of whom we were in search, which led us to apprehend that they had all fallen by the savage hands of the tribes who might occasionally visit the coast. Our apprehensions, however, in the sequel proved premature, for we found them to be alive. About four P.M., to our inexpressible joy, we could perceive a party of eight people, who appeared to have come from the eastern side of the bay, and had walked to Point Fynn. On their arrival at the Point, they planted a worn out Union Jack on a small hillock abreast of our vessel. The reader may imagine what were my feelings at such a moment, when I had been impressed with a conviction that no humanised being inhabited the coast; when I had imagined that we were cast upon a shore where civilised man had never dared to set his foot! They were enviable indeed, for few only enjoy them, and taste the sweets they give. The effect of such a signal was soul-stirring and irresistible; and, with the alacrity of an experienced tar, I descended from my station in the maintop, seized the first flag I could meet with, hoisted it in the rigging, where it waved gaily in the breeze. My delight was uncontrollable at having discovered something in the shape of civilised man, apparently manifesting a desire to shelter us in the bitter moments of calamity.

But the sudden ray of joy which thus beamed upon us, was soon overcast by a cloud of apprehensions. Much doubt followed our momentary gratification, and we soon discovered fresh cause for anxiety. On minutely surveying the group, six of them appeared in a state of nudity; one was clad in tattered European garments, and the other in a female garb, with her head tied up in a handkerchief. Our imaginations were now excited, and gloomy thoughts pervaded us.

We one and all concluded that the Europeans of whom we were in search had been massacred, and that the people we descried sought to decoy us ashore, where they would be joined by others, fall upon us, make us their captives, and devote us to the gratification of their savage propensities.

Lieutenant King, however, resolved upon putting an end to these doubts, by approaching the shore in the long-boat, and I, nothing loath, but rather anxious to know my fate, expressed a wish to accompany him, to which he assented.

Having equipped myself for the purpose, with a brace of pistols and a wallet of bread, I, like my companions, descended from the bowsprit of the vessel into the boat; we then made for the shore with as much speed as the rough state of the sea would permit. Approaching the beach, we lay on our oars until the strangers arrived at the water's edge. The man clad in European attire, and who turned out to be an Englishman, took off his cap, made of cat skins, and saluted us. We then, without hesitation, pulled through the surf and embraced the stranger, looking upon him as a guardian angel sent to snatch us from that destruction to which we thought ourselves inevitably doomed.

This individual proved to be Thomas Holstead, a youth about my own age, and belonging to Mr. Farewell's party. The rest of the group consisted of a Hottentot woman, in a dungaree petticoat, with a blue cotton handkerchief tied round her head; five natives, entirely naked; and a female with a piece of bullock's hide fastened round her waist, hanging to the knees, made black with charcoal, and softened by frequent rubbing. Her personal appearance was not attractive : she was ordinary and of middle stature, but her arms, from the elbow to the shoulder, exhibited one continued cicatrix, bearing dreadful evidence of some disease that had entirely consumed the skin. My curiosity was excited to know the cause of it. I subsequently ascertained that she had eloped from her husband, who had branded her arm with a fire-stick, and afterwards beat the burnt part, which had produced the forbidding appearance just described.

> " Withered and wild in her attire,
> She look'd not like a habitant of earth,
> And yet was on it."

Lieutenant King inquired of Holstead, if Mr. Fare-well and the whole of his party were living, and where the former resided. We found that he had gone accompanied by Cune, an attendant, on a visit to Challa, chief of the country; and that Mr. Fynn and another had proceeded to the district of the Amum-ponds—a tribe dwelling about two hundred miles to the westward—for the purpose of trading for ivory.

The tide was flowing when Lieutenant King returned to the wreck with his crew, to endeavour, if possible, to get her into deep water. Not being a seaman, and utterly inexperienced in all nautical matters, I found that I could render no material aid; I therefore accompanied Holstead and Rachel, the Hottentot woman, to Mr. Farewell's residence. We proceeded about two miles along the beach, where there grows a dwarf shrub, to the very margin of the sea, which here forms a spacious bay. It is of a circular form, and intersected by several small islands, covered with a species of underwood. After sunset we arrived at Mr. Farewell's house, when Holstead and Rachel advised me not to venture out after night had set in, as the wolves and panthers were numerous, and made considerable havoc in the vicinity of their dwellings; two natives and a dog having been carried off within a week or two by these nocturnal marauders.

On my arrival at Mr. Farewell's residence, a number of natives came to welcome me: having done so, and expressed their satisfaction at seeing another white man among them, they left me, and I retired to the dwelling of the Hottentot, where I regaled myself with milk and bread, a welcome repast to one who had tasted nothing since the previous evening, and had undergone much fatigue with no little anxiety.

Being left alone, an opportunity was afforded me of reflecting upon our miraculous preservation, and the subsequent discovery of those of whom we had come in search, as well as to ruminate on the scenes we had witnessed on reaching this but little-known country. The wild and savage scenery,

together with the peculiar habits and appearance of
the natives who had approached us, left impressions
which time can never efface from my memory : when I
took a superficial glance of the country, and viewed
only an occasional hut, the shape and construction of
which was not only singular, but " passing strange ; '
when night had closed in, and all seemed still around,
the solitude of the place awakened in me feelings not
easily described. The well-known lines of the poet
struck me as peculiarly applicable to the scene, and
being in unison with the sensations which at the time
pervaded me, I involuntarily exclaimed

> Oh solitude where are the charms
> That sages have seen in thy face !
> Better dwell in the midst of alarms
> Than reign in this horrible place.

Finding Holstead anything but intelligent, and
being somewhat exhausted, I laid myself down to rest
on a four-post bedstead of native manufacture, having
strips of bullock's hide as a substitute for sacking, a
mat to repose on, a bag stuffed with old clothes for a
pillow, and a blanket for my coverlet ; thus did I
enjoy the sweets of repose, such as even monarchs
might envy, and luxury covet.

After a short time, however, I was awakened and
much alarmed at the report of guns. I called for
Holstead ; but his movements not being of the most
rapid description, and the firing still continuing, I
forgot, in my anxiety to know the cause of this

c

nocturnal interruption, the caution I had received from him and Rachel, rushed hurriedly from my abode, and proceeding to the hut of Rachel, there found Holstead. The continued firing of muskets, the barking of dogs, and the distant howling of wolves, together with a dark, dreary night, made it, indeed, truly awful.

I concluded that the vessel had gone to pieces, that Lieut. King had got ashore with his crew, and been attacked by the natives. In this state of perplexity I remained for some time, and being without a musket myself, could not answer the firing of my friend; nor could I get any one to accompany me to the beach on account of the prevailing dread of wild animals. At last, however, after some persuasion I got my attendants to prepare some fire-sticks, when we made several large fires on the beach; and Lieutenant King and the crew, with the exception of the mate and another, came ashore. After mooring the boat, we all proceeded to the hut of Rachel, where my companions regaled themselves on the same fare, as I had before participated of with much satisfaction.

All hopes of getting off the vessel had vanished. The flood-tide, which had raised a little hope, had now began to ebb, and every plan that ingenuity could devise had been tried by Lieutenant King, with a zeal quite indescribable, but to no purpose; she was therefore finally abandoned, but care taken as the vessel went to pieces, to secure those parts of the wreck which might hereafter be serviceable.

The place selected by Mr. Farewell for his residence had a singular appearance, from the peculiar construction of the several edifices. His house was not unlike an ordinary barn made of wattle, and plaistered with clay, without windows, and with only one door composed of reeds. It had a thatched roof, but otherwise was not remarkable either for the elegance of its structure, or the capacity of its interior. The house of Cain was contiguous to that of Mr. Farewell, and about twenty yards from it, while that of Ogle was at a similar distance, and had the appearance of the roof of a house placed designedly on the ground, the gable end of which being left open served as a door. Opposite Mr. Farewell's house was a native hut, in the shape of a bee-hive, about twenty-one feet in circumference, and six feet high, built of small sticks and supported by a pole in the centre. It was thatched with grass, and had an aperture about eighteen inches square, through which the owner crept into his mansion, when he was disposed to enjoy the sweets of repose.

Oct. 2nd.—It was Sunday, but no sound indicative of the Sabbath morn assailed us, for

> The sound of a church-going bell,
>   These valleys and rocks never heard ;
> Never sighed at the sound of a knell,
>   Or smiled when a sabbath appear'd.

all seemed wild, gloomy, and revolting. At dawn of day all hands arose, when we refreshed ourselves with a scanty meal of bread and milk, and repaired to the point for the purpose of saving such goods as might have been washed on shore from the wreck, and of communicating with the two persons left on board. During the two succeeding days we were similarly engaged, and found that the water had reached the cabin floor; that most of our little cargo of goods and our provisions had been washed out, but that otherwise the wreck was in the position we left her. It being sunset, we returned to our huts (which we had constructed on the beach, with the vessel's sails) to enjoy some little repose after a laborious day, and under a tropical sun. The wolves, which were numerous, serenaded us with their midnight howls; and we were obliged to keep a strict watch, with large fires, as a protection against these rapacious animals, whose thirst for blood is prodigious, and whose quickness and sagacity are surprising. About nine o'clock in the evening we were alarmed by the report of guns, proceeding from the wreck. We pulled off to her, but not without difficulty, as our boat swamped several times in its progress through the surf. At length we got on board, and found that the vessel was turning on her beam ends. We brought off the mate and seaman, who reluctantly quitted her, though to have remained would have been destruction.

— 5th.—The wind had somewhat moderated; the

vessel had canted in shore and been driven nearer to the beach, so that at low water we could wade to her. The beach was completely strewed with pieces of the wreck, of which, with the assistance of the natives, we secured as much as possible.

— 6th.—While the crew were engaged at the vessel endeavouring to preserve all they could, I employed myself at Mr. Farewell's (where I considered myself at home,) in drying the clothes and other things saved. I was greatly mortified to find that the few articles of my own, which had been washed up, were rendered perfectly useless, so that, like the natives, I was almost in a state of nudity, having nothing but the suit I stood in, and that in a very tattered condition.

A number of natives came to see me; their gestures were so unsightly, that their presence was not in the least degree attractive; and, had it not been for the Hottentot woman Rachel, I should have felt some little alarm for my personal security, under the apprehension that they might design me for a repast. To assure me of her power over these rude and ignorant creatures, she administered to them a wholesome quantity of personal chastisement, and that, too, without much sympathy. Her argument was irresistible, and my unwelcome new acquaintances retired with a very significant proof of her authority; it was effective: it relieved me from annoyance, and caused my alarm to subside. She said they were servants of the establishment, and that they had been collected by Mr. Fynn in his travels. Another party of ten arrived, who she told me were strangers, and belonged to two Zoola chiefs stationed in the neighbourhood. They were curious in examining my person, and actually scanned me from head to foot with a suspicious scrutiny. They had several assagai, or spears, which they offered for sale, but, as I did not know if our little means would enable me to purchase, I hesitated, but was, however, compelled by their importunities to barter with them, in order to induce them to depart. I allowed them to make the best bargain, for which our good Rachel somewhat chided me, it being against that wholesome advice which she had given me, to make all I had scarce and valuable. I gave for seven assagai and two small calabashes neatly carved, a head of negro tobacco. Rachel said it was too much; but the natives were pleased; I was satisfied, and they departed. This being my *coup d'essai* in bartering with these people, I arrogated to myself no little credit for my adroitness.

— 8th.—The previous day I had been indisposed, but this morning I felt recovered, and took a walk, to survey the spot destined for my future abode.

The situation selected by Mr. Farewell for this purpose, did not exceed twenty feet above the level of the sea, it was a plain of a triangular form. Some parts contiguous to it were marshy, but it was upon the whole pleasantly diversified, being intersected with trees, and covered with a sort of dwarf shrub, peculiar, I fancy, to this part of the world. In the rear the land gradually rising to an ordinary altitude, is thickly covered with trees and underwood. On one side it is bounded by the River Umgani, and on the other, by the Bay and the Ocean, the whole skirted by magnificent trees, the timber of which would be, doubtless, invaluable, could it be applied for purposes of building either houses or vessels. The plain is about four miles long by two and a half broad, and resembles an English park. There is an ample supply of excellent water not only from the river before named, but from innumerable minor streams, and springs, which are here very abundant.

The house already described, was merely a temporary dwelling, and not designed for any protracted residence; Mr. Farewell having commenced building a fortress, which he purposes calling Fort Farewell. This is situated on the flat, nearer, by about a quarter of a mile, than his temporary habitation. It will cover a surface of about two hundred square yards, and is to be constructed in the form of a triangle. A ditch by which it will be encompassed was in progress; and palisadoes were being planted. To the house, which is to consist of one floor, and its dimensions to be about sixty feet by twenty, will be attached a store. A mud fort had been commenced, at each angle designed to mount three 12-pound carronades, which were lying there dismounted, with carpenter's tools, and other things, all indicating that something had been begun, but nothing completed. Near the ditch was a cattle-pound, partly finished, and at a distance of two hundred yards, a native kraal in a similar state, enclosing an elevated space of ground of about as many yards in circumference. The outer fence of this kraal was constructed of the mimosa tree; the inner of wattle, being designed for the security of the cattle. The streets were built between the two fences; and opposite the entrance a place was partitioned off for calves, a measure of precaution against wild animals which abound in this vicinity. In front of the fort, a square piece of ground had been fenced in, intended for a garden : it had been turned up, but nothing had been planted, with the exception of some mustard and cress, and a few ears of Indian corn. The whole space looked rich in verdure, and lacked only the art and industry of civilised man to render it endurable. With proper culture, it is evident the soil might be rendered productive, but from a people in a state of absolute barbarism nothing is to be expected beyond what nature spontaneously bestows.

Here I was destined to remain two years and nine months, an almost solitary European, wandering occasionally I knew not where, and in search of I knew not what. As I now and then sat reflecting on my own condition, a thought of home,

and of my dear friends, would irresistibly steal upon
me, and

> In a moment I seemed to be there,
> But alas! recollection at hand,
> Soon hurried me back to despair.

I must not dwell longer on these grateful recollections
—but return to my abode, which I reached after
having viewed Fort Farewell, just in time to escape
a violent storm. It rained heavily all night, accompanied with loud thunder, and incessant lightning. Our
hut, although impervious to the sun's rays, was not
proof against the torrents of rain that fell, and I was
obliged to get a bullock's hide to throw round me, as a
shelter against its unwelcome visitation.

At this crisis we began to consider for the future,
and to devise means for extricating ourselves from our
present position. Only one plan suggested itself as
at all affording us any reasonable hope, although the
undertaking appeared somewhat laborious, if not
nearly impracticable, namely, to build a small vessel with the materials saved from the wreck, with the
aid of such native timbers as we might be enabled to
procure suitable for the purpose. The remains of the
wreck could be of no further use, and as she was
sinking rapidly into the sand any attempt to break
her up for the materials would be abortive.

Any endeavour to reach the boundaries of the Cape
Colony, which were about 500 miles distant, or, on
the other side, to make for the Portuguese settlement

at Delagoa Bay, must have been attended with great
difficulty and hazard.   The course of the country to
the former had never been successfully traversed by
Europeans, those who were said to have made some
effort to accomplish it, having been massacred on
their progress.   We were also informed that war
was raging among the native tribes through whose
country we should be necessitated to pass.   Not long
before Mr. Farewell, on the other hand, had sent a
party to Delagoa Bay, not one of whom returned, and
the inference was that they had all been sacrificed by
the ferocious natives, or forced into the interior to
suffer every species of inhuman treatment, or to be
sold as slaves.   The plan determined upon, therefore, was to build a vessel, as before described, and
this we found, after a little consideration, the most
feasible one we could adopt.   Mr. Hatton, the chief
mate, who acted as captain of our late vessel, was
a practical shipwright, and had been brought up to
the trade, Lieutenant King consequently agreed with
him and the seamen, to add a little to their wages
during the performance of the work; and, as they
acquiesced in this arrangement, preparations were
made for commencing.

9th.—Sunday. This day Lieut. King assembled
his crew and read prayers, and, with much earnestness,
endeavoured to impress them with a due sense of their
obligations to God for their miraculous preservation,
entreating them not to forget that, by good and orderly

conduct towards the natives, instead of exciting them by any improper intercourse, they would be enabled to proceed with their labour without obstruction, and finally to retire from a country in which, in their present condition, they could derive no enjoyment. A good example to the natives, who sought to mingle with us, and to watch every action, might be productive of good; it could not do harm.

In the afternoon we crossed the Bay to view the country, and to select a fit place for building the vessel. The spot conceived to be most convenient, was situated on the declivity of the hill on the western side of the Bay, and in a parallel with the point of King's Island, so named after my gallant companion.

We proceeded afterwards along the brow of the hill, until we came to a small track that led to the forest; at this place we turned from the beach, and having Holstead with us, who spoke a little of the native tongue, we resolved on pursuing this narrow foot-path, which had several windings, and led us out of the forest. A cultivated country presented itself; several small hills had been cleared of underwood, and planted with Indian corn, which had been but recently gathered. On reaching the summit of one of the hills, we discovered a native Kraal, situated in a valley and surrounded by bush: we also perceived smoke to ascend from

several parts of the woody country, which indicated
the site of native towns and villages. Being five in
number, and our guide Holstead assuring us that
the people were friendly, we proceeded to the kraal,
which consisted only of a few straggling huts. The
pass thither being narrow only admitted one at a
time, so that we marched through it in single files.
There was something in the face of the country, as we
advanced, that demonstrated its wild and savage character, and indicated, every step we took, that precaution was imperative, lest we should be surprised by
the natives, or attacked by the wild animals that
infested the neighbourhood.

At one angle of the forest we came suddenly on a
native, who, when he saw us, darted into the jungle.
Immediately afterwards we perceived a number of
females, with their infants at their backs, running in
all directions, and evincing no little fear at our
approach. Continuing on the same pass, we shortly
came to a cross path, when we observed another Kraal,
to which we proceeded. Just before we arrived at the
place, a poor emaciated man approached us: he
trembled violently, and appeared to be in considerable
anguish; his body exhibited several scars. He at
first spoke to us in a low voice, but afterwards ejaculated, " Yoatee Bache wenna in qua-se-a-warmee !"
meaning, Oh my father, you my king! being the
usual salutation of the natives. Lieutenant King

gave him a piece of tobacco and a biscuit; the latter
he at first declined, but, seeing us eat it, he took
a piece, and thanked us repeatedly, as he preceded us
to the Kraal. He left us for a short time and then
returned with fourteen women, a number of children,
and four young men. Five of the women were his
wives, and, as he was the master of the Kraal, the
remainder he said were his people. The females
were all besmeared with red clay. Both sexes had
incisions in the lobe of the ear, in which either a piece
of reed, or a small vessel used as a snuff-box, was
introduced. It was some time before we could prevail
on them to approach us; but on making signs of friendship, and after giving them tobacco and some bread,
of which they seemed fond, the men soon mingled
with us and became quite familiar: the females,
however, continued at a distance, sat on the ground,
and hung down their heads, either from fear, or some
other impulse.

The sun was now fast declining, and we made signs
that we wished to return to our habitation, when they
manifested a desire that we should remain with them,
but, as we declined their offer, the females began to
cry, followed us a considerable part of our way to
the boat, and seemed indisposed to leave us,
until we assured them that we intended to visit them
again.

In crossing the bay, we asked Holstead, why these

natives, in their own country, were so terrified at
the approach of strangers; he informed us that they
were the remains of tribes who had been destroyed
by a powerful nation called Zoolas, whom I shall
hereafter have occasion to describe;—that they were
even to this day subject to great persecution,
and abode in the forests, as we found them, in
order that they might with greater facility make
their escape in the event of being disturbed. Their
cattle had been taken from them, and they were
often destitute of the means of subsistence. Were
it known that they possessed even corn, the Zoolas
would destroy them to obtain possession of it,
consequently, they seldom planted any, but sub-
sisted chiefly on fish, and such esculents as grew
spontaneously in the vicinity of their residence. At
sunset we reached our miserable abode.

10th. Our crew were engaged in securing every
thing that could be obtained from the wreck: this
occupied them several days, and we were fortunate
in collecting many articles of copper that afterwards proved to us inestimable. I experienced for
two or three days considerable indisposition, and was
necessarily confined to the only mattress we had saved.
On the 14th, at sunset, we were most agreeably
surprised by the appearance of John Cane, Mr.
Farewell's carpenter, who had left the dwelling of
Chaka, the Zoola chief, four days before, a distance

from our residence of about 120 miles. He brought with him a number of cattle, and gave us the pleasing intelligence that Mr. Farewell was on his way home.

15th. In the afternoon, Mr. Fynn arrived from the country of the Amampoatoes, a tribe inhabiting the banks of the St. John's River, a distance of about 200 miles from Natal. This gentleman had been trading with the natives, and had collected a great quantity of ivory. For eight months he had separated himself from his solitary companion, Mr. Farewell, and had associated solely with the people with whom he sojourned. We sat attentively to hear him detail his adventures—the many vicissitudes he had endured, and the obstacles with which he had contended, not only in having been often without food, and ignorant where to seek it, but in daily terror of being destroyed by wild animals, or massacred by the savage natives. He had from necessity assumed the costume of the latter while with them, but resumed his own on his return to his habitation. It is almost impossible to convey a correct idea of the singular appearance of this individual when he first presented himself. Mr. Fynn is in stature somewhat tall, with a prepossessing countenance. From necessity his face was disfigured with hair, not having had an opportunity of shaving himself for a considerable time. His head was partly covered with a crownless straw hat, and a tattered blanket, fastened round his neck by means of stripes of hide, served to cover his body, while his hands performed the

office of keeping it round his " nether man;" his
shoes he had discarded for some months, whilst every
other habiliment had imperceptibly worn away, so
" that there was nothing of a piece about him." He
was highly beloved by the natives, who looked up to
him with more than ordinary veneration, for he had
been often instrumental in saving their lives, and, in
moments of pain and sickness, had administered to
their relief. About a hundred had attached themselves
to him, so much so, that they were inseparable. He
apprehended no danger from such an intimacy, but
rather thought it a security, and that it relieved him
from the anxiety which at first harassed him.

16th. Proceeded to the head of the Bay with
Lieut. King. On our way we saw several hippopotami, basking in the sun, on sand banks surrounded
by water. We fired at them, without making any
impression; but the dog, whose exploit I have before
detailed, barked, which induced them to plunge into
the water. For twenty minutes we saw nothing of
them; they, however, appeared again on its surface,
and, after blowing and inhaling a little air, disappeared, by plunging into their favourite element.
We were alarmed for the safety of our dog, which
had fearlessly swam off towards these amphibious
monsters; he, however, returned to us in safety. The
next day being Sunday, Lieut. King as usual read
prayers, and we otherwise "kept holy the sabbath day."

18th.—This day we were visited by a Zoola chief

named Enslopee, who resides in the vicinity of our
abode, and who had been commanded by Chaka (his
king) to offer protection to the white people against
the remains of a conquered tribe of Bushrangers
scattered in the vicinity of our habitations. This
was, however, a mere pretext for watching our proceedings, not from any motives of a friendly kind.
Indeed, whenever the natives spoke of us it was
always with reproach. They called us "Silguaners,"
or beasts of the sea, and whenever they pronounced
this term, it was accompanied with a gesture of
opprobrium that could not be mistaken. for kindness,
for they

> Grinn'd horribly, a ghastly smile,

and excited terror, rather than appeased our apprehensions. Their motives for not destroying us, will
hereafter be made evident.

Enslopee appeared to be a good humoured sort
of a fellow, and was something of a mimic; he
amused us by many grotesque descriptions, and
ludicrous distortions, for which his countenance, not
unlike that of the baboon, was peculiarly adapted.
He did not appear to want any portion of native
address, but was very ready in extolling his king,
and in endeavouring to impress us with a sense
of his master's friendly designs. With no little
adroitness at flattery, he evinced a desire to imitate
my friend Lieut. King, whom he described as having
a bold and a commanding appearance, declaring that

he only required a black face, and an "umptcher *,"
instead of clothes, to qualify him for a Zoola warrior.
We knew well what he designed by this,—that he
only desired to obtain from Lieutenant King clothes
similar to those he had on; with these the latter soon
furnished him: upon which he became so enamoured
with the present, that he actually forgot the object
of his mission, and absolutely left us in admiration,
exclaiming that his wives would admire him in his
new attire, and that he could now show them what a
" Maloonga," or white man was like.   I accompanied
him across the plat, when he entreated me to visit
him at his kraal, (situated on the eminence before
mentioned, as commanding a fine view of the bay
and the ocean,) which I promised to do, and afterwards redeemed my pledge.

His kraal was similar to the one I had before seen,
and his hut like those of the natives generally.   I
crept into it in a horizontal position, when he assembled his wives, ten in number, who, by their gestures,
appeared to have some difficulty in determining which
pleased them the most, their singularly accoutred
husband, or myself laughing at his grotesque appearance.   The females were far from being ill-shaped
or forbidding; their dress, to be sure was not well
adapted to exhibit their persons attractively, being
nothing more than a piece of prepared hide tied round
the waist, and hanging to their knees.   Their

* A piece of hide, so fastened as completely to cover the hips.

heads were shaven, with the exception of a small tuft on the crown. Some of these tufts were of an oval shape, and some round, but all were besmeared with red clay and grease and designed to imitate rows of beads.

Enslopee made signs indicating his desire that I should point out the prettiest, which I did, when the sable damsel, in an exceedingly modest manner bent her head to the ground, while he, and the other females, put their hands over their mouths, as if surprised at my choice, although I understood that it was congenial with their own. The eldest of the females disappeared, but soon returned with an earthen vessel containing milk, which was thick and sour. She set it before me, and made me to understand from taking a wooden spoon, and eating a little, that it was intended as a refreshment for me. Although I was not indisposed for something palatable, I could not partake of the fare my sable hostess had so kindly offered me. The chief perceiving me disinclined to indulge in the repast thus provided, grasped the vessel, gave the females a small share, and with gestures that would have made a stoic smile, in a trice disposed of the remainder, to the no small astonishment of my comrades and myself. I now left the chief to his domestic enjoyments, and returned home.

CHAPTER III.

20th.—This being a fine day, I took the dogs
and rode for some distance on an ox, (which the
lad Holstead had broken in) and saw various birds,
such as the wild turkey, wild geese and ducks,
and others of a smaller kind. As their solitary
·abodes had not been much invaded by the sportsman,
they disregarded me, until I advanced near them,
when they took flight, but did not appear to go far.
The dogs started several deer, of a brown colour,
which darted through the high grass with great speed,
and I soon lost sight of them in the thickets of the
forest. The dogs quickly returned from the chase;
one belonging to Mr. Farewell had been severely
wounded, being covered with blood. I was then told
that the forest was infested with panthers and leopards,
which, until I saw the dog, I had forgotten; I therefore without much hesitation made a retrograde movement, to which my stubborn ox offered no opposition;
and the apprehension excited by the immediate vicinity of wild animals in a short time subsided.

At midnight we were awakened by the report of a gun; concluding this to be the one with which the wolf trap was charged, we arose, expecting to find one of these prowling marauders, suffering the punishment of his temerity: but we were all most agreeably surprised, for, instead of finding a wolf in the trap, we met Mr. Farewell in the kraal, who had fired his gun to announce to his people that he had arrived.

Anxious to see his old friend and companion, Lieut. King, of whose arrival in the interior he had heard, he travelled during that day from Ootoogale, a distance of eighty miles; and he had moreover been only two days on his journey from Gibbedack, the residence of Chaka. We congratulated each other at meeting in these inhospitable regions.

The meeting of two friends, under circumstances of so peculiar a nature, could not but be interesting to those who were witnesses of the scene; and the joy beaming in their countenances, was too evident to admit of a moment's doubt, that the principals participated in the gratification which their dependents manifested. For my part, I could not conceal those impulses which so sudden and unexpected an event usually excites; and the tear of pleasure involuntarily flowed as I witnessed the outpourings of unaffected joy at this happy meeting.

Although greatly fatigued, before we retired, Mr. Farewell gave us a brief detail of his journey to the residence of the Zoola monarch, as well as an account of the latter's cruelties to his subjects, and his hospitality to white people. He conjured us to be particularly cautious not to make it known that our vessel had been wrecked; but to state that we had been despatched by the government of the Cape in search of him, (Mr. F.) and his party; Jacob his interpreter and follower, having given Chaka a brilliant account of the Cape authorities, and of the extraordinary power of the nation to which we belonged. After having heard these little details, we retired to our respective places of repose; but, reflecting on the past, and predicting future difficulties, I was not disposed to sleep, and passed the night without much tranquillity.

The account I had heard of Chaka, and of his execrable propensities, raised in me apprehensions of no ordinary magnitude, which were greatly increased, when I considered the little chance we had of effecting our escape from so inhuman a monster. If indeed we should effect it, the period of its accomplishment must be protracted to a distant period. Every thought, every sound, seemed to encourage my forebodings, until

Grey eyed morn began to peep,

followed by the glorious sun in all his grandeur, diffusing his influence over the native wilds. I arose and made every effort to shake off the gloom with which I had been overcome, and which the lowing of the cattle, and the apparent joy of the herdsman numbering his flock, contributed in some degree to dissipate. I went forth and looked around, examined the quality of the soil, turned up a little, minutely calculated its capabilities, and concluded that the industry of man might make it fruitful. I determined on cultivating a space, as it might tend to alleviate the pangs of a pensive hour, and add a little in time to our scanty means of subsistence.

After breakfast, being provided with some seeds and tools, by Mr. Farewell, I set to work, attended by a few native boys, whom I endeavoured to teach to use the pick-axe and hoe, but who, not being gifted with very quick comprehensions, made but poor use of their tools, and seemed more to enjoy looking on than working, at the same time expressing their admiration of the " Maloonga," or white man's strength.

23rd.—To day, Mr. Farewell gave the natives, who brought him ivory, a cow for a repast. They slaughtered the beast with surprising dexterity, by means of a sharp pointed spear, which they plunged immediately behind the animal's shoulder blade; it instantly fell and expired. The tail was in a moment cut off, and became an object of contention. Some of them, having previously sharpened their short spears, began to skin the animal, which was soon effected, and the entrails, which I thought would become food for the dogs, were divided, their contents having been previously abstracted, when they were devoured by the people with surprising eagerness. Some of the most offensive parts, however, were burnt over a fire, which the boys had prepared for this purpose, while the men were engaged in preparing the flesh for dressing.

Towards evening they had consumed the whole of the cow, with the exception of the skin and bones; the latter became the property of the boys, as their share of the repast. The whole of them at this time began to sing and dance, after their wild and savage custom, (which was far from being either amusing or attractive,) continuing until a messenger arrived to say, that Jacob was about to kill Enslopee the chief of this district. This separated them; and each taking his spear or club, ran off exultingly to join in the affray. Mr. Fynn, who spoke the native tongue fluently, and who had a good deal of influence with the natives, followed, and prevented Jacob from carrying into execution his bloody design. The chief, whose countenance, even in the moment of joy, was never prepossessing, exhibited features with an expression scarcely human. His eyes rolling, his mouth extended across a face which none would envy, and in the attitude of fear, his tout-ensemble did not ill resemble the figure we have seen representing the "prince of evil." Jacob, like another Bobadil, was brandishing his spear, and ready to kill his man, but wanted courage to make the attempt. Mr. Fynn appeased the latter, and the fear of the former diminished when Jacob told us the cause of their nearly mortal strife.

It appears, that Jacob had become enamoured of Enslopee's sister, and had sent three head of cattle to "Lololer *," when it was understood, that the girl was to have been sent by the persons who drove the cattle. The girl was subsequently given to Jacob, and in time presented him with a pledge of their love.

25th.—The whole of this day was attended with heavy showers of rain. We were, however, busily engaged in making preparations for a visit to Chaka, king of the Zoolas. Out of the things saved from the wreck, we were enabled to select a tolerable present. Lieut. King prepared to accompany Messrs. Farewell and Fynn to see the Zoola Chief. I was anxious to join the party, but it was necessary that some one should remain in charge of our premises, to prevent that plunder which would otherwise have ensued, the vice of thieving among the natives having, as in a other countries, made considerable progress, and they being great adepts in the skill of abstracting.

* A remuneration for the loss of the girl's services, as the sister is considered to be property.

CHAPTER IV.

On the 26th of October at day-break Messrs. King, Farewell, and Fynn were ready to proceed, but wishing to make an imposing appearance before the Zoola sovereign, and not finding a sufficient number of people to carry their luggage, they were detained some time. At ten o'clock, however, my friends with two seamen and forty natives, were in motion. I accompanied them to the banks of the Umgani, where I took my leave of them, returned to my home, and employed myself in drying such clothes as had been washed on shore from the wreck, and brought to us by the natives.

The next day one of the natives arrived, and informed me that the first night the party had reached a small kraal to the north east of the river Umtangartie, a distance of about twenty-five miles, and that the sailors, being out of their element, were much fatigued by the journey.

From the absence of my principals, I was considered of some importance, and the natives, hearing that I was left in charge of Mr. Farewell's establishment, became intrusive and annoying, to which I submitted with as little appearance of uneasiness as possible.

The " Coptai," or chief of Mr. Fynn's kraal, came to report that one of the men was ill. The kraal being at some distance, I rode a pack ox and, accompanied by faithful Rachel, proceeded to visit the sick man, and, if possible, to administer relief. After travelling about two miles, we reached his abode, when an object presented itself which might have been mistaken for anything but a human being. A tall figure, with a head and neck longer than his body, and greatly disfigured by disease, sought relief from the " Malonga," or white man. It appears that he had been afflicted with a sore throat, which rendering him unable to swallow, they had used decoctions and other applications, to reduce the swelling, and had also resorted to a practice prevalent among them in all diseases of the human frame. In the present instance it had caused my patient to become the frightful object he exhibited. Several incisions had been made in the diseased part, with a view of extracting the blood, which operation is performed by applying a bullock's horn to the place where the incision is made, when the "inyanger," or native doctor, sucks the blood through it until he has got a mouthful; this he discharges, then fills his mouth again, and so on successively, until he has extracted blood enough. Should the blood not flow freely, the affected part is beaten with a stick;

this part of the operation they had freely tried in the present instance. All the old female natives evinced considerable concern at the patient not being able to eat, and, by their supplicating gestures, made strong entreaties for me to administer some relief, with which I complied.

I directed them to make some chicken soup, and give him while I returned home to examine my medicine chest which I had recovered from the wreck, when I sent a dose of salts, with directions to give it to the man. The following morning I visited him again, and rubbed his neck with a soap liniment, then tied a piece of a red woollen shirt round the diseased part. This operation and the attraction of the bandage had a novel effect on the bye-standers, who afterwards, as well as my patient, had great confidence in my skill, and faith in my prescriptions. My patient appeared to be recovering, and he himself thought so, when I received the flattering designation of " Malonga" doctor. But alas ! after all my rubbing, after all my embrocations, liniments, and inward applications, —my patient died ! and like his forefathers, his corpse was dragged to the side of the distant jungles; where it was left as a bonne bouche for the hyenas.

Nov. 1st.—This day I went with a few of the natives in search of native fruit, of which I had seen a good deal in various places. I found three kinds, all differing in appearance and flavour, as well as the shrub or tree that bore them. One sort was produced on a small twig of a slender form, which spread itself on the ground not unlike the branches of the vine; its fruit was similar in shape to the pippin; being mellow, somewhat acid, and stringy, with a thin skin. The other grew on a vegetable resembling the melon plant: this fruit was encompassed with a hard shell, the inside containing small stones of an oblong shape, covered by a soft and pleasantly tasting spongy substance. The third, which the natives called armatingoola, grew on the thorn tree, which throws out a white blossom exceedingly pretty; its fruit resembles in shape the European plum; its skin is thin, and it contains a great number of seeds. This fruit the natives consume with great avidity in their incursions where there are no kraals; it also makes a very rich and agreeable preserve.

At this period Mr. Hatton, and the crew of the wreck, took up their abode at the spot selected for building the vessel, designed for our escape: it was, of course, contiguous to the water, and in the vicinity of timber suitable for the purpose. This spot was named Townshend, after Lord James Townshend. It was, however, rather a dangerous spot for such a service, but being the only one which afforded timber, it was consequently fixed on, although greatly infested with panthers and leopards, one of which latter carried off our Newfoundland dog, a loss we greatly regretted, as he had been a faithful and watchful attendant, and had saved several seamen from being drowned.

Nov. 6th.—This day I proceeded to visit a native chief, named Mataban, accompanied by Messrs. Hatton and Norton with Ogle who was anxious to go. The tribe of which Mataban was chief, had been subdued by Chaka, but having rallied the remains of it, with them he had sought a settlement between the forests, where they took refuge from the incursions of the Zoolas. The innumerable persecutions to which they had been subjected by their more powerful and sanguinary neighbours had tended to render them timid and apprehensive. On the approach of strangers they would flee with their valuables into the innermost recesses of the forest; where they would seclude themselves until an opportunity occurred for emerging from their concealment. It was not therefore until after the lapse of some time, that the Europeans became acquainted with their neighbours; but when their retreat had been discovered, and the discomfited chief had seen the difference between the assurances of our party, and the predatory visits of his oppressors, he was not long in determining on a friendly alliance with us, and on living contiguous to our kraal. Our presence gave them confidence, and they became tranquil. They resumed their wonted avocations, and their cattle had their care without any fear of being disturbed. They looked up to us for protection, and solicited our aid in case of surprise; they were nevertheless subject to the laws of the Zoolas, who sorely oppressed them.

The customs of this tribe differed widely from those of their neighbours the Zoolas, particularly with respect to tatooing the face, and other incisions on the body. The Zoolas, contrary to what has been said of them by visiters who have written from report, do not tatoo the face. The tribe of Mataban, on the contrary, perform that operation, together with another more singular; they cut off the first joint of the little finger from the right hand of their children, to make them, as they say, grow up strong and brave.

Mataban is a tall athletic man, about six feet three inches high; active and muscular, and capable of considerable exertion. He is the only one of his tribe who possesses cattle. His tribe live principally on fish, which they catch in a peculiar manner, by enclosing square places in the water, into which they put pieces of the entrails of animals :—at high water the fish swim over the tops to obtain the food, and on the water declining are entrapped. In this way they secure large quantities, and are extremely fond of it. Indian corn, too, they use, which is prepared by soaking it in warm water as in other parts of the tropics; on these, with esculents and animal food occasionally obtained, they usually subsist in winter. Corn and monkeys, which they consider a great delicacy, is their summer food.

After walking round the kraal, we returned to our boat, and, on crossing some corn fields, gathered a head or two, which one of the natives perceiving, he ran towards us with his spear and forbade our plucking any more. Ogle, who understood him, took his spear, and on threatening to chastise him, he flew to the forest without his weapon. We afterwards ascertained that the poor fellow was impelled to remonstrate with us from a sense of duty, the laws of Chaka being severe against any one gathering corn without the king's permission, or until he himself had commenced cutting. This is a severe law, and injurious to the natives, who are deprived of the gratification which the green corn affords them, and in consequence of its being obliged to stand too long before it is cut, a great deal is often completely destroyed by rot. But on the other hand there is something salutary in this decree; for were there not a preventive against cutting the green corn, the natives, who care not for the morrow, but are satisfied with what the present produces, would consume the greater proportion of their produce in its growing state, and leave but little for that part of the year when they would mostly require it. To gather corn without the king's permission is punished with death.

Towards sunset it blew heavily from the westward, and the tide having receded, we were left between the forest and the bay; but notwithstanding the terrific gusts of wind, rather than remain all night in a position where we were likely to be assailed by panthers, we decided on crossing the frith. After some pulling, we got nearly over the western channel, but, just by the bank, the sea broke over us and filled our boat, obliging us to get out and discharge her contents. After the boat had been three times swamped, and all of us had got completely drenched, we arrived at our abode just in time to escape the rain, which set in heavily.

11th.—This afternoon Lieut. King, with Messrs. Farewell, and Fynn, and party, arrived from their visit to the Zoola chief: they appeared much fatigued, but expressed themselves satisfied with their reception on the one hand, and the pleasure derived from viewing the enchanting scenery on the other. Lieut. King's detail I shall now submit; as it will show my readers that this extraordinary man had already become somewhat familiar with us, at all events it demonstrates that Chaka held us to be individuals towards whom he was induced to extend his protection, and not indisposed to our residing in his country.

" Having collected from the *Mary* every thing we could, and made arrangements for building a small vessel, (which appeared an arduous undertaking, on account of our very limited means, the principal part of the carpenter's tools being lost,) I accompanied Messrs. Farewell, Fynn, and several seamen, with about forty natives, on a journey to King Chaka, of the Zoola nation. On the eighth day, after having travelled about 135 miles through a most picturesque country, and crossed several rivers,

CHAKA KING OF THE ZOOLUS.

London, Published by E.Churton, 26 Holles St.

we arrived at the summit of a mountain, from which
the view was particularly grand and imposing.
We could distinguish the king's residence, and
numerous other kraals, on an extensive plain,
encompassed by a chain of hills.   Shortly afterwards
we came to a brook, where we refreshed, and put
ourselves in proper apparel to meet the king.   At
about eight at night we arrived at the entrance of his
kraal, and were soon admitted.   Afterwards we were
taken to his private residence, and gave the customary
salute of the nation, which, not being answered, was
repeated.   A domestic now informed us, that the
king was holding an en-daba (a council) with his
warriors; we then proceeded in order, and soon discovered his majesty and his court, surrounded by large
fires.   We stood for a few minutes, while the chief
who accompanied us addressed the king relative to
our mission; after this we were desired to advance,
presented our presents, and seated ourselves on the
ground, about six paces from him.   During this
interview his discourse was principally on war, owing
to his enemies being at hand.   However, he soon
permitted us to retire to the huts which had been
prepared for us.   He shortly afterwards dismissed his
people, and retired to his private kraal; we then
received a message, requesting we would wait upon
him there.   Here our reception was very different
from the former; he now cast off his stern look,
became good-humoured, and conversed with us through

our interpreters on various subjects. A large basket
of boiled beef and several earthen pots of milk were
ordered to be placed before us, of which we ate
heartily. After this entertainment we expressed a
wish to retire, on account of being much fatigued,
to which he very readily assented. The following
day we again waited upon him, and found him seated
upon his mat, haranguing his people. We immediately withdrew, and having rambled about the greater
part of this day, in the evening were highly entertained
by his warriors singing war and other songs. At the
king's request we fired a train of powder to show its
effects; and, after several other entertainments, he
retired, expressing himself much pleased.

" The following morning proved excessively hot, so
much so that it was scarcely possible to stir about;
we therefore kept within our hut. The king, however,
feeling no inconvenience from it, sent for our sailors,
and proposed their going with him, and a number of
his people, to hunt the elephant. These men, being
aware of their inability, and having only leaden balls,
prudently declined, saying they could not go without
consulting us. The king desired the interpreter to
tell them they were afraid; this touched their pride
of the insufficiency of our arms (of which we were
equally aware) to destroy such animals. We immediately went in pursuit of them, and soon fell in with
the king, surrounded by his warriors, seated under a
large tree, and from which he had a complete view

of the valley out of which they intended to start the
elephant: we took our station about 200 yards from
him, under a smaller tree, waiting impatiently, yet
dreading the result. Two hours had nearly elapsed,
when a messenger presented to the king the tail of
an elephant, at which they all appeared greatly surprised; he was desired to bring it to us, and say the
white people had killed the animal. As may be
supposed, we could scarcely credit the fact, but
hastened towards the forest to join our people, and
met them almost exhausted; we, notwithstanding,
had the satisfaction of congratulating each other upon
what appeared to us almost a miracle. It appeared
that the natives drove the elephant from the forest
to a plain, where the sailors placed themselves directly
before the animal: the first shot entered under the
ear, when it became furious: the other lodged near
the fore shoulder, after which it fell, and soon expired.
Had this affair turned out differently, we should, in
all probability, have been held in a contemptible light
by this nation, and awkward consequences might have
resulted to the settlement.

"In the evening, at the request of the king, we
joined in their amusements, and could not ourselves
avoid singing: we commenced with 'God save the
King.' On our explaining its literal meaning, Chaka
was highly pleased; in fact, there was nothing but
good humour to be observed in the countenances
of every one present. The party broke up at a late

hour; and, as is usual, in the morning we paid the
king an early visit. We now expressed a wish to
see him in his war dress; he immediately retired, and
in a short time returned attired: his dress consists
of monkeys' skins, in three folds from his waist to the
knee, from which two white cows' tails are suspended,
as well as from each arm; round his head is a neat band
of fur stuffed, in front of which is placed a tall feather,
and on each side a variegated plume. He advanced
with his shield, an oval about four feet in length,
and an umconto, or spear, when his warriors commenced a war song, and he began his manœuvres.
Chaka is about thirty-eight years of age, upwards of
six feet in height, and well proportioned: he is allowed
to be the best pedestrian in the country, and, in fact,
during his wonderful exercises this day he exhibited
the most astonishing activity: on this occasion he
displayed a part of the handsomest beads of our
present.

"While sitting in our hut, at a late hour, we were
aroused by the shrieks of thousands of human voices;
we naturally concluded it was the enemy advancing,
being aware they expected them hourly: the real
cause, however, was soon ascertained,—which was
the death of the king's grandmother, supposed to be
between ninety and a hundred years of age. The
kraal in which she resided was about a mile distant.
Men, women, and children, having cried bitterly for
several hours, there ensued a profound silence; after

which thousands at the same moment commenced a
most doleful song, which lasted a night and the
greater part of the following day. It is said that
this is the only instance ever known of the king
having grieved. To give his majesty an opportunity
of seeing our respect for the deceased, we repaired
to the kraal where the corpse lay; but in consequence
of the excessive heat of the day, and it being surrounded by so many thousand people, with scarcely
a breath of air blowing, we were obliged to retire to
a more wholesome spot.

"To give an idea of the heat, hundreds were carried
away, having actually fainted, and were drenched in
a contiguous brook. The remains of the old lady were
conveyed to a particular spot, where they inclosed
her within a stone wall; an honour which is seldom
paid, except to the chiefs, who are similarly inclosed,
with their heads above ground: the others are
allowed to remain on the spot where they may have
died, unless it happens in a hut; in which case they
are removed a short distance, and in a few hours are
devoured by hyænas or wolves, with which the country
abounds. When a chief of a kraal dies, it is immediately burnt; and the inhabitants remove to an
eligible spot and build another. In consequence of
the death above alluded to, several days elapsed
before we had any communication with the king; at
length he allowed us an interview, when we thought
it best to acquaint him, lest he should hear it through

another channel, that our vessel had sustained some damage, and we were in hopes, in about three months, to get her in order. We were apprehensive he might take advantage of our unfortunate situation, had he known she had been an entire wreck. He expressed himself satisfied, and made the remainder of our stay in his territory tolerably pleasant.

"The day having arrived for our departure, Chaka made us a present of 107 head of cattle; we then took our leave, with a promise of returning as early as possible. On our way to Natal, we found the rivers more difficult to cross than before; in attempting one, my companions nearly lost their lives. Mr. Farewell, in stepping from one rock to another, was carried away by the stream into a most perilous situation: Mr. Fynn, with his accustomed bravery, being near, plunged in, followed by several natives, to Mr. Farewell's assistance; the current carried them all a considerable distance, until they came in contact with a body of reeds attached to the bottom, which caused an eddy: here they remained several minutes to rest, after which they happily succeeded in swimming to the bank. These rivers are infested with alligators, which are constantly destroying the natives.

"On the seventh day after our departure from Chaka, after an irksome journey, we arrived at our residence at Port Natal."

CHAPTER V.

THE account given by Lieutenant King of his journey to the residence of the Zoola king, at once raised in me a strong desire to penetrate a little into the interior, and I embraced the first opportunity of gratifying an anxious disposition to obtain some knowledge of this interesting portion of Africa, which was soon afforded me by Mr. Farewell.

That gentleman having collected a considerable quantity of ivory on the banks of the river Ootergale, required some confidential person to accompany his natives thither for the purpose of bringing it to his residence, for without the controul of authority they would abuse the privileges which the king had conceded to the white people, by wantonly taking the food of the settlers on their way, in cases when they were not offered any. The propensity to steal, so inherent in these natives, is too often practised on the petty chiefs tributary to Chaka, who seldom gave them redress, or punished the offenders. But it excited no favourable feeling towards the white people, and subjected them at times to considerable annoyance. For this purpose I volunteered my services to accompany the party on their journey.

29th.—Being equipped, provided with a fowling-piece, and a few rounds of ammunition, with a couple of loaves of Indian corn bread, at 10 A.M. I set out, accompanied by the youth Holstead, and about sixty natives, for the purpose of conveying the ivory.

I had rather an advantage over my company, for I was accommodated with a horse; he had but one eye it is true, with which he had seen "years a score;" he had two sound legs, and two imperfect ones, and from his appearance had been much accustomed to stumbling, his knees exhibiting indubitable proofs of such a failing. A blanket for my saddle was secured by a canvas belt, fabricated expressly for my journey. My bridle was of the same material, and the work of the same individual: some cord sufficed for reins, and an iron ring as a substitute for a bit. With my Rosinante thus accoutred, I started, elated with pleasing anticipations, and flattered with the importance of my mission. My steed seemed to partake of the joy which pervaded his rider, for he pricked his ears, and displayed a strong inclination to lead our party, proud, perhaps, of conveying so important a personage as the one that bestrode him.

At 11 A.M., we crossed the river Umgani about half a mile from its embouchure; it was about three feet deep, and about a hundred yards across. Its

banks, as far as I could perceive its course, presented
a pleasing and diversified scene; and the country
contiguous exhibited a variety of surface beautifully
interspersed with spontaneous vegetation. We advanced two miles over a country thickly covered with
underwood and jungles, and then approached the
beach where the soft sandy surface rendered the
travelling exceedingly unpleasant and laborious.
We proceeded onwards about eighteen miles, and
arrived on the banks of the Umtungartie, passing
previously two small streams which were closed at the
entrance. We halted for a short time and took some
refreshment, then proceeded again for the Kraal of
the Chief Osingales, where we took up our abode
for the night. Here, in the hut allotted to me for
my repose, the natives, men and women, entered
sans ceremonie, but the girls carefully avoided us;
and thus, as the object of their curious speculation
and surprise, I was obliged to submit to their visits
the whole of the evening.

30th.—Rose early, and pursued our journey as
soon as the heavy dew would permit. Travelled
about fifteen miles through a clear and rich country
of pasturage, and saw several small kraals, and occasional herds of cattle. We reached the residence
of King Magie in time to escape a heavy rain.
His majesty came to see me and behaved civilly.
He was a fine, stout, well-proportioned man, of a
commanding appearance, familiar, but not liberal.

He remained with me some time, when my fellow
traveller Holstead asked him for some food for our
party, with which he furnished us, but not without
reluctance, and then only in the first instance with a
little milk; but Holstead knowing the customs of
the country demanded a cow to kill, asserting that
we were on the king's business; this he could not
give us, but sent us a quantity of corn with which
our party made a hearty meal. I was obliged to do
as they did, and partook scantily of that which they
had prepared. I was amused with the chief's daughters,
seven of whom came to my hut, and remained
some time with me, until I indicated a wish to repose.

December 1st.—After a refreshing night's rest,
we arose and started on our journey. The sun beamed
on us warmly, and we found it advisable to halt
occasionally under the shade of the surrounding
foliage. We saw numerous herds of cattle as we
advanced, and several kraals on each side of our
line of march. We crossed the rivers Mafote and
Nondote; the latter is greatly infested with alligators, but we forded it safely and without seeing
one of them, though recently two of the natives
had been carried off by them in the act of crossing
one of its fords. We reached Tas' kraal about 4
P. M., having travelled about forty miles through a
highly picturesque country that presented many
interesting changes on its surface. The river Ootoo-

gale could be distinctly discerned from this place, and added considerably to the effect which the whole expansive scenery had created.

Tas the chief of this kraal had been formerly a king, but having been subdued by the Zooloos, had sunk into a tributary chief to that nation. He was remarkably liberal and hospitable, giving us corn, milk, and a few sweet potatoes; I partook of the latter with some eagerness, and made the only palatable meal I had eaten from the time I started from home.

2nd.—Commenced collecting the ivory which lay in this vicinity, and sent it off by the natives reserving six to accompany me. Crossed the Ootoogale, or Fisher's River. This river although very large is not navigable; in the rainy season it is impassable from the irresistible torrent of water that rushes down from the interior. For some distance from its embouchure the side rises twenty feet; it is infested with innumerable alligators and hippopotami. The former are destructive to human life, and take off many of the natives who are obliged to cross this stream. The banks of the river are exceedingly high, but the soil in its neighbourhood displays its richness in the verdure which every where abounds. Large and valuable timber grows on its margin, and altogether impresses the traveller with a favourable opinion of its neighbourhood for settlements.

Proceeding on, we passed several small kraals,

and saw in different directions herds of cattle indulging in luxuriant pasturage, and after ascending two or three hills of no great altitude we reached Moyarkee kraal. To the nation of this chief, Chaka the Zooloo king is indebted for his throne, and for those many conquests which I shall have occasion hereafter to detail. He received me quite friendly and gave me a bullock to kill, which afforded me a welcome repast, being the first animal food I had tasted from the hour of starting. His kraal was extensive, being about a mile in circumference, and comprising within it about four hundred huts, besides the palace of the chief and its appendages. Young females were numerous here, very pleasing, and tolerably good-natured. Cattle were also plentiful, and I saw several sheep, the first I had seen in the country.

3rd.—Commenced travelling this morning very early—the-chief accompanied me a short distance, appearing to be attracted more by my horse than any thing else; he wished to see it gallop in which I humoured him, after which he returned. I proceeded with as much rapidity as I could during the coolness of the morning. We passed two large kraals at no great distance from our course—crossed the river Armanticoola or Great Water, and proceeded afterwards over a fine, and apparently a richly productive plain, until we reached a small kraal, where we halted a short time to take refreshment. The course we pur-

sued lay over a mountainous country, and the sun
was declining, when I was informed that the residence
of Chaka was not more than three miles in advance.

We halted on the banks of a small stream to bathe,
and otherwise to prepare ourselves for entering the
capital of this barbarous sovereign. Our guide sent a
messenger to announce our approach, who shortly
returned with a request from his majesty, that we
would hasten our advance as much as possible. It
was not long before we arrived at the entrance to
the imperial kraal. It being dark, however, we could
not perceive much of its extent; from the great noise
which the people made by their shoutings, we concluded at the moment they were numerous. As we
walked on through the kraal we observed a great
many fires, round which the people were regaling.
It had a pleasing appearance, and relieved my apprehensions, which arriving at night had raised.

We now reached the head of the kraal, where a multitude of the natives had congregated and were seated
in the form of a half circle. Chaka sat by himself on
a large mat rolled up. Our natives saluted him after
their manner, and I did the same, according to our
European custom, and then took my seat among his
people about twenty yards off. He desired me to
approach him, which I did, when he immediately asked
me how Mr. Farewell was, whose people we were,
and if I had any knowledge of the Portuguese,
mentioning that he had a Portuguese with him; at

my expressing a wish to see him, Chaka sent for the
individual, and I was soon most agreeably surprised
to see a European in this wild and unfrequented
place. The king desired me to go away, and not
understanding him I was led about like a child. As
his orders must be instantly obeyed, my interpreter
had no time afforded him to explain the object of my
visit, he therefore pulled me about from one place
to the other, like a man confused and apprehensive.
My natives all appeared alarmed as they approached
the king, who sent for me again and presented me
with a piece of paper, on which he had made some
marks; these I was directed to decipher, but not being
competent to do so, and my interpreter not being
a very profound translator, we made but a sorry
figure, and Chaka turning towards his people said,
" he does not understand the ungnorty," or the letter,
and they replied, " Yubo Barlu," or, yes father we
see it. He then asked the Portuguese, who, as may
be expected, was as incapable of expounding his
hieroglyphics as myself. After amusing himself at
our expense for some time, he directed us to retire
to the hut, where the Portuguese had some ribs of
beef, on which I made a sorry meal, not because I
had not an appetite, but from the peculiarity of my
situation, for we could not converse nor administer
to each other any consolatory hopes of a more pleasing
interview than the one just witnessed. I ascertained
from my Portuguese inmate, however, though perhaps

employed by his government in some military office, that he had arrived there for the purpose of purchasing cattle. We then retired to our mats to repose, and to which kind of rest I had now become accustomed.

4th.—This morning I offered to his majesty the presents I had brought with me, consisting of twelve brass bangles and a bottle of sweet oil, the value of which he would be able to estimate when applied to bruises and swelled parts of the flesh. He desired me to rub his leg with some of it, an honour to which none but his subjects of rank are admitted; and during my performance none of his people dared advance to within twenty yards without danger of his displeasure. While thus engaged the Portuguese came up, whom he asked, " who were the greatest warriors," when he replied, that the English had subdued all the powers on the other side of the great water. I was apprehensive that this compliment to the gallantry of my country might incense Chaka, and lead him to fear that we might next attempt to subdue him; but to my great enjoyment he felt otherwise, and said to his people about him, " King George's warriors are a fine set of men, in fact, King George and I are brothers; he has conquered all the whites, and I have subdued all the blacks."

He asked me if " King George was as handsome as he was;" I told him, by way of flattering him, that I thought not. He then asked me to fight with the Portuguese, but I told him that, although our nation

had conquered the Portuguese, we were now not only
at peace with them, but were by treaties their pro-
tectors, and that were we to fight in our present
situations, it might be the cause of disturbing the
good understanding existing between the two countries.

"Well," said he, "what need you care? You have
once conquered, and may conquer again." My Portuguese new acquaintance sat all this time and heard
our conversation with concealed chagrin, and swelling
with rage; but when we had left the presence of
Chaka, we both laughed at the vanity of the savage.

I walked round the kraal, which is called "Gibbe-
Clackee," or "drive the old people out," from a ferocious act of this chief's, who murdered all the old men,
saying, "they were of no use as they could not fight."
We saw here a great number of persons called
Umpugarties or warriors, whose aspect was wild
and forbidding.

The circumference of the imperial kraal I should
think would exceed three miles, and it includes within
its space about 1400 huts. The king's palace, which
is situated at the head of the kraal, on an eminence,
comprises about 100 huts, in which none but girls
live, as men are not allowed to enter the palace.

As Chaka ordered me no food, I should have starved
had it not been for the generous Portuguese, who,
having a small piece of beef remaining, kindly shared
it with me. One of the chiefs offered me a pot of

E

thick and sour milk, which is with them a principal article of food. The people were all friendly, but importuned me so much for beads and other things, that it at length became very annoying.

5th.—This morning, the king's servant came to call me to his master's presence. When I approached, the sovereign, addressing his warriors, said, "Cannot you perceive a great difference between the people of King George and the Portuguese?" "Yes," said they, "as much as between us and a bush Caffre." One of the chiefs very kindly telling Chaka that I had taken nothing, and must be in want of food, he ordered a cow to be caught for myself and party.

Three boys came with water, carrying it over their heads with their arms extended, which I perceived was the usual way they bore everything to the king. One held a broad black dish before him, while another poured in water for his majesty to wash, and a third stood ready with a further supply in case of need, holding it in the position before described, without daring to put it down.

Chaka, while bathing from head to foot, conversed with his people near him. After this was concluded, another attendant came, bearing a basket, which he presented to the king at arm's length. His Majesty took from it a sort of red coloured paste, with which he ornamented, or rather besmeared his body, but kept rubbing until the whole had disappeared. After this another attendant came with some greasy sub-

stance, which the king likewise applied to his body,
over which he rubbed it, and this gave him a fine
glossy appearance.

At this period, a body of natives arrived, about
three hundred in number, every one saluting as he
went on, " Biet tu Barber ;" whilst some would say
also, " Whenua cong Caswa," or " you who are as
large as the world." On a sudden a profound silence
ensued, when his majesty uttered one or two words,
at which some of the warriors immediately rose and
seized three of the people, one of whom sat near me.
The poor fellows made no resistance, but were calm
and resigned, waiting their fate with apparently stoical
indifference. The sanguinary chief was silent ; but
from some sign he gave the executioners, they took
the criminals, laying one hand on the crown and
the other on the chin, and by a sudden wrench
appeared to dislocate the head. The victims were
then dragged away and beaten as they proceeded to
the bush, about a mile from the kraal, where a stick
was inhumanly forced up the fundament of each, and
they were left as food for the wild beasts of the
forest, and those carnivorous birds that hover near the
habitations of the natives.

After this savage execution of the criminals, the
cause of which I could not discover, Chaka having
given orders that his warriors should disperse, retired
to his palace, and I retired to my hut with feelings
not a little excited by a scene which sinks man to

a level with the brute.   Shortly after my departure,
a fat cow was sent to me, which I killed, and,
being somewhat hungry, it was a most acceptable and
timely present, and no time was lost in preparing it
for the table.   In the evening we were sent for by
Chaka, but this monster being more inclined to indulge
in sleep than in talking to us, I first amused myself with
the guards, and then retired to my hut for the night.

6th.—Having been honoured by an interview with
the king of the Zoolas, and not feeling quite so easy
from the exhibition of the day before, I went to take
my leave of him, when he desired me to stay, as he
had no cattle ready to give me.   I therefore returned
to my hut.   At noon a servant came to summon me.
I proceeded to the royal presence, and found the
king sitting outside his palace, with a number of the
natives round him, near a drove of cattle which
belonged to the wretched victims who had been so
brutally sacrificed the previous day.   He gave me
twelve head, and, happening to observe Mr. Farewell's
dog, which had accompanied me, he desired me to
leave it.   I told him the dog was a favourite one of Mr.
Farewell's, and that were it not to return with me,
that gentleman would be highly incensed.   He, however, detained it, and gave me two oxen for it.

I took my departure from the imperial kraal, and
journeyed on my return until we reached the residence
of Chaka's servants, about fifteen miles, when we
halted for the night.   The wolves were so numerous

that my horse narrowly escaped being eaten by these nocturnal prowlers. At this kraal we saw a number of young girls who belonged to the seraglios of the king.

7th.—I arose early this morning, being desirous of making a rapid and lengthened march, for the purpose of getting the sooner home; but my guide mistook the pass. This impeded our progress exceedingly; in fact, although we travelled a great distance, our advance was not more than twenty miles.   At sunset we reached a kraal near the river Amaticoola, where I purchased three goats for three small strings of beads. Here I passed the night, but most uncomfortably, from the rats and mice having evinced a great taste for gnawing my feet.

8th. — As the dew fell heavily during the night, travelling early was neither pleasant nor advisable. We waited, therefore, until the sun began to shed its influence a little; after which, we commenced the day's march, and at noon forded the Ootoogale. Feeling languid and disposed to eat, we killed a calf, and made a fire on the margin of the river in order to cook a portion of it, which we accomplished, and I sat down and partook of it with a zest that none but the hungry can enjoy. At three P. M. we again proceeded, soon crossed the river Nondotee, and reached the kraal of Nongasis, where we remained for the night.

9th.—We set off this morning early, and, after travelling about five miles, my horse, which had hitherto performed his journey prodigiously well, fell sick, and could not proceed. He seemed to have been attacked similarly to the animals about Graham's Town in the colony of the Cape. The poor thing first staggered, then foamed from the nostrils, and was soon covered with a continued lather; after which he dropped, and I was compelled to leave him.

I was at this time about sixty miles from my residence, and had only an old pair of shoes to walk in, which was as painful as walking without any. As necessity on this occasion made me a pedestrian, so it also drove me to every shift to get on as easily as possible. It was a hot day, I had tender feet, and the road was at times strewed with thorns, when we approached near the thorn-bush jungles. I, however, discarded my shoes, for I could not walk in them with greater ease than the poor pilgrim who was doomed to do penance by walking with peas in his. Every now and then, therefore, I was obliged to submit to the operation of extracting thorns from my feet, by operators not the most skilful in the world, though occasionally expert. After having extracted them, they tried to induce me to put the offending thorns into my mouth, and chew them, as a charm against future inflictions, which they averred would prove effectual. Their superstitious customs, however, I heeded not

on this occasion, and in a few minutes I had another
cause of conviction of their inefficacy, when my
attendants, with astonishment and the most imper-
turbable gravity, attributed a second misfortune to
my inexperience in travelling. Their feet, unaccus-
tomed to the shield of a shoe or sandal, are proof
against any substance, however hard or sharp; they
are, in fact, as impenetrable as horn. I travelled in
a most painful plight about ten miles, and reached the
chief Magie's kraal, where we halted for the night.
Soon after my arrival, my young friend, Magie's
daughter, with her usual sympathy and kindness,
brought me a pot of thick sour milk, a part of which
I ate, and thought it palatable.

10th.—Having heard that Magie possessed a unicorn, or, as the natives described it to me, " In yar
mogoss imponte moonya," "An animal with one horn,"
I had a great desire to see it. From my imperfect
knowledge of the language, and not wishing Holstead
to hear of it, lest he should purchase it, I misunderstood
the nature of the animal; but being unusually eager
to obtain so great a natural curiosity, I set out early
to another of Magie's kraals, to see the chief; here
I met him and communicated to him the object of my
journey. He confirmed what I had heard, and by
singular gesticulations and attempts at description, he
led me to comprehend that it was about three feet high,
and, from his taking my hair and pointing to it, I
understood that it had a flowing mane, he at the same

time exclaiming, " mooshly garcoola," which I knew
meant " very handsome." The more he particu-
larised this animal, the more my anxiety to possess
it increased, conceiving that I might attain some cele-
brity among naturalists, if I should be enabled to
produce the wonderful creature known only, like the
mermaid, to have existed in fable. To be the owner
of the " In yar mogoss," was an advantage not to be
lost, and I evinced an eager desire to see it; the chief
however told me it was at another kraal, some distance
in the interior, but that he would order it to be brought
up for me to see it some other time. My anticipations
of acquiring renown among naturalists and men of
science vanished at once into empty air. I gave up
all hopes of obtaining it, although the chief assured
me that he would dispose of it to no one but me.

After this I took my departure, and crossed the
Flats, an extensive plain running parallel with the
coast. At four P. M. we reached a small kraal, where,
feeling myself much fatigued, and my feet exceedingly
sore, I put up for the night. In the evening I was
joined by Enslopee, who had arrived on a visit to the
Cales (Magie's tribe), to make arrangements for a
wife, in which he had been successful, and was about
to return with his new spouse.

11th.—Continued our journey homewards, purchased some curiosities, and arrived much exhausted
at Osengale's kraal, where I met several natives from
home.

12th.—Early this morning I crossed the river Umtungartie, and came out on the beach. The tide being high our progress was greatly impeded, and though suffering severe pain from the state of my feet, I reached the river Umgani, where I bathed, and otherwise refreshed myself. Luckily, on our advance shortly afterwards, we fell in with Mr. Farewell's cattle, from which I took a pack-ox and rode the remainder of my way to our abode. I found all my friends well; they congratulated me on my return, and especially complimented me for my arrangements respecting the unicorn. I could not yet but feel that I was entitled to some little praise for my sagacity in an affair which would, in all probability, crown our adventures with considerable eclat.

I learnt from Lieutenant King, that Mr. Norton and three of the crew had taken our long-boat and put to sea some days before. This reduced our crew to half its strength, besides rendering the labour of building our vessel more difficult, and the time for its completion more protracted.

The reader will doubtless conceive that a journey like that which I had undergone could not have been performed without incurring considerable hazard, not only from the effects of climate and exposure to a tropical sun, but from the conduct of the natives, and the attacks of those ferocious animals which so numerously infest the whole country through which our route lay. Fatigue and hunger, and being barefoot, was enough to appal one; but having an irresistible desire to see the king, and to view the face of the interior, I was not to be deterred by any apprehension of disaster on my way. I was amply compensated for the inconveniences to which I had been subjected, and took no little pride to myself in having, unaccompanied, but by Holstead and a few natives, summoned resolution enough to appear in the presence of a chief, the ferocity of whose character made even his own subjects tremble.

CHAPTER VI.

For two or three days after my return I remained tranquil, to recover from the fatigue I had undergone, and to get my feet somewhat in order. Christmas approaching, we made some little preparation for amusements in Fort Farewell. I felt much disposed to engage in anything that might prevent ennui, and those depressions that would occasionally recur when reflecting on the condition to which we were reduced, and the lengthened period to which our extrication would be unavoidably protracted. I engaged in nothing, therefore, but a little gardening, sometimes hunting or shooting, or making short excursions in the vicinity of our dwelling, until the 31st, the last day of our untoward year, when all the enjoyments of its commencement flashed before me with inconceivable delight, but were soon lost in melancholy solicitude for our future escape from our inhospitable abode.

On this day, Lieutenant King summoned the natives to our dwelling, to dance the old year out

and the new one in.   We had the parties of Umsega
and Enslopee, who exhibited their respective skill in
dancing in opposition.   The two chiefs also displaying their individual qualifications ; one, flattering
himself with a decided superiority over the other,
provoked some little manifestations of anger, which we
prevented reaching to anything of a serious nature.
To obviate this, Lieutenant King directed a bullock
to be killed, which attracted their attention.   They
soon abstracted themselves from the dancing circle,
and eyed the expiring animal with savage anxiety.
On its being cut up and distributed to them, they
ate it raw with such extraordinary eagerness, that
in less than an hour the whole bullock was consumed : the company then returned to the circle
and resumed their dancing.   We gave them two
pails of grog, which they drank with avidity ; at first
it elevated them, but, finally, sank the whole in
slumber.   While the chiefs were asleep, some of
their people awoke and reeled homewards, taking with
them such pieces of the beef as had been hidden in
the grass.   The natives being thus tranquil, our crew
quite characteristically sang the seaman's soul-stirring
song, in which the author, as if to inspire them with
hope of protection from their guardian angel, has
written,

> A sweet little cherub sits smiling aloft,
> To keep watch for the life of Poor Jack.

All having regaled themselves, and the night having

been spent in great harmony and to the amusement of all, we retired, as day began to dawn, to obtain some little repose.

Nothing particular occurred at our residence at Fort Farewell for several weeks, and we employed ourselves variously. From the beginning of the new year, the weather had become exceedingly hazy, at times changing into heavy falls of rain, accompanied with loud peals of thunder and appalling flashes of lightning; we consequently passed most of our time under cover, with the exception of an occasional visit to our dock-yard, to see how our design of building was likely to be effectually accomplished.

February 7th.—Finding to-day that our cattle began to diminish, and that it was requisite to obtain a further supply, and not having means to purchase it, another visit to Chaka was seen to be unavoidable, and I, having a great desire to acquire the Zoola language, determined to accompany Mr. Fynn, who undertook the mission. The figurehead of the brig, which we had saved, and intended to present to the king, together with twenty large neck bangles, were got ready.

9th.—The weather having now the appearance of being settled, we started on our journey. Our party consisted of Mr. Fynn, myself, George, one of our seamen, and some natives. My luggage and accoutrements consisted of a fowling-piece, a few slugs, which answered as a substitute for shot, and a horn of powder, with a mat, a blanket, and a bag of clothes. Being thus equipped we started about ten A.M., soon crossed the Umgani, and proceeded about ten miles across the beach, where we were detained by the tide entering the Umslatee, or rapid river, which rendered it impassable ; we therefore kindled some fires and remained here until low water. At midnight, notwithstanding that the river was then deep, we forded it, although the force of the stream made it hazardous. We succeeded, however, and advanced rapidly until morning, when we arrived at Osingale's kraal, where we halted and refreshed ourselves with some milk and corn.

10th.—The day was beautiful, but having travelled the greater part of the night, we were more inclined to repose than to proceed; we consequently rested for a few hours, after which we resumed our march. Our way being in the immediate vicinity of thorn bushes, and not having any shoes, I was obliged to pick my road, which greatly impeded my progress; we managed, however, before sunset, to reach a kraal belonging to Magie in which we took up our abode for the night.

11th.—The rainy season had now apparently set in, and all the rivers were so much swollen, as to render them impassable. We learnt also that when the Ootoogale was once full, it was usually three months before it became sufficiently low to enable the traveller to ford it. Finding it therefore impracticable to proceed, we resolved to return, and leave our things here until we should be able to prosecute our journey. I desired Magie to send me the unicorn, which he promised to do the following day.

The rainy season in these hot latitudes is exceedingly heavy, and renders all intercourse with the interior quite impracticable, as the torrents which force their way down the large streams carry with them everything in their course, and make those rivers dangerous to ford. In fact, instances of the natives attempting it are not frequent, and when an effort is made by them it is often attended with the loss of life, as nothing can successfully stem the current. If we had pursued our journey to the Ootoogale, it would have rendered a retrograde movement altogether impracticable, as the rivers in our rear in time would have been impassable, in which case we might have been shut out from our friends, and left to seek an abode in the wilds of the forest, subjected to inconceivable danger and privation. To turn back towards our home under such circumstances was nothing more than prudence and foresight suggested.

12th.—As we retraced our steps, nothing worth recording occurred, except that a messenger came to announce the unicorn had arrived. I went unhesitatingly to see it, when lo! this wonderful production of nature, from which I was to derive fame and renown, turned out to be a he goat with the loss of

one of its horns! I predicted the ridicule to which
this circumstance would subject me, and made up
my mind to submit to the sarcasms of my friends
with the same fortitude as I bore the disappointment
of anticipated honours, from the possession of this
wonder of fabled history.

13th.—We pursued our way homewards, but by a
different route from the one we had taken in setting
out. This we did for the purpose of calling at some
hamlets and savannas, in our course, to obtain cattle
and curiosities. We succeeded in getting a few of
the latter, and, after journeying fifteen miles, reached
Osingale's kraal, where we halted.

14th.—Rose at dawn of day and commenced
travelling. Saw several wolves, which retired to
the jungles on our approach, but followed us after we
had passed, making a hideous howling. We made
a stand behind some bushes with the hope of getting an opportunity of firing at them, but they were
too wily, and kept at a distance. They at length
suddenly disappeared, apparently afraid to attack us.
We proceeded until we arrived at the rapid river, which
we had some difficulty in passing. Here we stopped
to rest, and then advanced to the Umgani, taking care
to wait until our natives arrived, so that we might all
cross together, on account of the numerous alligators
that infest this stream. After having forded the river,
we pursued our journey, and early in the evening
reached our residence, not, however, to the astonish-

ment of our friends, for, from the state of the weather, they had anticipated an interruption, and, consequently, looked for our return.

March 16th.—From the inclemency of the season we were confined many days until yesterday, and to-day we proceeded to our dock-yard, which, as before mentioned, we named Townshend; here we found that Mr. Hatton had laid down the keel of the vessel destined to convey us from this coast.

17th.—Some messengers arrived to-day from his Zoola majesty, who had reached the banks of the Ootoogale, requesting that Lieutenant King would send a boat to that river to enable him to cross, for the purpose of paying a visit to our habitations.

18th.—Availed ourselves of this opportunity to obtain cattle, and to show the king our superiority of conveyance over rivers. They are ignorant of the use of boats or canoes, and deem it impossible to cross the Ootoogale when the water is high. We immediately repaired the jolly-boat, and determined to employ natives to carry it thither.

20th.—Having, yesterday, got the aid we required to carry the boat, Mr. Fynn, myself, and George Biddlecome equipped ourselves for the journey. We despatched our natives before with their load, and started ourselves about 11 A. M. Nothing material occurred worth recording; and, in fact, the route being similar to that we had already pursued, we did

not anticipate anything to attract us. Having crossed
the Umgani, and overtaken the natives with the boat,
after a march of nine miles we halted near to a
spring, and remained there for the night.

Towards evening, as the sun disappeared, the whole
horizon was overspread by one dark and dismal
cloud. The wind, which had increased as we advanced,
now began to blow from the westward with some
force, and everything indicated an approaching storm.
We prepared for the worst by erecting a temporary
shelter.   This was accomplished by placing four
muskets on the sand, and raising the boat upon them,
keel upwards, securing it there and round the sides
by means of branches of trees cut for the purpose.
We also kindled fires round us to keep off the wild
animals, the whole of this part of the country being
infested with leopards, panthers, and hyenas. We
had no sooner seated ourselves in our newly constructed hut than the "pitiless storm" gave vent to
its fiercest rage. The thunder crashing in awful
peals, and the lightning incessantly spreading on the
surface before us, made our situations at the moment
far from being enviable. The rain also came down
in torrents and put out our fires, when the hyenas
surrounded us, howling most hideously, and keeping our natives in a state of perpetual apprehension.
The wind began at length somewhat to abate, but the
rain did not diminish, and the sand becoming quite

saturated with water, our boat sank on its pedestals into the sand, and left us to creep out of our temporary shelter the best way we could.

The dawn brought more favourable weather. The wind had sunk, and the rain had ceased; we therefore rekindled our fires, dried our clothes, and prepared to go on. The natives, not having had any repose, could not proceed, so we left them with the seaman George, and directed them to go in search of other natives to assist in the labour of carrying the boat. Having arrived at Osingale's, we made our first meal since we had quitted home, of boiled Indian corn.

22nd.—We waited some time for George and his party, and not hearing of their approach we feared something had happened. On returning to the spot where we had directed them to search for porters, we found that the natives had come there from all quarters to view the boat. They were so attracted and astonished by its ornamental painting, that men, women, and children followed us several miles, not being able sufficiently to satisfy their curiosity and surprise. Although they were thus so much attracted by the boat, nothing could induce them to approach it; nor would any of them step forward to touch it, not even after the strongest assurances from us that it could do them no injury. They persisted that there was some charm in it, which might eventually destroy them.

23rd.—This morning we had inconceivable difficulty in prevailing on the natives to carry the boat:
the sight of it seemed to alarm them. The fear,
however, that Chaka might put them to death, soon
made them exert themselves, and we kept them on
until we arrived at Nongasi's, about twelve miles from
whence we started. Here all the people ran away,
whether it was from the sight of the boat, or from a
disinclination to carry it any further, we could not
determine, but so it was; every one decamped and
left us in peaceful possession of the village. We
were now obliged to proceed to another kraal of
Nongasi's, in order to obtain porters to bring the boat
on. We arrived about sunset, and informed the chief
that his people had left the king's property, and that
we required hands to carry it in the morning. He
was incensed, and said he would send after them
and destroy them all. We thought this was merely
a boast and exhibition of his power to terrify us;
but when we saw him making preparations for carrying his threat into effect during the night, we
began to reason with him on the inhumanity of
killing men for doing that to which they had been
urged by their fears; telling him that the best punishment he could inflict, would be to compel them to return,
and proceed with the boat in the morning. He, however,
appeared inexorable, and persisted in destroying them
to the number of forty men and women, among whom
were his two brothers and five wives; on our telling

him however that such an atrocious act would occasion
the boat to sink in the water, and that our man would
go home if he saw a party arrive to attack the kraal,
he changed his resolution, and said he would send
to let them know, but that he could not suffer his
people to escape for leaving the king's property, as
Chaka would kill him for their bad conduct. We
assured him that Chaka would not hear anything
about it; at which he was pleased, and sent to order
those who had refused, to bring the boat on immediately. He gave us a cow to kill, and plenty of
corn, for which we were thankful.

24th.—The whole party, the natives having come
in, set out at day-break with the boat. After travelling about three hours over a level country interspersed with rich savannas, and diversified with agreeable and frequently striking scenery, we reached the
Ootoogale. The rains had swollen the stream prodigiously, and the impetuosity of the current made it almost
terrific to attempt crossing while the water remained
at such an altitude. The natives were deterred from
making any effort to cross, deeming it impossible.
The appearance of the boat, and the feelings its many
colours had excited, collected the inhabitants from
within a circumference of some miles, who stood
amazed at so singular an object. At noon we launched
the little bark destined first to waft us to the opposite bank of the river; and, secondly, to bear the
sovereign of Zoola to the western extremity of his

dominions. The strange and almost panic-stricken appearance of the natives, when it first buoyantly veered with its head to the stream may be imagined; but it would require a more descriptive pen than mine to pourtray the astonishment depicted on every countenance. Gestures and shoutings, and every demonstration of wonder, was to be seen among the ignorant and amazed concourse of assembled natives. We crossed to and from the opposite margin of the river repeatedly, and each time took several natives who had been detained from the dread of crossing. The moment they had landed, they shouted the war whoop of their tribe, danced with joy, and sang in praise of Chaka, who, they averred, had conquered the demon of the Ootoogale, and had added another glory to his reign. The simple and ignorant youth of either sex were heard to express their pleasure (from having been witnesses of such an event as that of crossing the water in a boat) at being now older than their forefathers, who had never seen the "great river crossed when it was in wrath."

We now moored the boat to a ponderous stone on the margin of the river, and proceeded to a kraal in the neighbourhood, where we intended to wait the king's arrival. In the evening, however, messengers came to inform us that Chaka had given up his design of visiting us for the present, not wishing to cross the river, but desired that we would proceed to his residence as soon as possible. Although somewhat chagrined at this, and left to conjecture the cause of such a peremptory summons, we determined on proceeding the next morning at as early an hour as possible.

25th.—The dawn had scarcely appeared, ere we accompanied the messengers, taking with us the figure-head, bangles, and medicines which we had prepared. After proceeding a few miles, we were compelled to delay our journey from the very unfavourable state of the weather. Having passed Gomany's kraal and reached Moyarki at one P.M., we halted for the remainder of the day.

In the evening the chief of the place arrived from the king to prepare his regiment for immediate service. He informed us that the enemy (Inconyarner) with whom they were at war had encamped within a day's march of the royal residence, that their force was large, and that he saw four vessels standing to the westward. He gave us a cow for our use, and some milk.

We now began to guess the cause of Chaka's sending for us and for the boat, and experienced some little difficulty in determining how to act. To advance would in all probability, we thought, bring us in contact with the force of the enemy with whom Chaka was at war. To retreat would incense him, and remove the high opinion he entertained of European bravery; we therefore resolved upon proceeding to his capital,—a measure we were induced to adopt

from the impression, that should he subdue his enemies, and should we not have obeyed his command to
visit his residence, he would at once turn his arms
against us, and subject us to every species of mutila-
tion and cruelty; while, on the other hand, we might
calculate on our personal security so long as he main-
tained his favourable opinion of the personal bravery
of Europeans. It rained in the evening incessantly;
this detained us the whole of the following day (Sunday), for which we were not sorry.

27th.—We travelled about six miles to the banks
of the Armanticoola, and found the river impassable;
our passage being likely to be obstructed for several
days at least, we proceeded to another kraal of
Moyarki, where we determined to remain until the
river was fordable. While here a Caffre came to tell
us that our boat had broken adrift from the increased
swelling of the river, and that he and others had been
in search of the boat, but could not discover anything
of her.

We were at this time most critically situated. To
return was impracticable, as the Ootoogale at
this period became impassable for the space of
three months, and should the enemy of Chaka
invade this part of his dominions, we had no
means of escape from the hands of a body of
rapacious savages. In this extremity the weather
favoured us. The rain fell in considerable showers
during the night, and the whole of the following day,

which occasioned every river to overflow its banks. We sent to Moyarka for food, who supplied us with a cow which we killed, and were thus enabled to prepare a hearty repast.

29th.—The weather cleared up a little, but the rivers still continued impassable. At noon we were surprised to see a single messenger arrive from the king. He had orders to hurry us to the royal kraal. He said that the king had sent him, and two others, three days before; as they attempted to cross the river, one of them was carried away by the force of the current, while the other two had great difficulty in reaching the shore, so as to return to Chaka to apprise him of the impracticability of crossing the stream. On the return of these two to the royal presence, this inhuman despot, in the moment of his rage, felt disposed to kill them, but for once stayed his merciless hand, and gave them their choice either to proceed again and ford the river, or suffer death upon the spot. He ordered another to take the place of him who was drowned, when the poor fellows proceeded, thinking there might be a chance of escaping death in attempting to ford the river, for they knew full well that to disobey would be immediate destruction. All three entered the stream together, but only one succeeded in crossing; the other two were carried off by the impetuosity of the waters. The man who had escaped, after having delivered his message, hurried us to advance, as Chaka was impatiently waiting

for us; stating that if we would not accompany
him, he must return immediately with the medicines,
and find a place which might be fordable further in
the interior.   We decided on accompanying him, pursuing our course inland on the banks of the river; but
the sun, the excessive heat of which was almost over-
powering, made us somewhat listless, and precluded
the possibility of our getting on very fast.   We soon
reached a kraal, into which we entered, and sought
shelter from the insupportable rays of the sun.   Here
we sat down in front of the chief's hut, who after a
short time accosted us roughly, and in rather a peremptory tone bade us proceed, " For," said he, " I
have no food to give you, you had therefore better
pursue your journey."   We told him we did not ask
him for food, neither did we wish him to present us
with any, and that we only sought a momentary shelter
from the sun's oppressive heat.   To this he replied
more peremptorily, " Go, go, it's getting late."   We
were not a little annoyed at the manner and treatment of
this chief, so unlike the Zooloos generally, and therefore resumed our route over a hill, leading to another
kraal, where we found a more hospitable reception.
The chief before alluded to, whose name was Ama-
sellanger, followed us, and on our asking his motive for treating us with so much incivility, as we
were not travelling for our own gratification, but to
oblige the king, who had commanded us to wait on
him, he made no reply, but left us.   Shortly after he

returned, and brought with him a fine fat cow as a peace-offering, and as an atonement for his incivility. He said he did not intend to insult us, and that he hoped we would not mention it to the king. At first we refused to receive the cow, although we were much in want of it, but on his renewing his entreaty that we would accept the animal, our people being in want of food, we did so, and promised him that we should look over his offence this time, but cautioned him against similar behaviour, for the future.

30th.—This morning we proceeded to another branch of the Amanticoola, and finding it also impassable, we returned to Quandalos kraal, where we had passed the preceding night, and where we remained the whole of the following day ; any attempt to ford the river being impracticable.

April 1st.—About 10 A. M., just as the sun was shedding its influence on the dew-covered foliage below, the "inyangers," or water doctors, arrived to take us across the river, which in parts was five feet deep, with a rapid current. It had an appalling appearance. Above us it was somewhat extended, but at the place of our crossing it became contracted, so that the force of the stream had increased to a fearful velocity. Several large rocks whose tops were visible on its surface, invited us to effect a passage by them, but we found that they increased the difficulty, as the current near them rushed by with much greater impetuosity. The bed of the river also had a most uneven surface; large stones, slippery and dangerous to tread upon, were strewed in every direction, making it dangerous to step. With all these formidable obstructions, however, the river doctors selected this place for our passing, because they said the unevenness of the course made it a likely place not for alligators to be found in. It gave us also awful apprehensions that it was never designed for Europeans, or any human beings to attempt to buoy themselves through its fearful and impetuous current.

The natives had congregated on its banks in great numbers, and with eager curiosity to see a white man without his habiliments, that made us smile. The women and girls in particular, were more than ordinarily diligent in scanning our persons on the moment of our stepping into the water. They contended, with some strife, to obtain the best situations for a full and unobstructed view, and in these efforts to maintain the nearest margin of the river contiguous to us, one of the females fell into the stream, and with great difficulty escaped being drowned. During this moment of confusion in securing the female, we entered into the water, having two stout able natives on each side of us, by whom we were supported, and after indescribable difficulty, and being driven against rocks and stones with no little pain and fear, we got safe over. The inyangers from their great muscular power, and experience in their occupation, kept us above the water, which no skill nor exertion of our own could have effected. Our supporters got severe bruises, but they disregarded them, and only asked us for a string of beads to buy medicines.

The females, though somewhat disappointed, hailed us as we crossed the river, and called on us to do as they did; thinking, however, that we might not understand them, they conveyed by gestures what they thought language could not accomplish. Although many of the young females were rather handsome, displaying much symmetry of figure and simplicity of feature, with a tone of voice which indicated tenderness of expression, yet I could not conceal my disgust at their general habits, and quitted the banks of the stream with as much haste as my situation would permit.

From the river we proceeded over a rich and luxuriant plain for about two miles. Nothing could exceed the verdure which spread round the hamlets scattered within its space. The pasturage grew luxuriantly, and the foliage of the mimosa tree rivalled in attraction the beauty of the savannas, on which they grew in great abundance.

On my march, I suffered exceedingly from the thorns entering my feet, but the small and sharp pebbles now began to be equally painful, and impeded my progress greatly. We arrived by a pleasant pass at the base of a steep mountain, which we ascended, and from the summit of it took a view of the surrounding country, as far as the eye could reach. The whole extensive surface was grand and imposing, and I viewed the landscape with sensations of admiration and wonder. During the short time we remained on this spot I could not help indulging in a strain of praise at the works of nature, and the design of Omnipotence. The interior exhibited a happy variety of hill and dale in pleasing undulations, intersected with many beautiful streams, affording a refreshing coolness to the wearied traveller. The round and regular clusters of thriving trees, which seemed as though they had been planted by the labour of man, added considerably to the interest which the whole scene created. At a distance, mountains of unusual magnitude raised their stupendous heads, and occupied a large proportion of the landscape.

As we journeyed over the plain, and at the base of some of the hills, we passed a great many antelopes, which seemed to take no alarm at our approach. We saw some deer also, of a small species, which evinced no desire to evade us. Birds of various kinds were seen as we advanced upon the base of the mountains, apparently of the vulture kind, together with wild guinea-fowls and wild turkeys in abundance.

After travelling some miles, the landscape changed its aspect; instead of a rich loamy soil of great depth, capable of being converted to agricultural uses, we arrived where we found a gravelly soil, without much vegetation. But even here the industry of man, if judiciously employed, might have reaped an abundant harvest. The sun being very powerful greatly incommoded us, and we observed, in a variety of places where the rain had washed off the upper surface of the earth, that a glittering species of mineral was very general, containing apparently some metallic properties. To us it appeared rich with ore, but we were incompetent to ascertain or describe either its value or its character. I was induced to dig about eighteen inches in depth, and found the whole of the ore richly spangled. I put a large quantity into a bag, but could not prevail on the natives to carry it, and found it unavailing to use either threat or persuasion. While in the act of digging, I observed that they looked with astonishment, but I was too much engaged to attend to their remarks. The reason of their stubbornness in refusing to carry the bag of ore, led to an explanation.

Some years back, they had been informed that the natives had dug from the bowels of the earth a mineral which, when melted in their crucibles, turned to a beautiful glossy white, and was worked by them into arm bangles. Before this, they had been accustomed to have them made of iron, with which the country abounds. The chiefs abandoned the black metal, and as badges of distinction between them and their dependents, the former wore the white bangles, and the latter were consequently obliged to wear the black ones.

At this period a number of the chiefs died; the inyangers, angus, wisemen or soothsayers, were ordered to assemble, and immediately discover the cause of their death. Several people were suspected of having administered poison to them, and were all killed without discrimination, or without proof of guilt. The prevailing malady by which the chiefs had been carried off still continuing, and innumerable natives having been destroyed under the impression of being the cause of their death, or being, according to their designation, "Umtugartie," that is, "evil-disposed persons," they decided that the white metal worn by the chiefs was the cause of the death of that class of persons, which put an end to further executions of the innocent. The individuals, however, who had discovered the metal, and those who had fabricated it into bangles, were condemned and executed. The bangles were also commanded to be returned to the earth whence they had been taken, and orders issued that in future no white metal should be dug up, without subjecting the offender to capital punishment.

The poor ignorant natives believed earnestly in the supernatural power of the metal having occasioned the death of the chiefs as had been traditionally related to them; they believed that even walking over it would be fatal; but they ingenuously observed, "as you

are a white man it may not have the effect upon you;
nevertheless it will make our king angry, and, in all
probability, he will order us to be killed for allowing you to dig it." I was, therefore, induced to
throw my prize away, yet determined to avail myself of an opportunity of speaking to Chaka upon
the subject, which I did, but shall revert to this
hereafter.

The sun being now exceedingly powerful, we
sought to shelter ourselves from its oppressive rays
under the foliage of some neighbouring trees, and
halted awhile, so that we might enter the imperial
kraal a little refreshed.

We soon resumed our march. When the abode of his
Zooloo majesty opened upon us, its appearance was
singularly magnificent, and the scenery imposing and
attractive. The kraal was situated on an eminence
forming an oblong square, within a circumference of
about three miles, and partly encompassed by a deep
ravine. The whole was surrounded by high and irregular land, covered with lofty and thriving timber, the
shading branches of which added much to the interest
excited by the landscape.

We were now about three miles from Gibbeduck,
where we stopped to bathe and refresh again. While
we were here, a great number of natives passed to
and from the king's residence; most of them were
crying bitterly, but not one of them would notice our
importunities to know the cause of their grief. We

began to be apprehensive; but on meeting with an elderly man, who stopped to converse with us, he informed us that the sorrow of the people was occasioned by the death of an old chieftain, who had been a great favourite among them.

Apprehending previously that the enemy advancing near might have induced all this sorrow and bustle, but finding it was not so, our fears subsided, and proceeding, we soon arrived at the gate of the kraal. Here we were for some time detained by the crowd of people who were lamenting with hideous sounds and gestures, and whose wild looks greatly discomposed us. We observed a number of people dragged away and instantly executed, for, as we were told, not shedding tears in the imperial presence on such an occasion. Poor wretches were immolated, who perhaps inwardly felt, what they could not outwardly manifest—the want of a tear; that

Tear which they could never shed,

doomed them to feel the inhuman monster's wrath, and to be sanguinarily butchered to appease his savage rage.

It is a barbarous custom among the savage tribes superstitiously to contend that their chiefs cannot die naturally;—that they are destined to live until they fall in battle; and that death, proceeding from age or disease, is occasioned by the power of the Umtugarties. This sanguinary superstition is carried to the fullest extent by Chaka, who, on such an occasion as the death of a chief, endeavours to find out those held to possess the charm, and supposed to manifest it by not being able to shed a tear. Then follows a number of most inhuman massacres; and we had a lamentable proof that these were not confined to a few. After forcing our way through the dense crowd, we met one of the domestics, who informed us that we could not have access to the king, on account of his being in the act of mourning. He pointed out a hut to us, to which, he said, we had better retire, as it was dangerous to appear in the kraal in the present frantic state of the people. As we made our way from the crowd towards the hut, several of the native warriors asked us if we were not afraid of death, and offered us some snuff, which they were forcing up their own nostrils in prodigious quantities. This they generally resort to on all similar exhibitions, and the tears, usually forced from them by the power of the snuff on the olfactory organ, demonstrates their excess of grief on the melancholy occasion.

That the king himself does not feel any loss in the death of a chief, and that he never grieves, were pretty evident to us. The present is merely a usage or barbarous custom, instituted to enforce sorrow on the people for the death of a principal native, and cause them to use every means to protect him and preserve his life, or prevent their having recourse to charms to destroy him. This custom is prevalent among the tribes on the Gold Coast, who practise Obeah, which finally brings the individual, on whom it is practised, to a lingering end. The hideous yelling of the natives continued until a late hour, and we were not without some apprehension of being molested. Several of the people were knocked down in our presence and killed; all the huts were searched, and those found within were forced out to share the fate of those who had been previously killed for not weeping. Our lives were alone held sacred amidst this scene of sanguinary executions, for it appears that a general feeling pervaded the natives, even in the moment of terror and unrestrained massacre, of our being the king's white people, and that our presence was a most favourable omen.

Our ignorance of their customs, was assumed as an apology for our not crying in consequence of the chief's death. It was admitted, indeed, by their wise men, that it could not be expected white men should mourn for the death of a person, for they never killed any one, and being, moreover, ignorant of charms, they could not be suspected of having been accessory to the chief's death.

Such a sacrifice of human life was truly revolting, and made the became painful to us from the alarming position in which we stood. That there should be a spot on the globe disgraced by such inhuman customs is deeply to be regretted, and it is much to be wished that such a dissemination of more civilised notions should be attempted, among the natives of this part of Africa, as may eventually root out these savage and brutal propensities, which deluge the earth with blood, and urge man to prey on man. That something has been accomplished will, I think, be seen by my readers, as they advance in their perusal of these pages, and a final attainment of so desirable an end I trust may yet follow, for the sake of humanity and civilisation.

2nd.—The king sent for us, and gave us a letter addressed to Mr. Farewell. It had been sent from Delagoa Bay by Captain Colledge of the Brig Salisbury. The tenor of the letter was, that, having heard of our being wrecked on the coast, he would, when homeward bound, call off Natal. This gave me some hopes of getting away from a country where such savage customs existed, and where human life was held in so little estimation. At this moment the letter impressed us with feelings of no ordinary acuteness, it seemed like something dropped from heaven to administer comfort to us in the hour of danger and affliction.

The king produced a quantity of medicines, and desired to know the use of them, as well as of those we presented to him. Having described their properties, he called all his girls and began so distribute them by wholesale. On our cautioning him that they were not to be used in that way, he asked if they were not good for the several diseases to which his

people were liable; we answered in the affirmative.
" Well," said he, " you cannot give too much of a
good thing, and if a small quantity will cure in a
short time, a large quantity must cure in less time."
It was vain to argue with him, and we therefore
adopted the Caffre custom by saying, " Yes, father,
you know best," which elicited a momentary smile
of approbation.

After delivering a teaspoonful of calomel to one,
and half-a-dozen purgative pills to another, and so
on, until he had supplied all the sick and expended
all the medicines, he asked the chiefs if they did not
consider him a good "inyanger" or doctor, when
they responded "y-abo, barber," meaning "yes,
father;" although it appeared to me that fear alone
induced them to take the medicine thus given to them,
and that they looked at it more as a poison, than as
a remedy for disease. Chaka gave us a cow, and
told us to go and eat, which we did with a tolerably good appetite.

3rd. We walked about the kraal and entered into
conversation with several chiefs, from whom we understood that Chaka contemplated going to meet his
enemy at the full of the moon. In the evening we
went to see his majesty,—he was in his palace amusing himself with his girls. He inquired of us " how
old King George was, and if he was as great a king
as himself ; whether he possessed as many cattle, and
if he had as many girls." To the latter question I

replied it was the custom of our country to have but one wife, and that our king set the example. He laughed, and said, " that King George was like him, who did not indulge in promiscuous intercourse with women, which accounted for his advanced age." Chaka, however, notwithstanding this declaration of his purity, made evident signs, that he preferred the society fo his girls to our conversation, for he directed us to retire to our hut, to which he had sent some beer for our refreshment.

4th. This morning we proceeded to call on the king: we found him surrounded by about 2,000 of his people, discussing affairs of a warlike tendency. As soon as we had taken our seats on the ground, as near as we could discreetly, we heard him give orders for the execution of seven men, all of whom were taken from near the spot where we were seated. They were instantly seized and beaten to death, with other barbarous cruelties too revolting to detail, and which operated on me so painfully, that I was compelled to retire from so horrible and inhuman an exhibition.

5th. Our natives, whom we had left on the road with our present, arrived late in the afternoon; they could not advance more rapidly from the state of the rivers. The king was too much engaged with his people to afford us a chance of showing him the several articles we desired to present.

6th. We gave the king the present we had brought

for him. He took no notice of us, but seemed highly pleased with the present. We all remarked it to be a peculiar feature in the conduct of Chaka, that, however he might be delighted with any offering from us, and pleased with the object, he never evinced it in our presence before his people. And we also observed it to be his invariable custom, whenever he was informed of the approach of " his white people," as he designated us, that he never failed assembling a large body of his warriors, for the pretext, we conjectured, of impressing us with a due importance of his power and dignity, to display the awe in which we held him, and to show his subjects how little value he set on anything we introduced to him.

He appeared elated at the surprise and astonishment of his warriors, when they first beheld the figurehead of the Mary, while he preserved his usual assumed indifference ; and displayed a carelessness quite in character with his general usage, during the whole time their curiosity led them to examine our present ; but no sooner had his warriors dispersed, and the goods had been removed, at his command, into his palace, where we were ordered to accompany him, than he opened himself in admiration of our present, threw off all restraint, and evinced the pleasure which our few trifles gave him. His inquiries as to the use and quality of every thing manifested a shrewdness which we little expected to find in an unlettered savage. Anything in the shape of an implement of war always irresistibly caught his attention, and he would attend to any explanatory description with the most intense anxiety.

At noon our man, George Biddlecomb, whom we had left in search of the boat, arrived: he could not return, from the state of the rivers, so he followed us.

7th. Early this morning we' saw the king sitting outside his kraal with his warriors. Their conversation was mainly on the power of fire-arms. Chaka desired us, when we approached him, to go and shoot some vultures that they might see the effect of our arms. Jacob, having his musket with him, on hearing the command went out instantly and shot one of these carnivorous birds; the effect which this produced was astounding—they were at once, in a measure, paralysed. Jacob's fire had made the birds wild, and therefore, determining not to be outdone by him, we pursued them, but were stopped by a messenger from the king, who required our presence. We perceived him following, accompanied by a body of his people, and we soon found that his object was to try the effect of our fire-arms on another species of the animal creation. By this time a body of from 4,000 to 5,000 people had congregated, when the king halted, and the warriors formed a circle round him, at the same time enclosing us.

Chaka addressed us, and asked " if our nation were as numerous as the body of men now about him ?" We told him that it was, which he doubted, and

then inquired " why we came so few at a time ? "
We replied that we were perfectly aware of his
friendly disposition towards us, and consequently
did not require to be numerous. He laughed, and
asked me our mode of warfare, and said " he thought
it would be no difficult matter to conquer us, as our
muskets, when once discharged, took some time to
reload, during which they might make a rush, and
the losing a few men by the first discharge would be
nothing to him who had so many."   We now showed
him the position of the square, one of us kneeling in
front, and the other two in their respective positions,
which proved to him that, according to the system of
firing in that manœuvre, the position was invulnerable to an irregular force. He saw it, but his warriors being inclined to flatter his military genius, observed that by charging in a body, in the way to which
they usually resorted, especially under his bold and
judicious command, they thought it would more than
overbalance the strength of our positions, and the
force of our arms.

The king had sent a body of his people in search
of buffaloes while he was thus engaged with us, who
returned and said that they had discovered a drove ;
he then despatched four parties in different directions,
at the same time giving them instructions how they
were to hunt. We now proceeded over a strong
country covered with thorn-trees, which was painful to
us, travelling without shoes, although by this time we

had got a little inured to going barefooted. As we were advancing through the bush and jungles, Chaka suddenly started back, exclaiming, "there are the buffaloes close upon us." We did not see them, but had the presence of mind to stand firm, ready to fire. He laughed heartily, and we soon found, from our native boy, that it was a ruse played off by the king to try our courage.

After this we ascended a hill, where we had a fine view of the country. We had walked about twelve miles: Chaka sat down; we soon saw some buffaloes, when he desired us to accompany the party then present and hunt them, but not to return without killing one. We were already fatigued, and my feet were greatly injured by thorns, but we could not abstain from proceeding, fearing that he might attribute it to cowardice. We therefore jumped up with all the activity we could command, and commenced running, until we got fairly out of his view, when the chief of the party sat down. In a short time we saw the buffaloes making towards us, and we began to flatter ourselves with being able to carry a tail of one to the king (the custom for announcing the death of a wild animal), but we were disappointed; for the people, who had stationed themselves on each side of the drove, had so harassed the animals that we could not get a chance to fire, unless with an uncertainty of hitting them, and at great risk of hitting some of the people. We therefore stood and looked

at them, when presently we observed the warriors
disperse in all directions. The buffaloes had tossed
one man upon the top of a thorn bush, and after
trampled him to death; another had had his thigh
dislocated. They, however, killed one, carried the
tail to Chaka, and reported the accidents, to which
he evinced great indifference, saying to the man who
had his thigh dislocated, "it shows the weakness of
your limbs," and in a laugh, in which all the people
joined, he continued, "you are like an old woman
now, I must find a husband for you." By this time
he was interrupted by another party coming with two
tails, the chief of whom reported one man to have
been killed and two seriously hurt. Several others
were killed by these animals.

The buffalo is a powerful, fierce, and very active
beast, ferocious and not easily subdued. They herd
in large droves, and are formidable not only from their
numbers, but from their strength and courage. The
natives who go in pursuit of them are obliged to use
great precaution, and to single one out as the object
of their attack, if they possibly can accomplish it;
they may then succeed in securing the beast, but not
even then, in all probability, without one or two of
the party falling a sacrifice to the animal's rage,
and several receiving severe wounds and contusions.
Those who unfortunately fall in the attack, or are
severely wounded, meet with no sympathy from their
king: the unfeeling savage, when told of several

having been trampled to death by the buffalo, evinces no sorrow, but says, with an air of indifference, "it was the best way to get rid of cowards."

We returned from the buffalo-hunt not a little fatigued; my feet had undergone some severe lacerations and punctures from the thorns, which made them exceedingly painful, and it was too late to extract them.

After arriving at our hut the king sent us some beef and a jug of beer, of which we partook with much eagerness, made a hearty meal, and retired to rest.

CHAPTER VII.

THE day succeeding the buffalo-hunt we were exceedingly languid; my face had been burnt by the heat of the sun, and my feet were in great anguish from thorns and other injuries; at noon, however, we waited on the king, to ask his permission to return to our homes. He said that, as the enemy was near, and the rivers had considerably swollen, we had better remain with him for a while. This was far from being agreeable to us, and we retired to our huts to reflect upon our condition, and to give me an opportunity of having the thorns extracted from my feet.

Sunday, 9th.—The king sent for us—he was sitting in his palace;—we seated ourselves on the ground before his door. We observed a large quantity of small white flowers, blown from the shrubs in the vicinity, floating in the air, covering the whole space of the kraal, and

Light as thistle down moving,

which were carried off by the first ripple of breeze that

sprang up. The king asked us the cause of this, when we being at a loss for a plausible reason, he observed, "that it was a sign the enemy had retreated from his position." While we were communicating with him, messengers arrived to announce the fact, and that they had encamped two days' march nearer the confines of their own country. Chaka immediately gave orders for his warriors to hold themselves in readiness for an immediate attack.

In the night his majesty sent for us; we entered the palace and saluted him;—he came out and ordered a fire to be kindled with reeds. He asked us what the skies were composed of, and if they were not a mass of stone, or the smoke which had ascended, and from time to time collected into a compact body, as it appeared always to be borne upwards by the wind. As he could not comprehend the opinion we advanced, he turned it off, and introduced the subject of religion.

We explained to him that the religion of our nation taught us to believe in a Supreme Being, a First Cause, named God, by whom we swore, in whom we believed and trusted: that he created all things, and was the giver of light and life. To this he paid marked attention; and when we adverted to the origin of the world, he seemed as if struck with profound astonishment. He turned, however, from one subject to another in such rapid succession, that we found it impracticable to confine him to our explanation of the foundation of the world, and of our notions and ideas of divinity.

We told him that we had not brought any doctors with us (missionaries) to instruct the ignorant in the ways of God; this he appeared to regret, and expressed a wish for them to come and teach his people, observing, " that he had discovered we were a superior race," and that he would give the missionaries abundance of cattle to teach him to read and write. His warriors now made their appearance, and we availed ourselves of the opportunity of retiring to rest when he entered into conversation with them.

12th.—The two preceding days the king had amused himself by dancing with his people, and superintending the driving of his cattle to the rivers, the latter being a favourite recreation. He again asked us if King George had been married, and to how many wives. We told him that he had been married, but that his queen was dead, and that he was now living single. He said, " I see it is the custom of all warriors to abstain from cohabiting with women." This was remarked with a smile, and indicated that he did not accord with the precept, nor profit much by the example, for immediately afterwards about fifty of his girls appeared, saluted him, and went into his palace; he soon followed them, when the doors were instantly closed, and we retired to repose, the night being somewhat advanced.

This morning three regiments of boys arrived to

be reviewed. There appeared to be nearly 6000, all
having black shields. The respective corps were
distinguished by the shape and ornament of their
caps. One regiment had them in the shape of
Malay hats, with a peak on the crown about six inches
high, and a bunch of feathers at the top. Another
wore a turban made of otter-skin, having a crane's
feather or two on each side; and the third wore small
bunches of feathers over the whole head, made fast
by means of small ties. Thus accoutred and distinguished, they entered the gate, ran up the kraal,
halted in front of the palace, and saluted the king.
One boy stepped in front and made a long harangue.
When the orator had concluded, the whole of his
comrades first shouted, and then commenced running
over the kraal, trying to excel each other in feats of
agility and gesture, regardless of order, regularity,
or discipline. After this exhibition, which lasted
three hours, a regiment of men arrived with white
shields, having on them one or two black spots in
the centre; they saluted Chaka, then retired to put
away their shields, and assembled again in one body
to dance.

They formed a half circle; the men in the centre
and the boys at the two extremities. The king
placed himself in the middle of the space within the
circle, and about 1500 girls stood opposite to the
men three deep, in a straight line, and with great
regularity. His majesty then commenced dancing,

the warriors followed, and the girls kept time by
singing, clapping their hands, and raising their
bodies on their toes. The strange attitudes of the
men exceeded anything I had seen before. The
king was remarkable for his unequalled activity, and
the surprising muscular powers he exhibited. He
was decorated with a profusion of green and yellow
glass beads. The girls had their share of ornaments;
in addition too they had each of them four brass
bangles round their necks, which kept them in an
erect posture, and rendered them as immoveable as
the neck of a statue. This ceremony was performed
with considerable regularity, from the king giving,
as it were, the time for every motion. Wherever
he cast his eye, there was the greatest effort made;
and nothing could exceed the exertion of the whole
until sunset, when Chaka, accompanied by his girls,
retired within the palace, and the warriors to their
respective huts. Many, however, first went to the
river and performed their evening ablutions.

13th.——Early this morning we saw the king with
his warriors. There was also near them a large herd
of cattle, upwards of 1000 head. We conceived this
to be a most favourable moment to apply for permission to return home. Chaka was then engaged
in conversation with his chiefs on the subject of the
last war, and commanded them to point out all those
who had proved themselves to be cowards, as they
had now to contend with a brave and formidable

enemy. The chiefs assured him that all of them had
been killed, not one having been spared who had so
disgraced himself. A pause ensuing, we embraced the
opportunity of telling him that we were about to return
home: he consented to it reluctantly, and gave us
three oxen and three cows. This present was much
inferior in value to the one he had led us to anticipate, and infinitely below his gifts to others; but
having his permission to leave, which was of more
importance to me than any consideration of cattle,
we quitted him at noon, and proceeded about nine
miles over a mountainous and stony country. My
feet were so bad that we were obliged to halt for
the night in a small kraal on our route.

15th.—Yesterday we journeyed onwards, but
met with nothing worth notice. We crossed the
Ootogale and arrived at Nongasi's kraal to-day,
where we met messengers from home with a letter
from Lieutenant King, stating that his majesty's
sloop of war Helicon had been seven days off Natal:
that her boat, with Lieutenant Wood, had been
on shore, and seeing it was impossible I could
arrive in time, from the state of the rivers, he had
deemed it advisable to take a passage in the ship,
conceiving that it would be for the advantage of us
all, and recommended me to make myself as comfortable as I could until his return.

I felt much grieved at this untoward event, and
regretted having lost so good an opportunity of

returning to the Cape, and leaving an abode which daily became extremely distressing to me. I could not, under such peculiarly unfortunate circumstances, condemn the step taken by my friend and companion, because I was impressed with the strongest conviction that he had not left me without a design of making an immediate effort to extricate me from my miserable situation. I felt, however, no ordinary depression of spirits, and although, before I had been apprised of the cause that occasioned it, I was about to indulge in an inviting repast for a wearied traveller, namely, some substantial beef, I could not eat; my appetite was gone from the effect of disappointment, and I looked on the objects around me in silent anguish and despair.

> Straight towards heaven my wandering eyes I turned,
> And gaz'd awhile upon the ample sky.

Recovering a little from the momentary effects of so sudden a shock, and from the dejection which it had occasioned, I returned to my party and endeavoured to dispel the gloom which had pervaded me, by expressions of hope for the future, and by encouraging the conviction that my adventures would yet terminate favourably.

16th.—Anxious to reach home, we commenced travelling early, regardless of the heavy dew and the effects arising from it. We met with occasional obstacles at the several rivers, but eventually crossed them. Having arrived at the rapid river at eve, we halted on the beach for the night; and after setting a watch, we lay down to repose,—" the *leaves* our bed, our canopy the skies."

17th.—After a sound sleep we rose and pursued our journey until we reached the Umgani, where we were momentarily opposed by an alligator; our party coming up we commenced firing at the voracious monster when he departed, and left us to cross the river without obstruction. In the evening we arrived home and received the congratulations of Mr. Farewell, with whom, and my companion Mr. Fynn, we spent the evening with much amusement, detailing our adventures, commenting on their strange variety, the vicissitudes we had met, and the difficulties we had encountered.

I understood from Mr. Hatton, on whom I called at Townshend, that His Majesty's Ship Helicon had arrived at Natal expressly to take off the crew of the Mary, the wreck of which had been known at the Cape through Mr. Norton and the seamen who so cowardly deserted us and took away our long-boat. They arrived, it appears, after some difficulty, at Algoa Bay; and the circumstance of their desertion after all ended favourably for us, as, in all probability, without such an effort to escape, our disaster might have remained unknown much longer.

CHAPTER VIII.

NOTHING material occurred until the tenth of June: the weather had been cloudy, and rain had fallen heavily, attended with thunder and lightning. The night before we had been greatly annoyed by hyenas, which we had some trouble to drive away. To-day the weather cleared up, the wind having shifted to the eastward. Observing two natives run towards the signal-post and try to hoist a signal, I sent our boat and crew over, and they brought me a note from Mr. Farewell, requesting Mr. Hatton and myself to come over to the Fort, as Mr. Fynn had arrived with unpleasant news. We accordingly proceeded thither. On our arrival we found Mr. Farewell and his party assembled in his bed-chamber. He said, on our entering, that he had sent for us respecting an affair between Mr. Fynn and the Hottentots. Mr. Fynn then related that he had been to the king with Michael and John (two Hottentots), that on their arrival he had furnished them with abundance of food, and cautioned them not to take any victuals from the Caffres by force, as they were in the habit of doing. This, however, had no effect, for Michael took some of their beer and got intoxicated; he afterwards took their provisions, and finally beat one of them, when the latter threw a stone at the former, and immediately proceeded to the king to complain. This trifling matter had like to have ended seriously, but Mr. Fynn, who explained the affair to Chaka, put an end to the fray which these fellows had created, and which might have been of serious consequence. Chaka pursued a very impartial course, and would, on hearing the charge, and the explanatory account given by Mr. Fynn, have inflicted summary punishment on the offending Hottentots. These fellows made a serious attack on Mr. Fynn, and knocked him down with great violence; and the king hearing of it, immediately came, and would have had the Hottentots put to death forthwith had not Mr. Fynn assured him that their master, Mr. Farewell, would administer to them a well applied punishment for their cupidity.

Mr. Fynn returned from the king's residence without the Hottentots, who had designed to stay there; but he was surprised, on his return, to find they had got home before him. The object, therefore, which Mr. Farewell had in sending for me and Mr. Hatton was, to hold a court-martial on these offenders, which was immediately done, when the verdict was, that Michael should have his kraal destroyed, his cattle and his people taken away, and that he should receive a dozen lashes; that John should receive thirty lashes, and have his people taken away, which sentences were carried into execution upon the spot.

13th.—The last two days we amused ourselves at home. This day I went over to Fort Farewell, where I found, from Messrs. Farewell and Fynn, that messengers had arrived from the king to request all the white people to proceed to him with their fire-arms immediately, to accompany him to war, as he had resolved on attacking Isseconyarna at his encampment. I walked up the beach with them, and sent the boat back for Mr. Hatton and our party. In the evening we all assembled and discussed the subject. Mr. Farewell observed, that, on a former occasion, he had refused to go when the king had sent for him; it was now however evident, from Chaka sending us a peremptory order to visit him, that he never took notice of a refusal. After some deliberation we agreed to go, as it would be better to accompany him to attack his foes, than excite him to approach and attack us as an enemy.

For several days we were engaged in making preparations for our march: our fire-arms occupied a good deal of our attention and care, so as to have them in proper condition for those active operations for which we were destined. Moreover I took great pains to prepare cartridges for our muskets, and to have a sufficient quantity of them for us all.

I took opportunities during several days to teach my boy to shoot, and be otherwise expert with his arms.

25th.—This day messengers arrived from the king to inform Mr. Farewell that he need not hold himself in readiness to proceed to the imperial residence till the full of the moon, and that his majesty did not require him to bring his gun, as he had originally requested him to do. During several successive days, I attended Mr. Hatton at the dock-yard, and assisted in any way I could to forward our work of building the vessel.

11th July.—Other messengers arrived with a request from Chaka that the tent should be sent on to him. Mr. Fynn and Cane being absent, Mr. Farewell was regretting that he had not an individual under whose charge he could confide the convoy of it. He could not trust the Hottentots, nor the natives, by themselves, I therefore offered to superintend the delivery of it, which he gladly accepted; and the next day I prepared to undertake my mission.

13th.—This morning, being equipped for the journey, I set forth with John the Hottentot, Frederick my interpreter, and ten natives, and pursued a course which I had not gone before. Instead of the pass leading by the beach, we went immediately inland, by which the fatiguing part, over the sandy surface, was avoided. I was also anxious to ascertain the characters of some of the interior tribes. The morning being one of those brilliant and serene ones so peculiar to the tropics, which encourage and enchant the traveller, buoy him up to persevere, and enliven him by hopes of success, I certainly entered on my charge quite elated, and contemplated the pleasure I should derive from the new scenes that might occasionally break upon my view; nor was I disappointed.

We soon arrived at Umsegas, where I refreshed myself with a pot of thick milk, and, after procuring a guide, proceeded. We were not long reaching the banks of the Umgani. This river now took a serpentine course, unlike its appearance near its embouchure, and where we crossed it on our former journeys. We followed its course contiguous to its banks, in a north-west direction for about four miles, until we arrived at a broad but shallow fording, by which we crossed. Continuing our journey through a pass which apparently had not been trodden for many years, I found it not only tedious, but fatiguing, and not congenial to my tender feet; the high and thickly rising grass, together with the thorns on the surface of the ground, rendering it at intervals almost impassable.

I at last mounted a young pack-ox that had not been properly broken, and, after some labour and a little management, I induced him to go on at a tolerable pace. We passed the remains of several old kraals, and discovered that the vicinity had been a scene of some strife, from the innumerable fragments of human skulls and bones we met with in our progress. The whole scene showed that this district had, at one time, been thickly populated.

Nothing could exceed in grandeur the surrounding herbage, and the rich vegetation which displayed itself on the whole face of the country. A more charming spot cannot well be imagined. Clear and limpid rivulets, green hills, and clusters of trees studding the whole, attracted our attention on one side; on the other the river Umgani, whose banks exhibited a richness of verdure beyond description beautiful. In the distant ground to which our road led, we could perceive that our course lay over mountains rising gently from the sea, and intersecting our way; and ever and anon, at a distance, the river gliding majestically before us, formed altogether a landscape of no ordinary magnificence.

The soil appeared to contain properties highly congenial for cultivation, and in many places we discovered the work of the natives who had prepared it for Indian corn and tropical esculents and vegetables; but depopulation had stayed the hand of the cultivator, and that which might now have afforded food for man was left to be the haunts of wild animals, and the resort of carnivorous birds. The calabash and castor oil trees were seen growing in splendid clusters, and the pumpkin spreading its tendrils on the surface, in innumerable and extensive patches. We discovered one or two fires at a distance, but not a solitary inhabitant could be seen the whole of our journey through this part of the country. My pack-ox now began to show symptoms of fatigue or laziness, and I was obliged to dismount and drive him; for this consideration I received a kick in a dangerous place, which for some time fixed me on the ground. It was now noon, and feeling a want of refreshment I began to look for my boys with my provisions, but they had not come up. In vain did we search for them, and not knowing how far we should have to travel before we reached a kraal, I was compelled, although suffering from the pain of the kick, to continue on foot the remainder of the journey. Fortunately, by this time, my feet had become inured to the thorns and stumps, and my stomach to fasting, so that I was insensible to the attacks of the one, and could tolerably well endure the other; walking, therefore, was not so much regretted, nor the want of food lamented. I was greatly attracted by the surrounding scenery, and so much engaged in contemplating the advantages of settling on this spot, that trifling obstacles made no impression. We had some difficulty in finding anything like a path or vestige of one, and, consequently, advanced in a very irregular course; at last, however, Providence, in his goodness, led us to a spot that appeared to have been recently.

occupied, though it was now deserted. Here were the remains of a kraal, near to which was a plot of ground planted with sweet potatoes, then just fit for digging up; of these we partook with a ready and keen appetite. There were several remains of pots in the huts, and near to them a spring of delicious water. We soon began to cook, and made, on the whole, a very comfortable and hearty meal. Just as we had finished our repast, we discovered on an eminence, at a distance, three natives, whom my party wished to stop for the purpose of conversing with them; but not being able to accompany them on account of my accident, I declined communicating with them: as they, however, seemed to be approaching us, and had shields, I began to apprehend something hostile, and that they might be the owners of the hut we had occupied, and of the ground and vegetables with which we had made so free. As there is nothing more just than that " a bold front half gains a battle," I directed my three men who had fire-arms to meet them, and, if possible, gain them over to our interest, but on no account to molest them, nor give them battle, although it should even seem to be their design to engage us. In the latter case, my men were ordered to return to us. I looked on with intense interest to see the two parties come in contact, and fancying that if I could get the three strangers into my possession, I might obtain from them some information respecting the natives who frequent these parts, and live by hunting

the elephant, subsisting on the flesh of that animal;
but to my surprise, I saw my party and the strangers
cordially meet, and shortly afterwards the whole
approached me, when, to my astonishment, I found it
to be Umsegai and two of his men, who had followed
us, fearing that we might be molested by the bush-
rangers, who at times infest those parts, and that Chaka
might kill him if he suffered us to pass by his kraal
without affording us some aid.

We now proceeded until we came to a position
where the paths intersected each other in various
ways, and where we might have had some difficulty
in selecting the right one, had not Umsegai been
with us, he being the only person present who knew
the country, having traversed it before in search of the
bush-rangers, for the purpose of enriching himself by
adding their females to his establishment (who were a
valuable property and disposable at the will of the
possessor), and for the pleasure of killing the males
—a pleasure in which he delighted to indulge.

We continued to advance from one eminence to
another, through valleys of great beauty, from the
peculiarly rich herbage that overspread the surface, and from the surrounding vegetation of all
kinds, growing in splendid luxuriance. We here
met with trees indigenous to this quarter of the
globe, the timber of which appeared of a very
solid and close texture, and admirably adapted
for ship-building. Our track was pleasant, but some-

times irregular : night beginning, however, to spread
his dark mantle over the horizon, and the buffaloes
making their appearance, emerging from the thickets
of the forest to indulge in the grateful herbage
it afforded, we sought to find an asylum for the
night, but apprehending danger from these animals, we were obliged to make a circuitous movement to avoid them; and at midnight, when we
halted, we found that although we had travelled full
fifty miles, we had only advanced about seventeen
from our bivouac of the preceding evening.

After a sound sleep I arose, but found myself
exceedingly stiff. I looked round in admiration of
the spot we had selected for our halting-place for the
night : it was impossible to fancy a more enchanting
country, or one in which a settlement could be
established with a better chance of making it valuable
for all agricultural purposes. A soil with a depth and
texture surprisingly inviting, and well watered by small
clear tributary streams to the rivers Umgani, Isse-
loache, and Umslatee; fine forest trees, whose leafy
branches afforded a delightful shelter from the sun's
meridian heat ; all united, presented an invaluable
site, not only for agricultural experiments, but no
less advantageously situated for the purposes of inter-
nal traffic with the natives who go in pursuit of the
elephant and buffalo. Here also we found the
country thickly inhabited by three tribes, who possessed
numerous herds of cattle, but who had greatly suffered

from the incursions of Chaka. He had taken from them their most valuable stock, and otherwise subjected them to inconceivable loss and annoyance, from their predatory propensities. As I got up very stiff, I was not in a condition to travel, but necessity, dire necessity, made it imperative that I should move onwards, and on our progress we fell in with our boys with our provisions and the tent. It appears that from loitering a little on their way the day we missed them, they had unexpectedly lost sight of us, and having fallen in with a drove of elephants, they had been driven to pursue the road to the beach, through a forest, where they came out on the regular pass to the imperial residence.

15th.—To-day we moved on and reached Mazie's, where we halted. The chief was out hunting, but hearing of our arrival, he sent us a bullock to kill for myself and people. Next morning we set off early, advanced thirty miles, and on the 17th reached the Ootoogale, which we crossed, observing at the time a great many hippopotami in the river, and alligators basking in the sun on the banks. I fired at them with leaden balls, which produced no impression, and only made them reluctantly quit their warm position to seek security in the deepest waters of the stream. We pursued a track leading over the Loonghie mountains, the ascent to the summit of which was tedious and fatiguing. The path was a difficult one, from its occasional acclivities and acute angles; and from the ravines and other obstructions, with many dangerous interstices in the rocks, our passage was one of no easy accomplishment.

These mountains are remarkable for their mineral properties, and the geologist might find here much to attract his notice, and afford him materials for future contemplation. Iron and copper are to be obtained in prodigious quantities, and evidently much silver ore might be discovered by a little labour in excavating the various parts of these elevations.

The forests at their base, though they are magnificent to the eye, are yet terrific to the traveller, as they contain every species of wild animal indigenous to Southern Africa, and are therefore much frequented by the natives, who go in search of the elephant for the sake of his teeth, and of the buffalo for his flesh and his hide.

The day was excessively hot, and being unusually fatigued, we halted at the kraal of Umpungwaas, the principal domestic of the king. While we were here a great number of warriors passed to and from the imperial residence, which had now been designated " Umboolalio," or "a place of slaughter," from the circumstance of the king having recently ordered one of his regiments, with their wives and families, to be massacred for supposed cowardice. They had been defeated in battle, although they fought with great bravery, having been overpowered by superior troops and greater numbers, and compelled to retreat.

It is one of the inhuman customs of the Zooloo
kings to put all to death who are supposed to have
evinced any symptoms of cowardice, and in their selec-
tion of objects they are not nice in their discrimination.　In civilised countries, cowardice is punished
by the death of the offender, but testimony of his
guilt must first be established before conviction can
ensue; but the Zooloos are not so distinguished for
minutely investigating the charge; for merely from
suspicion, the poor object of it is led away to suffer
a cruel death by impalement, at the mere nod of a
tyrant.　From the horrible exhibition, therefore, that
I have detailed, the residence of the king has been
changed from the old name of " Gibbeclack " to the
more appropriate one of " Umboolalio," or " place of
slaughter."

19th. The morning being cool, I took advantage
of this favourable circumstance for proceeding, and
marched on rapidly, so that by ten A. M. we reached
the king's residence, and fired a musket to announce
our arrival.　He sent a messenger to meet me, who,
entered with me, at the lower gate and proceeded to
the palace, where his majesty was sitting.　He expressed much surprise at my party, who had remained
at home, not coming, and said that he intended to
go to war on the return of his spies, whom he expected in three days, and made no doubt that I would
accompany him.　I mentioned that I had no objection, but regretted that I had not come prepared

for such an event: that my visit was merely to present to him the tent which he had expressed a desire to see, and which I had brought for the purpose. He evinced a wish to see it fixed; accordingly we erected it, and it gave him inconceivable gratification, for he thought the sight of it would strike his enemy with dismay and panic. Chaka seemed confident that his appearance before the enemy in the tent would give his warriors an easy victory.

He gave me but little hopes of getting any cattle unless we went to war; he therefore proposed that I should return home and prepare my companions for it, and that he would protract his designed attack until the next moon. He gave me a mess of boiled blood and beef, directing me to go to my hut, and promising to send me a pot of beer.

20th. To-day and several succeeding ones I was detained by a boil on my foot, the pain of which was so acute, and it became so highly inflamed, that I was unable to commence my journey home before the 28th; but during this detention I had an opportunity of witnessing some Zooloo military spectacles of an interesting character.

One day the king reviewed about four thousand Amabootoes or young warriors, had them drilled, and gave them orders to prepare for immediate war. On the following afternoon five or six thousand other warriors came in, when the king sent for me to see them drilled. He asked me to give one of them my straw hat, which I did, and he seemed much elated with the present. The king seeing my foot so bad, sent me a doctor, who applied some vegetable to it, and, to do the native Galen justice, his application gave me considerable relief. He also ordered out the regiment of Sofancimbo (his favourite corps) to drill, and a number of oxen were directed to be killed for his warriors. He sent for me to his palace, and asked me to teach his boys how to make straw hats; I attempted it, but they could not comprehend, and, therefore, made no progress. My foot, though improving, still continued sore, it having broken, thanks to the skill of my doctor. His majesty sent for me again to the palace, and I had an opportunity of seeing a large body of his troops, consisting of seventeen regiments of Amabootoes with black shields, and twelve regiments with white ones, at drill on the hills around us. There appeared about 30,000 fighting men, and I understood that every man carried about him some badge of a warrior, there not being one among them who had not been wounded in battle. After a few loose evolutions, they moved in a compact body by the base of the mountain, and had a very martial appearance.

The king was exceedingly solicitous to know if king George could bring as many fighting men into the field as I had seen manœuvring the other day; at the same time he observed, that I had not seen half the number he intended advancing with against

Isseconyarna. I led him to understand that my sovereign could bring as many soldiers into the field
as he possessed, cattle and men together. He seemed
somewhat astounded at my communication, and turning to his people near him, remarked, that he feared
King George, who was so great a monarch, would
next attack his dominions and conquer Zooloo, when
they would lose all their cattle, and perhaps not escape
themselves.

The warriors would not heed the king's apprehension, but said they were willing to try it, because
they were confident they should be able to repel
any invader of their country. This caused great
arguments with the king, and ended by his killing
eight of them. The cause for this I could not comprehend, neither could I elicit it from any of the
natives.

27th. To-day my foot enabling me to proceed on
my journey home, I was disposed to set out, but the
king being engaged with a regiment of recruits, he
requested me to postpone my departure until the
next day.

28th. I went this morning to take my leave of his
majesty, who did not appear pleased at my going,
but gave me permission, and desired that my Hot_
tentot and interpreter should remain; they objected,
and said that they would rather accompany me.
Chaka was silent and got up to leave, when the Hottentot and the interpreter followed me. Just after

we had got outside the gate of the kraal we met Umsega, who went and informed the king that we had
departed, and then came running after us to command
us all to return to the palace.   I remonstrated with
him; finding, however, I had no alternative but to
return or excite the king's wrath, I chose the former,
when his majesty began to abuse us, and told me that
we were liars, and were afraid of war.   I said we
feared nothing but our king, who had sent us to get
ivory, and to make friends; we therefore did not like
to disobey his orders.   " Well," said he, " if you
want to make friends you will go with me to engage
my enemies, and then you will have me for your friend,
but if otherwise, you will make me your enemy."
I saw that he was determined I should accompany
him to meet his opponents; I, therefore, told him
I was willing to go with him, but that I must first
return home to prepare for the expedition.   He agreed,
telling me to return with Lieutenant King's party,
and that he did not wish Mr. Farewell to come, as he
was too much like an old woman.   He desired Jacob,
his interpreter, and Umsega, to accompany us, and to
see that all Lieut. King's party came.   He gave us
three head of cattle to eat on the road.   Having thus
arranged, we took our leave, and marched about eleven
miles, when we halted for the night.

29th.—This morning as I arose to pursue my journey, I found the Hottentot and my interpreter had
quitted me in the night.   I suspected their villany,

and travelled rapidly to overtake them, and demand
the cause of their desertion. I arrived at Sotoby's,
where they had slept, and were waiting for me. I
admonished them, when the interpreter became inso-
lent, which induced me to chastise him; and apprehending that he might act towards me as he had
towards Mr. Fynn, I took his musket from him, and
made both walk before me. At about 3 P. M. we
arrived at Moyarkie's kraal, where we met some
people, who informed us that Messrs. Farewell and
Fynn were coming, and had probably, by this time,
crossed the Ootoogale.

30th.—I rose early, and travelled briskly to Mon-
goses, to be there before my friends should arrive,
fearing they might advance from thence on another
road. I crossed the river, and reached the kraal at
noon, and in about an hour afterwards those gentle-
men appeared. We halted here for the night. Mr.
Farewell expressed a wish that I should return with
them to Chaka; this, however, I declined, as his majesty commanded me to bring all our party with me.
Mr. Farewell said it was a great folly for the sailors
to attempt to go to the king, and advised me not to
say any thing to them, and that he would become
responsible for their not appearing. At his sugges-
tion, I returned home to take charge of the premises
in his absence, leaving every thing to be arranged
with Chaka by him and Mr. Fynn. I became ill on
the road, and reached home, on the 2nd of August,

with some difficulty, where I found Mr. Hatton attend⋅
ing to his ship-building duty.

11th. — I received a communication from Mr.
Farewell, stating that he had arranged matters with
Chaka, respecting myself and the sailors not going,
on condition, however, that he and Mr. Fynn should
advance with him to war, which they expected to do
daily.

August 12th.— Having been indisposed for several
days, I kept myself principally within my dwelling,
occasionally communicating with my companions at
the dock-yard, and receiving an account of the progress they were making. To-day, being recovered,
I proceeded with a party of natives to bring planks
for the vessel, which had been sawn in the forest.
In the evening Hatton and myself went to the head
of the bay to hunt the sea-cows, where we met with
John Cane, who had killed one, which he offered to
us, and we gladly accepted it.

13th.—Engaged in attempting to preserve the sea-
cow; all our Caffres went to obtain the flesh, which
they ate with great pleasure. I made them carry the
skeleton and the skin home, when I placed the latter
on a tree to preserve it from the wolves.

16th.— Hearing from the people that they had seen
a sea-cow on the Flat for a week past, I started off to
the place, about five or six miles, with an intention of
shooting it; but it appeared that the natives having wor-
ried in attempting to kill it, the animal had pursued

the Caffres, but afterwards disappeared among the reeds and swamps, where I could not go after it, without incurring considerable danger, so I returned without success to Townshend, about 3 P.M.

18th.—To-day I visited our sick, and regretted to find they did not improve much, and that there were no convalescents.

24th.—I went in search of people to fence my garden, which I had brought into a tolerably flourishing state. The men whom I expected to get at Matuban's as soon as they saw me ran into the bush. Having sent my own boys after them, I heard one of them telling the people not to come, as I only wanted their work. I said nothing until I reached home, when I chastised the lad for his duplicity. He ran away, and I sent two others to bring him back, who went off together with the delinquent. The following day I went in search of them, but could obtain no tidings of them. In the afternoon I set a musket trap to catch a marauding wolf, and in the evening hearing a report of the gun, went to the trap, and found the animal dead.

26th.—Last night the wolves came and eat part of their dead companion. The natives had given me strange accounts of these animals, of their partaking of the nature of the male one year, and of the female the next; I opened the one we had killed, which was a male, and found what I might have supposed without the trouble of making such an experiment, that the

H

account was unfounded. I secured my runaway
boys at Fort Farewell, brought them home to Townshend, punished the one for his criminality, and reproved
the other two for their treachery, when they promised
well for the future.

27th.—It being Sunday, I read prayers to my
people, who attended with great order and becoming
decorum. The natives seemed attracted by the scene,
and noticed its solemnity.

29th.—The previous day I had been engaged in
attending to my sick, and administering to them medicines and nourishment, such as we could command.

Our corn and provisions now getting scarce, I
resolved on proceeding to the tribe of the chief Magie
to purchase, and therefore set about preparing two or
three things to barter with the people for those articles.
Accordingly John Cane, Rachel his woman, John
Ross (the apprentice of Lieut. King), and myself,
attended by some of our natives, started off on our
journey.

31st.—After having visited about fourteen kraals
yesterday and to day, situated in the vicinity of the
river Umstato, we only obtained a basket or two of
corn, and therefore returned to our quarters.

Sept. 1st.—Set off again with Cane on another trip
in search of provisions, and knowing that to return
would only be to endure the pangs of hunger, we
took an easterly course, resolved on obtaining something. We travelled about six miles, and arrived

at Hacacazing, where we succeeded in purchasing about fifteen bushels of grain. I gave the chief two arm-bangles for it, and about a pound of beads, which satisfied him exceedingly; we then returned to the kraal we left, to rest for the night. This place was so infested with rats that it was impossible to sleep: they actually gnawed my feet, and bit off the toe-nails of some of the sound-sleeping natives who disregarded them.

2nd.—It rained incessantly all night, and continued this morning a little, we however sallied forth again although the wind blew from the westward in strong blasts that made our journey laborious. Cane and myself advanced rapidly (leaving our natives to proceed with our corn at their leisure), and soon got home. The rain continuing, we were drenched, while the natives who only got on slowly, did not arrive until some hours afterwards, and were suffering severely from the cold.

3rd.—Got up early and proceeded to the point with Jack; the natives with part of the grain followed· Waited a considerable time for the boat, at last saw it, but as it did not make for the spot where I was, I fired to let them know my position. The persons in the boat, from some pretence or other, disregarded my signal several times, I at last fired a shot astern of them, which brought them to, when they rowed towards me, and on landing not only behaved with considerable insolence, but threatened violence. On the part of my comrades,

for such they were, and sharing in the inconveniences
of being left with little chance of escape from these
shores, such conduct was unmanly, and illiberal, and
could only have emanated from individuals insensible
to the common feelings of our nature, which teach us
benevolence towards each other.   During this extraordinary collision, Mr. Hatton came over in the jolly
boat; he, having noticed them pull away from the
point, proceeded to me.   It appears the fellows had
taken the long boat to go on a party of pleasure, but
Mr. Hatton took their boat to convey me and the corn
over, and left them to proceed with the jolly-boat
whither they liked.   Read prayers to-day as usual.

4th.—I engaged the natives to fence in my garden,
which had been much injured by the wild hogs, of which
we had a great many in the neighbourhood.   Our
fish kraal that we had constructed as before described,
had caught us sixteen fine fish, which led us to anticipate better living for the future, the past not having
been very palatable nor enviable.   We had been
obliged on many occasions to endure the inconvenience of fasting, and often to partake of meals which
were far from agreeable; but the shipwrecked mariner
meets with many privations, and has to contend with
elements not very congenial.   Misery being for a time
his lot, he submits with calm resignation, and finds as
Trinculo has observed :—

" Misery acquaints a man with strange bed-fellows."

CHAPTER IX.

THIS morning, October the 6th, having risen with the design of proceeding to bring home the remainder of our purchased corn, I was taking, as it grew clear, a view of the sea, and perceived, approaching the harbour, a vessel, which, by her making a tack, evidently intended to enter. About 10 A.M., she came into the bay, got safely over the bar, and anchored immediately opposite to our tents; I instantly went on board, and found there my companion Lieut. King, whom I shook cordially by the hand: he had brought with him Captain Dunn and Mrs. Farewell, and I was not a little surprised to see a female venturing to these inhospitable shores. We congratulated each other, and our satisfaction at meeting was manifestly mutual.

I received letters from my family and friends, and hearing of their being well gave me some consolation, though I confess at the moment I felt an unusual anxiety to be with them. The clothes I had saved

from the wreck were now nearly all worn off me, and
I made but a sorry figure in the company of a lady
however, through the kindness of my friends on
board, I soon became a new man; they replenished my
stock, and I had the pleasure of escorting Mrs. Farewell to the residence of her husband. I was now
placed in an awkward predicament, for the natives,
all in a state of nudity, were congregating near the
house for the purpose of seeing their mistress. I knew
not how she felt in such a situation, but could not
help sympathising with her. Being determined to avoid
as much as possible their intrusion, I got into the
house and fastened the door to prevent their ingress.
In the afternoon I went on board " the schooner
Anne," to obtain a few necessaries for Mrs. Farewell,
returned in the evening with Mr. Hatton, drank
tea with her, and afterwards retired to Mr. Fynn's
house, where I passed the night and caught a severe
cold, having slept without any covering except the
clothes I had on.

7th.—This morning I breakfasted with Mrs. Farewell, and afterwards accompanied her on board the
schooner, taking with us a Zoola native to shew him the
vessel and the present intended for his king. The sight
of a looking-glass pleased him exceedingly, so much so,
that he exhibited some curious and grotesque features,
which frightened our fair friend. He, too, not unlike
the monkey, kept feeling behind the glass for the

object that imitated him, or, as he said, " was having a bit of fun with him at his expense."

8th.—After breakfast this morning I took a walk with Mrs. Farewell, accompanied by Lieut. King, Mr. Dunn, and Mr. Hatton. We visited several kraals near to us, and returned by our saw-pits at the head of the bay. Lieut. King was much pleased at the quantity of plank prepared. We passed through the gardens and reached the dock-yard late in the afternoon; where we were obliged to remain, the wind being too strong to attempt crossing the bay. In the evening too it rained heavily.

14th.—For several days we had deliberated on the propriety of proceeding to the imperial residence. Lieut. King seemed much disposed to visit the king, but it was considered advisable to remain for the present as a protection to Mrs. Farewell, who, in a society so new, strange, and not very agreeable, might not feel quite so comfortable as it could be wished, nor have so much confidence in her personal security as would easily reconcile her to being left without some one of the confidential friends of her husband. We therefore determined on delaying a visit for the present, conceiving it possible that Messrs. Farewell and Fynn might soon be returning. We sent off John Cane to the former to announce the arrival of his "better half," with his friend King; in the mean time we tried to make his absence as light as possible to his amiable partner, and contrived to divert her as

well as our peculiar situation and circumstances
would permit. We had our little morning peregri-
nations and evening conversaziones, our visits on
board the schooner Anne, and occasional trips to the
dock-yard, all designed to divert our female friend,
and remove the gloom which the not finding her
husband at home very naturally generated.

14th.—I wrote several letters to my friends in St.
Helena and in England, and arranged with Capt.
Dunn of the schooner for taking charge of a cow,
which I was anxious to send to the former island. I
selected one and prepared the necessary food for it
on its passage, and employed myself in collecting the
purchased corn for our consumption until the

19th.—Having finished my business, and beginning
to entertain some hopes that the vessel we had on
the stocks would be soon finished, my friend King
too having brought us articles for barter, I made
up my mind resolutely to weather the gale with
my shipwrecked companions, and buffet the storm
with them, though it might be one of some
duration. Accordingly, perceiving that we should
require another supply of corn and provisions, I
equipped myself to collect the remains of our last
purchase, and obtain more whenever I could meet
with any. On my way I rested for the night at a small
kraal, where the rats not only gnawed the fat * from

* It is usual, after walking barefoot, to anoint the feet with a thick fat,
as it relieves them exceedingly.

the soles of my feet, but eat off two of my toe-nails so effectually, that, in consequence of the pain, it was with some difficulty I could proceed.

The wolves during the night also were more than usually troublesome, and made a most hideous howling. The next day, and after so bad a night, with my feet in the condition I have described, I rose without being much disposed for travelling; but some Caffres coming up, and mentioning to me that Mr. Farewell had passed in the night, I summoned a little resolution, and got to Hucacazing, where I loaded the natives with corn, and sent them on their return home.

21st.—My natives being gone, I went with my two native boys to the Cayles (the tribe of the chief Magie), and purchased a quantity of natural curiosities. After being absent ten days, I returned home, which I reached on the 30th, and found that Mr. Farewell had arrived, that a serious quarrel had taken place between him and Lieutenant King, but that it had been adjusted.

November 2nd.—In the morning Lieutenant King visited Mr. Farewell to arrange about conveying the present of feathers to Chaka, as it was the custom to send everything in the name of Mr. Farewell, for the purpose of making him appear the principal. As Lieutenant King had arrived at Natal with the view of assisting Mr. Farewell, he had no wish to act in opposition, or do anything that might be in the least prejudicial to that gentleman. It appears, however, from the selfishness of the latter, that they could not arrange or determine what was best to be done; Mr. King expressed therefore a wish that I should take charge of the presents to the king; on the receipt of which the latter had promised to reward us with a drove of cattle. I, who had only so recently come off a journey, consented to go, prepared myself accordingly, and two days after went to sleep at Farewell's residence.

5th.—To-day, I set off on my fourth journey to the Zoola king, accompanied by Lieutenant King's native servant Nasapongo, who had been at the Cape of Good Hope, and some other natives. I had, as a present for his majesty, a handsome brass crown, a quantity of beads, some blankets, and a plume of red feathers, with a quantity of peacock's feathers which he wanted for his warriors. My road thither being the same as the one of my preceding trip, and no incident having occurred on my way, I have nothing worth detailing that would be new to my readers, and a repetition of similar scenes would neither afford interest, nor convey much information. I arrived at the imperial residence on the

8th.—In the evening, after sunset, and the next morning, while his majesty was sitting in the palace, I proceeded thither, and gave to him the several articles under my charge. He viewed them with astonishment, and desired Nasapongo to put on the crown. He then called several of his chiefs to look at it, who praised its appearance and quality. The feathers, however, he did not seem to estimate, but rather received them with indifference, and thought them not at all suited for his warriors, for whom he intended them. He made particular inquiries after Lieutenant King, and seemed more than ordinarily anxious to see him, that he might obtain from him information of what had taken place " over the water." After questioning Nasapongo relative to the Cape of Good Hope, whether he had seen any soldiers, and if we had plenty of cattle, he permitted me to retire to my hut, and sent me a quantity of patconger, a preparation from ground corn and soap, which, to a hungry and wearied traveller, is not an unenviable dish.

9th.—The king sent for me this morning, and asked if Mrs. Farewell was a pretty woman, and if she had any children; but did not express any desire to see her. He seemed more to regret that Lieutenant King had not come with me than anything, manifesting his great solicitude to see my gallant companion, and wondered what could have prevented him from making a journey to the palace. He evinced some surprise at Nasapongo's account of the " other side of the water," and at times appeared in better spirits than I had ever seen him before, which I attributed to his recent conquest, having now de-

stroyed the most powerful tribe with which he had
ever contended; and, in fact, the only one that could
have held out so long.　They had often come in
collision, and each party had been successively defeated.　He appears to have destroyed in this last
encounter nearly every human being of the tribe,
man, woman, and child.　The king, Isseconyarna,
with a few men alone escaped; for security, he fled
to a pit within the bushes, and was there secreted
until the merciless Zoolas had retired from the field.
Isseconyarna had, in his time, been an inhuman
tyrant, and had now received the punishment due to
him for his many vices and cruelties.

　10th.—The king sent me a bullock, desiring me
to thank the spirit for Lieutenant King's safe arrival,
as customary with them.　Towards evening, and
during some part of the night, he was engaged in
teaching his people some new songs which he had
been composing, and requested me to sit down and
attend to their melody, which I did until near midnight, when he permitted me to retire.

　11th.—His majesty rose early this morning and
collected his warriors belonging to Umboolalio, formerly Gibbeclack.　He told his people that he was
going to select a spot on which to build a kraal, but
he had no such design; he sought only to carry into
effect one of his usual inhuman executions, or horrible
butcheries.　I suspected his design, and sought to
learn his purpose, because, having before been wit-

ness to similar proceedings, I could distinctly perceive by his manœuvres, and judge from the arrangements, that he no more contemplated seeking a site
for a building, than he did of being merciful to an
unfortunately offending native. The poor wretches
who were to be sacrificed that day being selected,
were sent under pretext of viewing the parts adjacent,
and to report a congenial spot for building. Chaka
then sat down, and desiring his people with great
earnestness and precaution to be secret, stated that he
had had a dream which greatly concerned him. He
dreamt that a number of his boys had had criminal
intercourse with his girls in the palace, and that while
he was teaching them songs last night, many of them
were debauching his women, and had thus polluted his
imperial establishment. This offence he declared
himself determined to punish with rigour; his
people applauded his resolution, and said, "father kill
them for they are not fit to live." The revengeful
and unappeasable Chaka, seeing his subjects partake
of his feelings, and hearing them demand that he
should execute summary punishment upon the supposed violators of the purity of the imperial seraglio,
said, "that the spirit of an old and favourite chief,
Umbeah, had visited him several times, and warned
him against the designs of his people, who, when he
called them out on public purposes, took advantage
of his temporary absence, entered into his palace,
and polluted his females;" that this had been done

last night he protested he had every proof, confirmed
by the communications of the spirit of his forefathers.
That it was so now he had no doubt, for many of
his people yet remained in the kraal who ought to
be present at the conference, but were indulging in
amours with the girls of the palace. "Look" said
he, "at the Maloonga (meaning me), you see he is
a man, he knows that it is improper to stop at home
in my absence." The people reluctantly acquiesced
in all he said, fearing the awful consequences that
might befal the girls, not that they esteemed them,
but because they were property. Meanwhile, two
or three of the men got up and went towards the
kraal, not, it was thought, with any criminal design,
but for the purposes of nature, when they were immediately killed.

The king now arose, and the people followed him,
keeping about twenty yards in his rear; and every
time he stopped they kept bending to the ground,
agreeably to their custom. "Now let me see," said
he, "if there be a man among you: how are we to
secure the people in the kraal?" Some said by
surrounding it. "Well," said he, "how will you
manage it, will they not see you, and many of the
guilty escape?" Here the people appeared at a loss,
or were most probably willing that those in the kraal
should escape. Chaka, therefore, conceived that the
best plan would be, when his followers approached the
kraal, for a few of them to run on each side and the

remainder shortly to follow them, and then, while those within stood unsuspectingly looking on, for all to unite again suddenly, and surround the whole kraal. A party was directed to remain with the king, lest something should be apprehended, who also might be employed in taking the people out of the huts and putting them in the cattle kraal. The people about Chaka were unanimous in applauding so ingenious a stratagem, and, declaring themselves ready to execute orders: this diabolical tyrant immediately marched his party into the kraal.

I went to secure my boys as I feared the approaching massacre,—the inhuman tragedy about to be performed, and was extremely anxious that they should not take a part in it. The king at first beat his aged and infirm mother with inconceivable cruelty, and to the astonishment of all, as he had ever manifested towards his parent a strong filial affection. He then became in such a violent and savage rage, that, knowing his want of temper to discriminate objects, and apprehending something for my own personal safety, I withdrew to my hut.

When all the poor unoffending creatures were collected in the cattle kraal, many of them being sick, their number amounted to one hundred and seventy girls and boys, a great many of whom were his servants and girls from his seraglios. Nothing could equal the horror and consternation which pervaded these poor miserable and devoted wretches, who, surrounded and

without hope of escape, knew they were collected
to sate some revengeful feeling of their tyrant,
but were nevertheless ignorant of the cause, for they
felt that they were innocent. Chaka, in an instant,
on missing me, sent to call me, and rebuked me for
leaving him, when I mentioned that I had been to
drive the strangers out of my hut, and secure my
boys; he shook his finger a good deal at this, as a
mark of his approbation. Every thing being ready
for the bloody scene, to complete this unexampled
sanguinary massacre of unoffending beings, he called
his warriors, that had surrounded the kraal, and told
them that his heart was sore, and that he "had been
beating his mother Umnante, because she had not
taken proper care of his girls."

He then ordered the victims intended for destruction to be brought to him, and those whom he selected
his executioners immediately despatched. He began
by taking out several fine lads, and ordering their own
brothers to twist their necks, their bodies were
afterwards dragged away and beaten with sticks until
life was extinct. After this refined act of monstrous
cruelty, the remainder of the victims in the kraal
were indiscriminately butchered. Few of the poor
innocent children cried or evinced any sorrow, but
walked out as if inwardly conscious they were about
to be removed from a state of terror to " another and
a better world."

There being so many of the victims, it took the

warriors a considerable time to perform their inhuman duty, and thus fulfil the bloody order of their savage master.

The tyrant was left alone, with the exception of the interpreter and myself, who were forced to witness the tragic scene, when, with a smile, he asked me " why I did not assist in killing the Umtaggarties," or people not fit to live, and otherwise appeared to exult at the success of his stratagem, and at the destruction of the innocent.

The warriors, after having done their infernal work of extermination, returned to the monster, and saluted him in their accustomed manner, by squatting on their hams. His majesty then addressed them, saying : " You see we have conquered all our enemies and killed a number of Umtaggarties, I shall now consult Umbeah, and find out the rest." Meanwhile he told the chiefs to kill some bullocks, and to thank the spirit, and then observed, " To-morrow I shall kill all those who have offended since I have reigned, there will then be nothing wanted to make you and me happy." After this, he arose and went into his palace, and the people after paying the usual respect retired to their huts, to take certain roots, for having killed their relatives ;—these, they say, prevent their grieving, which is punished with death.

I have known several instances of people having been suspected of crying for the loss of relations, who were, by the king's order, put to death on the instant.

In the evening, I asked his majesty's permission to return ; he would not grant it, but desired me to remain, and get the cattle which belonged to the Umtaggarties. I returned to my hut, but could not rest, dreading the sight of such another scene.

12th.—After a heavy shower of rain in the night, it cleared up, and this morning the king came out to bathe at the usual hour. He sent for me, and desired his servant to give me a cow to kill. He appeared much more lively and in better spirits than yesterday. The warriors soon assembled, when he told them that they had hitherto witnessed the deaths of common people, but they would soon behold that of chiefs. The sun being excessively hot compelled me to seek shelter in my hut, where I remained the whole day with the interpreter. The wolves were to be seen in large droves, making hideous and deafening howls immediately round the kraal, attracted thither by the blood so inhumanly shed the preceding day.

13th.—I was disturbed early this morning by the cries of a man, knocked down just behind my hut and taken away to be killed : he was the king's chief domestic. I could hear him distinctly thanking the savage monarch as they were beating him to death.

At noon two of the adopted daughters of this execrable monster, and one of his chiefs, were dragged through the kraal and executed with similar barbarity. The king, after these horrible spectacles, spent the afternoon in dancing with his people ! Towards sunset a drove of cattle arrived, which had been taken from the kraals of the people who had been sacrificed the day before, and were distributed among the persons present. The warriors returned thanks, and drove off their respective shares, when the king retired to his palace. The principal chief, Umslanker, gave me six head of cattle in the shape of a present, although I had doubly paid him by the different presents I had given him.

14th.—I applied to the king for permission to return to my companions, which he granted; but would not give me any cattle, saying, that "Lieut. King must come up," when he would give him a large quantity. I took my leave of him at noon, and in about four days arrived at home, and found my friends all well.

About this period, to our great regret, our two chiefs, Mr. Farewell and Lieut. King, had disputes of a personal nature, which tended to interrupt the little harmony that had previously existed, and which alone rendered our stay on this inhospitable coast supportable. This dispute, having arisen on matters of a pecuniary nature, between two formerly warm and inseparable friends, was a source of inconceivable regret to those who were with them, partaking of the fatigues and inconveniences of our common lot. For my part, I perceived, what I had long anticipated, that the warmth of friendship between my two companions was not of a durable character. I had heard much; and often elicited from each party enough to

convince me that a rupture would ensue, and that
their good fellowship was not likely to continue for
any protracted period.

To enter into the merits of the cause which ended
in the division of friends, would be foreign to my
purpose, I can only observe that I regretted it, and
the death of Mr. Farewell subsequently precludes my
commenting on his conduct, as I conceive it my duty
to abstain from remarks on those who cannot appear
to defend themselves.

One thing, however, became evident : this contention, which brought on a division of sentiment,
interest, and operations, was in the sequel detrimental
to the general good; as petty jealousies and envious
feelings increased so much, as to render it somewhat
difficult for either to carry on a communication with
the king, without perplexing or exciting a man so
sensibly alive to conflicting representations.

Lieutenant King, on his first landing and meeting
his old companion, Mr. Farewell, doubtless confided
every thing to the management and experience of him
who had become conversant with the caprices of the
Zoola Chief; and imagined that any traffic or intercourse that he might design, had better be conducted
through the agency of his friend, than by himself as
principal.   This was not only advisable, but, when
the character of the chief is seen, it will be said to
have been discreet also; the opinions of men coming
in collision would be likely to exasperate a savage,
who, without discrimination, might not only blast

their united interests, but subject us all to danger and destruction. There was evidently too great an assumption of power on the part of Mr. Farewell, and that gentleman demanded it as a right that the last presents of the crown and feathers should go in his name as usual; but this could not be agreed to by Lieutenant King, who now thought there would be no danger in making it known to Chaka that these presents were unconnected with Mr. Farewell.

This being, therefore, the result of the unhappy dispute between two old friends, I proceeded, as I have before detailed, with the presents for Chaka, and on my return Lieutenant King and myself agreed to trade together for ivory, conditioning that I was to receive one-fourth of the property collected by our party.

From this period I commenced operations quite distinct from Mr. Farewell; and although I had not to complain in the least at my success, yet I could not but perceive that each of our party sustained a considerable diminution of advantages by such a collision of interests, and that the king was greatly perplexed how to determine on many points, when he found there was such a difference of opinion prevailing among the respective white people with whom he communicated. Nothing could be more detrimental, because it was evident that each would endeavour to promote his own designs, to the injury of his opponent, and thus make it not only injurious to the whole, but even dangerous to our comforts and security.

CHAPTER X.

In the preceding chapter I mentioned the injurious effects that I anticipated might ensue from the disunion of our little party at Fort Farewell; and, in the subsequent pages of my work, it will be made manifest, that this difference, dividing our interests as it did, tended much to perplex Chaka, and to make him doubt, when he might have been convinced, that we only designed to open an intercourse with his country, and trade with his people on a reciprocal footing. But, unfortunately, there succeeded a collision of interests, although it was highly gratifying to me to find, that my gallant friend, Lieutenant King, was still held in high esteem by the king, and possessed his greatest confidence.

To resume my diary. I proceeded on my return, on the 30th of November, by way of the sea road, to the mouth of the Ootoogale, when I had an opportunity of observing that this river is not navigable, from a bar that runs across its mouth; at sea its entrance has a fine appearance, from its width, and

from the varied scenery on its lofty banks. It is at
all times dangerous to ford, from the great number of
alligators and hippopotami which infest it.   I arrived
at Gomarny's kraal, where I heard that Lieutenant
King was on his way to Chaka, who, by this time,
I concluded, had removed to his residence, Toogooso,
to the westward of the Ootoogale, and to within fifty
miles of Natal.   This new kraal of his majesty was
only of recent construction, and received the designation of " Toogooso," (or hide-away,) as appropriate to
his design of occasionally being absent from his palace
of Umbulalio, or from a wish of his people that he
should retire, while they attacked his enemies.   I
set off to meet my friend King, and was received by
Chaka with great civility, although he told me that he
did not like my trading, as it was a custom he did not
sanction: nevertheless he directed me to take the
ivory from any one whom I saw had any.

December 5th.—Lieutenant King, Mr. Hatton, and
George Biddlecomb, arrived, and I found from them
that " I had lost a day," not in doing good, but, I fear,
differently, from having been too much engaged in
matters neither of interest nor of moment.   The fact
was, that from travelling perplexities, and nearer objects
every hour engaging my attention, I had forgotten my
journal, omitted a day, but could not conceive that I
had done so, until my friends told me of my oversight.
It was unimportant ; had I been another Titus, it might
have been worthy of record. I had now been a month

from home searching for ivory, and was glad to meet
my friends.

The king evinced great pleasure in seeing Lieutenant King, and held a long conversation with him
respecting " the other side of the water." He had
heard from Kasapongo, who had been to the Cape of
Good Hope with Lieutenant King, that we made
bullocks draw waggons, and took no care of them.
His majesty observed, " that bullocks were intended
for their pleasure, and that clothes and trinkets were
proper for white people, who knew not how to take
care of bullocks." He gave us a cow to kill, when we
retired to our huts, and made a most hearty meal.

6th. To-day the king collected his people, to finish
a cattle-kraal he had begun. He superintended the
labour, and gave directions to his builders personally.
He ordered bullocks to be killed for them, and in the
evening sent forces to his palace; but when we
went, we found him engaged with his girls; so we
retired, after talking with the sentinels.

8th. To-day, as I was walking through the kraal,
I noticed a venerable-looking man washing his feet
with a calabash of water. His appearance attracted
me : he was tall, and of a yellowish complexion, much
lighter than the natives; this, with his washing his
feet within the kraal, a thing which I thought was
forbidden, drew my attention, and I accosted and
saluted him after the custom of the Zoolas. He
was evidently surprised, and looked at me with asto-

nishment, and hurried into his hut apparently alarmed. I followed him, and as I had by this time acquired a fair smattering of the Zoola tongue, and was competent to converse with the natives without the assistance of an interpreter, I soon found that he was the king of an inland tribe which had been subdued by Chaka, and was remaining with him as a dependant; because, no tribute having been agreed on, he had not become tributary to the Zoolas. He, as well as others similarly circumstanced, are compelled to accompany Chaka to war, and to furnish people to carry the baggage of his army, which consists only of mats to repose on. They are not permitted to fight as auxiliaries, because it is a Zoola custom that a subdued enemy is an " egguallor," or coward, and that he is at the command, and, which is far worse, at the mercy of his conqueror.

Their principal study is to please the savage into whose grasp they may fall, so as to appease his wrath, and obtain the unenviable rank of a tributary chief. In the course of my conversation with Sischlanslo (the name of the individual before mentioned), I ascertained that he had never seen a white man before; and that near his territories, there was a nation, or tribe of Bush Caffres, who exist by killing the elephant for its flesh, and that, in the event of conquering, they eat the dead bodies of their enemies as well as destroy their prisoners for a similar purpose: they are " Anthropophagi—men who do eat each other."

I had a desire, and sought, as will be seen, to meet with them.

The chief said that he had occasional intercourse with this people, but from their ignorance of white men, he thought that they had no knowledge whatever of trade. I therefore resolved to go to the country of Sischlanslo, to negociate with these cannibals as well as with his own people. He seemed much pleased at my proposition, as he had hopes of trading with me, and of procuring some beads, an article quite new to him. He appointed me a guide, and requested me to wait a day or two, when he intended to ask permission of Chaka to quit him. I took my leave of this unfortunate chief, and could not help pitying his fallen condition. It gave me the more concern, when I reflected that he had become dependent on an insatiable savage, a ferocious unrelenting tyrant, an inhuman monster. I returned to my friend, Lieutenant King, who readily approved of my design, and thought it might be advantageous in opening an intercourse for future traffic; or, at all events, I should see a country which had never been trodden by a white man.

9th.—I prepared a party of six stout boys, and equipped myself for the expedition to the country of Sischlanslo. I took fire-arms, although I had no danger to apprehend from the natives, so long as I was friendly with the Zoolas, who were the terror of the neighbouring tribes; but I found it would be

judicious to provide against the wild animals, which
are numerous on the route we were about to take :
besides, I found that fire-arms caused great consternation among the natives, and commanded respect. My
luggage consisted of a Caffre mat, a blanket, two duck
frocks, and two pair of duck trousers, which, when
rolled together, sufficed for a pillow.   I had no other
incumbrances than the foregoing apparel; as for food,
we made it an invariable rule to trust to Providence
and our own good fortune, to meet with provision on
the way.   In obtaining sustenance we never found
any difficulty, after having become friendly with
Chaka, who would direct any of his people to be
killed for refusing us aid when we required it, and
that too without any equivalent.

10th.—This morning Lieutenant King left the residence of Chaka to return home, whilst I, equipped
for my interior tour, set off with more than the ordinary
anticipations of a traveller.   I advanced about twenty
miles over a fine, clear, and regular country, exhibiting some pleasing scenery.   We passed only one
forest, which had nothing either attractive or otherwise   The country, at a distance, seemed irregular,
undulatory, in some instances mountainous, and of
a wild and terrific aspect.   My route, however, led
me to a more rich and fruitful part, abounding with
verdant savannas and innumerable hamlets, in all
which we could perceive cattle and provisions.   We
arrived at Amapamellow in the evening, at which

kraal I took up my abode for the night, having
sustained some fatigue from travelling twenty miles
under an oppressively hot sun. Here I was received
well by the natives. The chief, although poor, killed
for me a young heifer, as he said that I was the
first white man who had ever visited his part of the
country, and he could not imagine what induced me
to come; he was sure, however, that the Spirit would
reward him for having killed a cow for us. I spent
the night very comfortably here. The good old natives
thought that the Great Spirit could not do too much
for me. I had a tolerable night's rest, though the
mice, which were numerous, made sad havoc with my
toe nails; but I was so wearied on lying down, that I
was not awakened by them.

11th.—Early this morning I took leave of my
hospitable host, and pursued my journey. The chief
accompanied me a short distance and then took his
leave. After travelling three or four miles over an
irregular and somewhat rugged plain, we reached a
more elevated site, on which neither underwood nor
any description of bush or jungle was to be seen.
This exposed us exceedingly to the sun, the beams of
which shot down with oppressive warmth, making our
journey in this vicinity anything but agreeable. At
noon we happily arrived at a place where there
were a few huts, built by Sischlanslo, to halt at on his
journeys to and from the Zoola monarch. I reclined
here for a short time, enjoying the refreshment which

the shade afforded. We resumed our journey, and
arrived, after having crossed several rivers of no moment on our way, near to a cataract of much grandeur,
and of a picturesque character: its water falling over a
rugged surface of rocks, which divided it into a variety
of courses, gave it an appearance of singular beauty.
The contiguous scenery added much to the charms
of the fall, by its verdure and rich foliage; the trees
afford a shade under which the worn-out traveller
might rest his wearied limbs, and recruit himself
for further fatigue. The water from the cataract
falling into a spacious basin, I plunged into it, regardless of my heated condition, and after a short
bathe again equipped myself, exceedingly refreshed,
and vigorous to renew my march. Our course from
hence led to the summit of an eminence, on each
side of which there was a declivity of three to four
hundred feet. My guide hurried me on, as he said
we had some distance to go before we should be able
to find a shelter for the night, and the sun was fast
declining. After some little time we reached a most
dismal-looking spot, near to which we descried two
kraals below. It was fortunate we arrived here before
night, as the situation we were in was anything but
pleasing, being on the edge of a precipice of at least
four hundred feet perpendicular. We had to survey it,
and to discover the most secure way of descending
to the kraal at its base. It being a solid mass of
almost impenetrable rock, and my feet being tender,

I was obliged to pull off my trousers to put round my
feet, one after the other, as I took a step.   I got down
at last, but not without great trepidation.

We reached the kraal just before dark.   When
I looked on the scene around me, it was indeed a
dreary one; the stoutest heart might have been appalled
at the sight of the precipice, and at the wildness of
the spot.   It seemed as if designed for the abode of
banditti.   Gil Blas' cavern must have been a palace
to it.   Here for the night we had our hut

"In a deep cave, dug by no mortal hand."

The part of the country through which we had
passed had once been thickly inhabited, but now, alas,
scarcely a habitation is to be seen, or a solitary
native to be found!   The Zoola king had subdued
the chiefs, and depopulated the whole district, tribe
after tribe, in quick succession, so that of the original
inhabitants scarcely any remained.

Dismal and almost secluded from the haunts of
men as the kraal is, at which we had arrived at the
foot of the precipice, it had symptoms of being inhabited not to be mistaken, for the natives had congregated in a large body, to gaze at me as something
supernatural.   Their remarks on my person were
highly amusing: one of them said, " He is like us;
look at his hands and feet how pretty they are."
Others again said, " What a pity it is he wears clothes,
I should like to see his body: I wonder if it is like

ours." Another wanted to see my hair, and at last they became troublesome, which compelled me to retire to my hut.

The chief gave me a calf to kill; when, after making a meal of the roasted entrails with some corn, I retired to repose for the night, first taking care to secure my toes against another attack.

12th.—At about 10 A.M. I set out, accompanied by the chief of the kraal, and travelled about twelve miles over a very irregular country, exceedingly mountain-ous, remarkable for a dark and stony surface, and a sort of dwarf bush with but little herbage. We past several kraals, the inmates of which came round us, excited by my appearance, and followed us until we reached the kraal of Armansinne, the brother of Sischlanslo. Here we halted for the night. The chief had gone to another of his kraals on the opposite side of the river Ootoogale, whither I did not feel inclined to go, as the alligators in this part of the stream are exceedingly numerous, large, and destructive.

My chief sent to inform Armansinne of my arrival; he in the mean time gave me a cow to kill, and filled my hut with other provisions. I had seen this chief at the imperial residence. In the evening my hut was filled with young natives of either sex, who amused me with their dancing and singing, and in many other agreeable ways.

13th.—Some messengers arrived from the king Sischlanslo to acquaint me that he would send

people to look for ivory where the bush Caffres had
been killing the elephant, and requested me to remain
where I was until I heard from him again.   At the
same time he gave his brother directions to kill me a
cow every day, and to be particular in seeing that I
wanted nothing in the way of food.   The following
day I sent the messengers back with one of my boys
to thank my hospitable friend for this manifestation of
his care for me, and to express a hope that he would lose
no time in collecting the ivory he spoke of, nor in finding the cannibals, that I might see them, as my object
was mainly to have an interview with them if possible.

While residing here, I was much entertained at
times, by the extraordinary congregation of natives,
who had been induced to assemble from all quarters
for the purpose of seeing "the white man."

Their attitudes and expressions of amazement,
which my appearance excited, were so irresistibly
grotesque, that I could not abstain from smiling
at them, and, occasionally, from laughing aloud.
All ages and sexes, the hale and the infirm,
gathered round me; some afraid to approach me,
others placing their children at my feet, entreating me
to touch them, conceiving that my doing so would be
a good omen.   The young exulted, inasmuch as, they
said, it made them wiser than their forefathers, who
had never seen a white man among them.   They were
friendly without being offensive, and curious without
being troublesome.   The youthful seemed delighted,

and the aged pleased; the one danced, the other sang; all manifested their gratification at my being in their country, and their regret when I left it.

In the evening of the second day after my boy had gone with the messengers, he returned to inform me that Sischlanslo had sent a party of men to look for ivory, and another in search of the cannibals, and that he would, in all probability, arrive on this side of the river in a day or two. I was quite anxious to ascertain the result of this speculation, particularly as I had been led to expect a large quantity of ivory.

In the interim I amused myself shooting hippopotami, which were here very numerous. The Caffres were much surprised at my killing one of these animals, and the report of my gun had a singular effect upon them. They never before saw one, but had often heard the Zoolas speak of them with terror. At every discharge they fell on their faces to the ground, made a hissing noise, at the same time shaking their fingers, as they observed, to prevent the "issebum," or musket, doing them harm.

Upon a conspicuous hill, about ten or fifteen miles from this place, there dwelt the remains of a tribe who had been subdued and nearly exterminated by the Zoolas; about twenty men, with their women and children, only remained, who had sought the summit of this hill as a place of refuge. The hill itself was remarkable, having four sides, and each being perpendicular, rendering it almost inaccessible without some aid; it therefore was a place of security for these poor persecuted beings. They ascended and descended by means of a ladder, which they had constructed for the purpose, and, when all their party were up, the ladder was drawn up also. They grew corn around them; and a party occasionally, as they were required, sallied forth to seek wild esculents and other food. While on this service, there were always some left to look out for the approach of an enemy. In case of alarm, they all retired to their fortress, and drew up their ladder. In this way also they got their water, which was handed up in earthen pots upon a pole. Thus situated, they became unassailable, and considered themselves invulnerable.

Being in want of people, I repaired to this hill, although I was told they were a desperate body of people, and would most likely attack me, as my force was so inferior. My object was to try to get them to engage with me in a compact of friendship, to leave their secluded abode, and take up their residence under my protection.

I set off to this extraordinary spot, and after travelling over a hilly, stony, and disagreeable country, arrived within a mile of the abode of this persecuted tribe. I sent two of my boys to reconnoitre and hail them, and, if possible, induce them, or some of them, to come and meet me; but all would not do. They were apprehensive that it was a design to entice them from their abode and security, as had

been done before, when, under the cloak and assurance
of friendship, they had been induced to send people to
their neighbours, who always massacred them. Finally,
however, I went myself, when they all came to the
margin of the precipice, and exclaimed that I could
not be a human being, as they had never seen one like
me before. All my efforts to induce them to come
to me were unavailing; and, on my attempting to
approach a part which I thought I could ascend, they
told me that they would destroy me, and make me food
for the hyenas. I said I wished them to understand
that I was a friend to the distressed, and came to offer
them protection; but, if they were hostile, I could kill
them every one as they stood. At this they appeared
to be jocose, or to treat with indifference what I said;
consequently I fired a musket over their heads which
occasioned a panic, and they retired without my having
been able to bring them to converse with me. I returned therefore to the kraal of Armansinne, rather
chagrined at the unsuccessful termination of my day's
excursion.

The next day my friend Sischlanslo crossed the
river, and in the afternoon sent for me. I went,
accompanied by his brother, to his kraal, called
"Inyarkaneya," or "the old year," about two miles off,
where I met his majesty* sitting at the head of his
kraal, surrounded by a multitude of people. On my

* Although subdued he retained his royal dignity.

arrival he sent them all away, and invited me into his hut, where he asked me a number of simple questions about my country and my king; and, finally, wished me to give him a present, which I did, of two pounds of different sorts of beads. At this he was much pleased, and called a number of his wives to look at the beads, each of whom tried to excel in her remarks on their beauty. The evening being now advanced, he ordered his servant to show me a hut to repose in, and afterwards sent me beer, corn, and sweet potatoes, in abundance.

At noon the following day some people arrived with two decayed elephants' teeth, saying that these were all they could find, and that the cannibals had fled further into the country, consequently it would take some further time to find them. This information was rather disagreeable, after the hopes with which I had been buoyed up; yet I could not help thinking there must be ivory in this neighbourhood, as the whole of it abounds with elephants. I suspected also something from the manner of the chief on the occasion; he seemed anxious to know if Chaka was acquainted with my being in this quarter to obtain ivory; which led me to suspect that he had ivory, but was afraid to part with it on account of that monarch, it being an article he always took to himself for the purpose of making presents to the European party. In this I was not wrong, as messengers had arrived from the Zoola king to ascertain the quantity of ivory that Sischlanslo had collected, which was, he said, eleven teeth, and which he had intended to present to me, but, being afraid of exciting the wrath of Chaka, he begged me to accept of four bullocks; with these I departed, returning home by a different track.

This tribe was once a very powerful one, until Chaka subdued it, and took away all the young warriors belonging to it to complete his own regiments. The natives are a tall, stout, athletic and fine-looking people, much lighter in colour than their neighbours, and approaching to something between a yellow and a copper complexion; their manners and customs are similar to the Zoolas. They are superstitious, but honest and hospitable; and indolent as well as indifferent and slothful. They can, however, on any sudden stimulus, be as active and as supple as their neighbours.

The country they inhabit has an imposing appearance; its mountainous tracks are wild, terrific, and not easy of access; but the lowlands and the savannas exhibit a degree of luxuriant vegetation exceedingly gratifying to the traveller. The soil is very productive, being of a rich marl, approaching to a deep black mould, which produces the most abundant crops, and would amply pay the labour of tilling, had the natives the industry and skill of the European husbandman.

Their principal productions are corn, both Indian and Caffreloopoco, (a small grain, from which they make their beer,) sweet potatoes, and beans, or pulse, which they plant only for their own sustenance. The females attend to their little husbandry, and do all the laborious work, while the men attend to affairs of war. They are always ready at the pleasure of their king or chief. The boys are usually employed in superintending their cattle.

The road I travelled on my return was not so agreeable to a bare-footed wayfarer; it was exceedingly thorny, the thorn-bush, or gum-tree, being a general shrub on the whole line of march. It was also surprisingly infested with tigers and other wild animals. I saw three of the former, though neither of them showed any disposition to attack us, but retired rather quickly, which prevented my getting a shot at them. We passed several Zoola kraals, the natives of which had lately removed from the other side of the river Ootoogale; they were the people belonging to the new regiment, Toogooso, and were taking possession of the kraal appointed for them, driving the Cayles (the original possessors of it) farther to the westward.

After leaving this place, I journeyed on leisurely until I arrived at our dockyard at Townshend, the latter end of December.

This tour had occupied me about two months, during which time, having traversed a large portion of the Zoola country, I could easily perceive, through every district, the devastating power of Chaka, and the horrid depopulation he had occasioned. His power seems to have stricken the tribes with terror, ;—they were alarmed even at the sound of his name.

It is evident that population here, from what I could discern, would increase rapidly, were it not for the scourges of war, and the savage custom of extermination; for in the small tribes which have escaped the ravages of the Zoola tyrant, the increase is considerable, notwithstanding that they are mostly, in fact all, polygamists, and are otherwise unrestrained in their sexual intercourse.

CHAPTER XI.

AFTER my return to Townshend from my long tour into the interior, I remained there about three weeks, to recover from my fatigue, and confer with my companions on the subject of our ulterior operations. Inactivity became painful to me, and made the scene too sombre for one accustomed to roam in search of new objects, as I had been. For want of some change, or employment to occupy my attention, and to keep *ennui* from my too susceptible mind, I resolved on taking a trip to the river Umlallas, about ninety miles in a north-easterly direction from Natal, with a view of accompanying Lieutenant King to survey the mouth of that river; likewise for the purpose of trading in that district, and to shoot hippopotami. Mr. Fynn had just returned from that neighbourhood, where he shot about fifty of those animals, and had obtained seven hundred pounds weight of ivory.

January 18th, 1827.—On this day, being equipped for the expedition, Lieutenant King and myself set

off, accompanied by my six natives, whom I had
trained to the use of fire-arms, and some others to
carry our luggage. After travelling two days on our
old beaten track, we arrived at Toogooso. The king
was glad to see us; we made him acquainted with our
design of surveying the river, and of making a settlement there, if we should find it navigable. He quite
approved of our object, seemed much pleased with
it, and promised Lieutenant King a large grant of that
part of the country, with an exclusive right of trading to his dominions. We remained with him two days,
set off again on the 22nd; crossed the lower drift
of the Ootoogale, and pursued our course over a fine
plain,—a sort of Arcadian country, rich in verdant
pasturage, and herds indulging in the repast they
afforded. Some sheep we saw resembled those of
the Cape, having thick hair instead of wool, and
being broad-tailed. We passed on our way the posts
of two Zoola regiments,—those of Umtontalen and
Madadas,—situated on this plain, where they were
stationed, surrounded with every thing they could
desire for food, and with water of the purest quality.

Having arrived at the Umlallas, we repaired to the
kraal on the opposite side of that river, which belonged
to the queen, and there took up our abode. The husband of this woman died a short time back, and his
death the whole country had just cause to regret. He
was Chaka's principal minister, and to him the Europeans were indebted for his Sovereign's protection; he

having been the individual sent by Chaka to negociate with Mr. Fynn, the first white man who had
ventured to travel in the country.

His son, Sedunger, now inherits the rights of his
father, and has the same predilection for the whites as
his father had before him.

We proceeded the next day after our arrival along
the banks of the Umlallas, and after travelling about
ten miles, often up to our middle in mud and water,
and amidst thick reeds, at times almost impenetrable,
arrived at the mouth of the river, the appearance
of which amply rewarded us for our toil. We waited
until low water, and then sent two natives across
the course, in order to ascertain the depth, which
we found to be about four feet and a half. This
would have been water enough for small vessels to
come to anchor in spring tides, but we perceived
a bank about half a league distant from the mouth,
over which the sea broke moderately in a gentle
breeze. The river inside was broad and deep, affording fine shelter for vessels; and the coast contiguous
to the banks of the river being picturesque, presented
a most eligible site for a settlement. Nature had
been bountiful in supplying this district with innumerable objects of an attractive kind. Splendid
scenery and magnificent landscapes, a luxuriant soil,
and rich vegetation, animal food in abundance,
fish very plentiful, and water from innumerable
springs, were to be found through the whole district.

The forests in the neighbourhood, which are very
extensive, contain almost every species of animal
indigenous to Southern Africa, and called by the
natives Loonggoie.

Lieutenant King had an idea that this place would
be an eligible port for communicating with the Zoola
country, its proximity to it rendering the journey to
the interior much easier, and of shorter duration;
and that, eventually, a most lucrative trade might be
carried on with the natives, and afford a fine opportunity of communicating with Madagascar, the Isle
of France, and the Cape of Good Hope, it being
sufficiently central for an intercourse with either or
both of those places.

By the desire of Lieutenant King I planted the
Union Jack on an elevated and conspicuous sand-
hill, to the eastward of this river, taking possession of
it as a grant to us from Chaka to inherit, for the
purposes of trading under the auspices of the Zoola
monarch.

We afterwards returned to the kraal, whence
we set out by a different route to the one we
followed on going thither, our guide preferring a
shorter cut, but having led us through many swamps
occasioned by the overflow of the river in the rainy
season and at spring tides, which made it more
irksome than before, we endeavoured to escape it on
our return. At the mouth of the river the hippopotami actually seemed, from their number, to occupy

the whole bed.   We also saw a great many alligators, some of which were of enormous size, living on very friendly terms with their amphibious neighbours.

Being now again lodged safely in our kraal, we were relieved from the fatigues of the day by a sound sleep.   When we awoke in the morning, an elderly woman entered our hut with a large body of attendants.   We were a little surprised at receiving so early and unlooked-for a visit, particularly from a female apparently of consequence, of whom we had no knowledge, and whom we had not seen before.

She came, as it appeared afterwards, to allege charges against two of our Hottentots, Michael and John*, in the employ of Mr. Farewell, who had been left at this kraal to shoot elephants.   These fellows while out hunting one day, met the young wife of a great and favourite chief (of whom the female, our visitant, was queen), and offered her some beads to induce her to comply with their impure wishes. The faithful and indignant female boldly refusing their proffered present, Michael accomplished by force what he could not obtain by persuasion or bribe, John the while holding his musket over her head. Of this we were afterwards informed.   These two villains successively violated the unwilling girl, who immediately afterwards made the people of the kraal acquainted with the circumstance, and messengers were

* The reader will understand that our personal attendants were Hottentots, not natives.   The natives were only engaged occasionally.

despatched to the chief to apprise him of the circumstance. He immediately ordered the unhappy wife to
be sent away. All we could say to our royal visiter we
knew would be productive of no good effect, because
the whole affair had been communicated to the king,
nor did she wait upon us with the view of censuring
us; she merely complimented us by informing us of
the atrocious conduct of our men, in order to prevent
a recurrence, and that we might not be brought into
disrepute with Chaka, who was deliberating what
steps to take. Lieut. King and myself now determined upon proceeding to the king, but before we
started, Michael and John presented themselves.
They denied part of the charges, but admitted the
main fact. Lieutenant King having reprimanded
them, and desired them to return to Mr. Farewell, and on no consideration to go to the king,
fearing that their presence might incense him, when
he would not only order them to be killed, but the
lives of the whole European party might be put in
great jeopardy.

Having set off briskly, in two days we arrived at
Toogooso. Chaka received us very coolly, which
was an unusual thing with him; he talked to us on the
subject of our visit with a good deal of wrath, said he
would kill all the white people in Natal, and then send
to inform the Governor of the Cape the cause of it.
We acknowledged that the Hottentots had done
wrong, and deserved severe punishment, but endeavoured to persuade him of the injustice of punish-

ing the innocent for the offences of the guilty. To
this reasoning, however, he would not attend; and
at once observed, "if he killed one, he must kill all,"
as it was the maxim of his law and the practice of his
country.

Our situation was now somewhat critical; the stubborn Hottentots, in direct opposition to our instructions, had arrived at Toogooso, but, fortunately for us
all, they did not enter into the king's presence, as he
was much enraged, and frequently said to the chiefs
that were sitting around him, "Would you not kill
them if I told you?" It was in vain to attempt to
appease him, and Lieut. King, from not knowing the
language, and not being so well acquainted with Chaka
as myself, felt a little alarmed for our personal security.

I was not so much alarmed, thinking that his rage,
as on other occasions, was only assumed; nevertheless I
felt apprehensive that he might, in the moment of his
passion, utter the words "kill them," or even make a
sign without an intention of its being carried into
execution, when many near him would instantly rush
on us, and massacre us on the spot, not waiting to
receive more peremptory commands before they did
the deed.

During this state of indescribable suspense, it was
impossible not to perceive that we were on the brink
of destruction. Whilst we were fearing that there
was only a short space between existence and eternity,
and that in a moment we must be sacrificed to appease
the wrath of a savage, I, having my eye intently fixed

on the monster, saw a gleam of hope favouring us, although eventually it might be fleeting. The inhuman Chaka began to pause; he seemed deliberating between inclination and fear; he was disposed to execute us, but reflected on the after consequences; he feared that our death might be avenged; he was a savage tyrant, but an arrant coward; and though he could exult at our death, he trembled with apprehension lest it might entail on him endless persecution, and final destruction.

He suddenly began to change his manner. I saw it; he relented, and sent us to our huts under a guard of thirty warriors, with instructions to prevent our escape.

In the evening we were commanded to be brought before the king, and conducted to the palace by his servant, who remained outside while we were ordered in. This excited our suspicion, as did every movement at a moment pregnant with so much danger. We entered the gate and saw Chaka lying in his apartment; he addressed us in a milder tone than he had done in the morning, which gave us an opportunity of speaking to him, and reasoning with him on the subject, when he observed " that he was still our friend; though if he could get the Hottentots he would kill them, and that the cause for his being so enraged in the morning was to gratify the chiefs, who had met to consult him on the subject of the insult to the violated girl."

At this time John Cane arrived with a communica-

tion from Mr. Farewell, expressing his extreme regret
at the conduct of his Hottentots, and assuring the
king that he was exceedingly anxious to make his
majesty every satisfaction for the outrage they had
committed.   About fifty girls now entered, when
Chaka observed " that his heart was so sore he could
kill all the girls present." The assurances of Mr.
Farewell somewhat relieved him, but he said " something must be done to appease the chiefs, or they will
say I am not fit to command; you must, therefore, go
and fight the Umbatio." This was a small tribe in
the rocks, with whom Chaka had been at war for some
time, and whom he could not conquer, being so secured in their fastnesses that all his efforts to reach
them had proved ineffectual; they had successfully
repelled every attack of the Zoola chiefs, and had
recently destroyed a whole regiment of Chaka's
bravest warriors.

We did not hesitate, being glad of this alternative
to appease the monarch, and soften the wrath of
his people; and more especially as it was to save our
own lives, which otherwise might be forfeited. To
go to war with such innocent people, however, was
painful; it was, however, not a measure of choice, but
one of necessity, and we were led to hope that, instead
of any protracted contention, we might be able to
parley with them and bring them to terms. The next
morning we returned on our way homewards to prepare for the intended war   We took our leave of the

king, who said "that he did not expect either Lieut. King or Mr. Farewell to go," and that he thought about ten people with muskets would be quite sufficient.

/ Having arrived at our residence, we began to make preparation for our expedition against the Umbatio, as it was the command of Chaka that we should return without delay. After, therefore, making the necessary arrangements, and equipping ourselves for the occasion, we set off for the residence of the king, accompanied by two of Lieut. King's seamen, three of Mr. Farewell's people, our two interpreters, and two natives, all of whom had been used to fire-arms. Lieut. King did not wish me to go, but as I was an idler, and the seamen were wanted to get on with building our vessel, I was resolved to be one of the party.

On our road we called and took the cattle of Michael, one of the delinquents, as a peace-offering to the king (as is the custom of the Zoolas), and as a punishment to the offender for his criminality. Having our party assembled, ten in number, armed with muskets, with about twenty rounds of ammunition for each, and collecting here twenty of the natives with shields and their assegais, or spears, we proceeded to Chaka's residence at Toogooso. We saw his majesty, who was pleased at our return, and then conversed with us respecting the mode of attack, commanding us not to leave alive even a child, but exterminate the whole tribe. We remonstrated / against the barbarity and great impropriety of de-

K

stroying women and children, who, poor unoffending innocents, were not culpable, and could do no injury. "Yes they could," he said; "they can propagate and bring children, who may become my enemies. It is the custom I pursue not to give quarter to my enemies, therefore I command you to kill all." We remained here two days, when he directed a chief named Martarbalala to accompany us, and to provide us with food on the road. In the evening of the sixth day after leaving home, we took our departure from Chaka's residence, and arrived at another of his kraals called Cheeabanto, where we halted for the night, killed a bullock, ate heartily, and lay down to repose. In the night it rained heavily, but the morning having opened favourably for our marching, in two days we arrived at the country of Sischlanslo. My companions being more fatigued than myself put up at the first kraal, while I, accompanied by John Cane and Brown, went on to Urmansinni, to meet my old friend, and waited the arrival of the rest. The next day they came up, when we all proceeded about five miles on the border of the Oetoogale river, where we were obliged to remain for the "Inyangers," or "water doctors," the river overflowing and being quite impassable. The next day we descended a mountain, the declivity of which was enough to intimidate us; after which we arrived at the place for fording the stream, and where the natives performed their usual ceremony of first chewing the excrements of the alligator, and then spreading it over the body as a charm to keep off those voracious animals so numerous in this stream.

The native doctors, with their usual skill, exerted all their nerve and ingenuity to conduct us over the river; and to do them justice, we arrived safe on the opposite bank, to the great joy of ourselves and to the credit of our ferrymen.

The Ootoogale, in this part, is about 800 yards wide, and its current rapid, making it formidable to cross by any individual not accustomed to the fordings. We rewarded our conductors, the inyangers, and afterwards proceeded to the kraal of Sischlanslo, where we halted for the night. This kraal was situated on the summit of a mountain, and it being rather early in the afternoon, we had an opportunity of indulging in a little rest after the fatigues of our march, and the crossing of the river. The next morning early we commenced our journey through the country of Sischlanslo. We had some difficulty with our native boys, who, feeling that they were now on an expedition, assumed the right of being considered warriors, and, as it was a custom of the Zoolas, in all their predatory excursions, to ravage and plunder the neutral and unoffending tribes in their progress, they conceived they were warranted in pursuing a similar course. They did so until they were stopped, and had a salutary chastisement administered for their refractory conduct.

After this, we travelled onwards in some order, and without incurring any hostility from the tribes through whose territory we passed, until we arrived at the encampment of the Zoola forces, about two miles from the enemy to whom they were opposed.

We had now reached a point to which we had never penetrated before, some miles to the north-east of the river Ootoogale. Our first advance was through a champaign country, undulatory, but highly productive as far as natural vegetation went; the art and industry of civilised man had not been applied to assist nature in her works, nor could we perceive that anything like cultivation had made a stride. Every thing we descried seemed spontaneous, and nothing like human industry could be discerned. With a soil rich in everything tending to invite culture, with a climate congenial to vegetation, a bountiful supply of water, and with seasons that caused nature to outstrip the anticipations of man, nothing could be seen in the character of the husbandman pursuing his avocations for the benefit of himself and his offspring, but the native boys attending their herds and " ever and anon"

> Plodding homeward their weary way.

The plains were rich with herbage; and the um-brageous foliage of the various trees afforded to the cattle a shade from the sun's meridian blaze, while

the springs of pure and transparent water, issuing
from a thousand sources, and meandering through
the wide expanse, gave to the wondering traveller a
landscape of an enchanting appearance.

Arriving within half a day's journey of our enemy,
the face of the country changed into an irregular,
rugged, and sterile tract, without aught to indicate
comfort, but with much to inspire terror. Nothing
like a habitation—nothing exhibiting the least vestige
of a human haunt could be discerned; all seemed a
wide and wild forest, without any living creature but
beasts of prey as its occupants, or the carnivorous
eagle and vulture pursuing the small deer, scarcely
bigger than a hare, occasionally pouncing on the little
creature, and soaring with its prey.

Being encamped with the Zoola forces, we consulted with the chiefs (who came from all quarters
to see us) upon the best plan of attacking their
enemy. They, like ourselves, had no inclination to
fight, but our disinclination proceeded from distinct
causes; they apprehended defeat, we wished to avoid
the shedding of innocent blood. The Zoolas, also,
were living with more comfort in camp than at their
homes; in the former they were provided with sustenance without labour, in the latter they had to
perform no little labour to obtain it. They had,
doubtless, a desire to exterminate their foe, but they
greatly feared their ability to accomplish this; they,
however, thought, as they were sent to make an effort,

something must be done, and that quickly, or the
rage of their savage king would be provoked, and
the consequences terrible. We sought to bring
the enemy to terms, and our Zoola chiefs led us to
hope that we might succeed in effecting our object;
but they deluded us by inventing reports, and deterred
us from pursuing a conciliatory course by false representations. These chiefs, who had been encamped
with their troops in the face of their enemy for three
months, conceived that we should strike a terror by
the application of our fire-arms in the attack, and
thus at once subdue the tribe opposed to us, which
would enrage their king at their want of skill, or, as
he would call it, their want of courage, and subject
them all to his implacable resentment. We conjectured, as I have said, that the chiefs were deluding
us, and we soon had a full demonstration that our
conjectures were well founded.

Having been three days inactive in the face of our
enemy, without effecting anything, we began to
think of attacking them ourselves, if the Zoolas should
not be disposed to assist us; while, however, I was
reclining in my hut facing the position of our enemy,
I observed them herding their cattle; at this moment
Brown came in to inform me that our party were
going to engage the enemy and take their cattle,
while the latter were herding; that if we did not now
make an effort we might lose the most advantageous
moment for attacking them successfully. At this mo-

ment, seeing my comrades rush out at the gate of the kraal, I seized my musket (putting on also my accoutrements — a small leathern wallet with cartridges fixed round my waist), and ran after them. I soon overtook them, and we proceeded slowly to enable the chiefs to overtake us, which they did, and pressed us much to delay the attack until next day; but while they were engaged with me, a party of our men rushed forward and took possession of the cattle of the enemy, who had fled to the forest to summon their friends to their aid. The Zoolas, seeing what had been done, now came up to the number of five thousand men, formed in front of the enemy's position, and began to perform the usual superstitious ceremonies of their nation,—such as the anointing of the body with a preparation made by the war-doctors from roots only known to these inyangers, who, with an ox tail attached to a stick about two feet in length, sprinkle the decoction upon the warrior, who rubs it over himself, and immediately not only conceives that he is likewise invulnerable, but certain of achieving a victory over his enemies. Our interpreter, who had been long with us, and whom we hoped to have somewhat divested of such superstitious notions, was the most elated among the whole host of barbarians. I could not help smiling at his absurd apprehensions one moment, and his confidence another.

At this particular juncture, I felt no ordinary sen-

sations of anxiety and apprehension. I was young
and inexperienced, and had never yet been in an engagement. I did not feel the want of courage, but in
physical power I knew my own inefficiency, and
regretted it. I reflected also that on the cast of the
die all our hopes depended—that if we were triumphant, the lives of my companions and myself would
be no longer in jeopardy; but, on the contrary,
should we be discomfited, we should be condemned
to immediate death. These were very serious considerations, and, at such a moment, enough to generate
apprehensions and forebodings of no pleasing description. I, however, recovered my wonted confidence,
and, in the hope of being victorious, shook off the
depression with which I had been assailed; and
in the warmth of a grateful impulse for the many
blessings I had received, I fervently ejaculated,—
"in Thee, O Lord, have I trusted, let me never be
put to confusion."

The enemy having taken up their positions in
small detachments on the several heights, we advanced and ascended the hill that led immediately to
them, expecting the Zoolas would follow in our
rear, but in this we were deceived, for we observed
them getting off as fast as they could to the opposite
side of the river, about a mile from our station.
This was a critical moment to us, but we did not
want resolution, and with one accord we pushed on
for the summit of the hill, or rather the large rugged

rocks, behind which our enemy had taken shelter.
In front of us we saw a small party of about fifty,
whom we attacked and defeated. The report of our
muskets reverberated from the rocks, and struck
terror into the enemy; they shouted and ran in all
directions, and the Zoolas were observed all lying on
the ground with their faces under, and their shields
on their backs, having an idea that, in this position,
the balls would not touch them. This singular
manœuvre of the Zoolas had a terrific effect on the
enemy, who, on seeing the others fall at the report
of the musquetry, concluded they were all dead,
and ran off to avoid coming in contact with us.
We had just finished loading, when we perceived
a large body of them approaching us, in the height
of rage, and menacing us with destruction: my
party for a moment felt some doubt; on perceiving it, I rushed forward and got on the top of a rock;
one of the enemy came out to meet me, and at a
short distance threw his spear at me with astonishing force, which I evaded by stooping. I levelled at
him and shot him dead. My party also fired, and
wounded some others, when the whole ran off in
great disorder and trepidation. We now felt some
confidence, exulted at our success, and advanced
along the side of the rocks to dislodge some few who
had halted with a design to oppose us again; they
had got behind the bushes and large trees, and hurled
stones at us with prodigious force, the women and

children aiding them with extraordinary alacrity. I
received a contusion on my shoulder from one of their
missiles, and Frederick, our interpreter, had his foot
injured by another. Advancing a little further, we
reached some huts, which we burnt, and killed their
dogs; this we did in order to induce them to surrender
without further bloodshed. We continued on their
track, however, encountering occasionally their missiles, which did us no injury, until we arrived at the
place where their cattle usually stood; from hence,
like the women and children, they had dispersed in
all directions, there being occasionally three or four
only to be seen at a time. The position of the enemy
was of a triangular form, one portion of it protected
by rocks, and the other by a swamp; the former
were almost inaccessible, and the latter was difficult
to get through. The whole besides was greatly
sheltered by trees and bushes, making it not an easily
assailable point.

The commander of the enemy's forces came from
the thicket to view us, and then said to his warriors,
" Come out, come boldly : what are you afraid of?
They are only a handful?" Thus encouraged, his
warriors came from the bushes. When it appeared
that they had reassembled for the purpose of deciding
the battle, both parties paused a little; the chief
showed great anxiety, and, urging his warriors, ran
furiously towards our Hottentot, leaving his people
at a distance. Not having sufficient confidence in

my own skill in firing, and knowing that if every
shot did not tell we must be crushed by their force,
now one thousand men, I allowed the chief to approach Michael, while I aimed at one of the main
body, thinking that if I missed him I might hit
another. The Hottentot's piece missed fire at first,
but at last went off and shot the chief as he was
preparing to throw his spear. Just as I had pulled
my trigger, and saw the man fall, and another remove
his shield, I felt something strike me behind. I
took no notice, thinking it was a stone, but loaded my
musket again; on putting my hand however behind, I
perceived it to be bloody, and a stream running down
my leg. Turning my head I could see the handle
of a spear which had entered my back.   John
Cane tried to extract it, but could not; Jacob and
four others tried successively; I, therefore, concluded
that it was one of their barbed harpoons. I retired
a short time in consequence, when my native servant,
by introducing his finger into the wound, managed
to get it out. All this time I felt no pain, but
walked to a small stream at a short distance, and
washed myself, when I found that the wound made
by the spear had lacerated my flesh a good deal. I
now was more anxious than before to renew the
attack, but felt myself getting weak from loss of
blood; I therefore descended the hill, and got to the
position where a regiment of Zoola boys had been
stationed. I requested some of them to conduct me to

the kraal, as I had to go along the side of the bush where the enemy had small parties, but they refused to lend me the least assistance. I took a stick and began to beat them, and levelled my piece at them, but not with the intention of firing, at which they all ran off in great confusion. My party now came up, the enemy having retreated, and we proceeded towards the camp in a body, but I had not gone far before I was compelled to drop, and my wound being extremely stiff and painful, I was obliged to be carried on the backs of my boys.

At sunset we arrived at the kraal whence we had started. All night I endured excruciating pain, and was weak from the loss of blood. On the morning of the 8th February, it being clear and fine, and the enemy quite still, and not to be seen making any disposition to annoy us, it was deemed advisable, as my comrades thought the attack of the day before had terrified them, to advance, and show them that the loss of one person's services could not deter us from following up our success; this we thought might have the effect of bringing the enemy to terms. The Zoolas at this juncture, seeing us determined on making a second attack, assembled their forces, and at 10 A. M. the whole repaired to the enemy's position, leaving me at the kraal to be doctored, or rather to undergo a superstitious ceremony, before a wounded man can be permitted to take milk. For this purpose, the inyanger, or

doctor, has a young heifer killed as a sacrifice to
the Spirit for the speedy recovery of the patient; or
rather, as I conceived, for the purpose of having the
beef to eat. The excrements are taken from the
small entrails, which, with some of the gall and some
roots, are parboiled and given to be drunk. The
patient is told (quite uselessly, I think) not to drink
too much, but to take three sips, and sprinkle the
remainder over his body. I refused to drink the mixture ; my olfactory organs were too much disturbed
during the process of preparing it to render partaking of it practicable. The inyanger, from my
refusal, broke out in an almost unappeasable rage, and
said, " that unless I drank of the mixture, I could not
be permitted to take milk, fearing the cows might
die, and if I approached the king I should make
him ill;" expostulation was vain, and being too
weak to resist, I took some of the abominable
compound; he then directed me to take a stick in
my hand, which he presented to me, told me to
spit on it, point it three times at the enemy, say
" eczie " every time, and afterwards throw it towards them. This was done in all cases of the
wounded, as a charm against the power of the
enemy. After this I was directed to drink of a
decoction of roots for the purpose of a vomit, so that
the infernal mixture might be ejected. The decoction
was not unpleasant, but it had no effect in removing
the nauseous draught, the pertinacity of which to

remain baffled the doctor's skill. I, however, had is
permission to take milk, the only thing in my situation
the least palatable, the more so, as it indicated the
doctor's foolish ceremony to be at an end, which gratified me, as I wanted repose. He brought me some
powder, which he wished to apply to the wound, but I
resisted, and he did not force it, but left me to sleep,
if possible.

In the afternoon I was roused by the noise of the
warriors who had returned; and my comrades amused
me with a detail of their successful operations. Our
forces had arranged themselves for the attack, and,
as they thought, in front of the enemy, — but it
turned out to be in front of the forest, for no enemy
was to be seen. The Zoolas became then apparently bold, and began a disturbance among themselves.
The Armabooters, or young warriors, being jealous of
the success of my comrades, and seeing no enemy,
anticipated an easy victory; they set off, therefore, without the concurrence of their chiefs, and ran
towards the enemy's position; the chiefs followed,
overtook them, and beat them back; and while they
were engaged in debating on the subject of their
conduct, three people from the enemy made their
appearance, unarmed, on a conspicuous part of the
mountain. Some of the Zoolas went towards them,
and our party soon ascertained, to their great joy,
that they were chiefs sent by the enemy to announce
to the king's white people, that they had surrendered,

and were willing to accept of any terms of peace, as they did not understand our manner of fighting; or, in their terms, " they did not understand the roots or medicines we used, therefore could not contend with people who spit fire as we did *." This was an agreeable parley, and my comrades directed them to descend from the rock, which they were afraid to do; but after some persuasion they came down and approached the Zoolas; when, however, the white people went near them, they seemed to be struck with inconceivable terror. After a short time, their fear subsiding, they addressed us, and said, " that they would be glad to join Chaka; that they were now convinced of the power of his maloongos, or white men, and rather than encounter them again, they would submit to any conditions that might be demanded." The chiefs did not wait to hear our propositions, as they have only one term, namely, to give up their cattle, and become tributary to the conqueror. They did not hesitate to comply with this, but promptly brought forward their half-starved cattle and goats. One of our seamen proposed that they should give ten young maidens by way of cementing their friendship by nuptial ties. To this they also assented with the same willingness as they gave up their cattle.

The affairs being settled to the satisfaction of all parties, my comrades accompanied the chiefs to their

---

* They ignorantly supposed the fire from our muskets came out of our mouths.

quarters, where they had an opportunity of observing the lamentable condition of the enemy, who were in strange consternation respecting their dead and wounded; not being able to discover the cause of death, and attributing it to some unnatural power of the Spirit*, whom they might have offended; and as they could not discover any other cause, they determined not to contend with us any more.

* The Spirit of their forefathers, whom they always invoke.

CHAPTER XII.

HAVING completely subdued the tribe with whom we engaged, messengers were sent off to announce it to the king; and I wished to have availed myself of the opportunity of writing to Lieutenant King to inform him of our triumph, but found myself rendered incapable of writing, and much worse than I contemplated I should be from the wound. Whether this was caused by the infernal compound that had been administered to me, or was the effect of the state of the wound itself, I could not conjecture; but so, however, it was; and as I could not write, I was obliged to send off two of my boys to relate the particulars. At the expiration of three days I found myself better, and my party contrived to invent something on which I could be removed. This was accomplished by means of a bullock's hide, fixed on poles for me to recline on, and natives to carry me. In this manner I set out, leaving my party to attend the Zoolas, and to arrange about bringing off the captured cattle. The journey was exceedingly tedious

and painful, and the weather excessively hot, which
dried the green hide, and made it uneven and injurious to my wound; the Zoolas, moreover, not having
been accustomed to carry people, made but an awkward and bungling effort of it, and gave me a considerable degree of pain and uneasiness; for, in ascending
and descending the hills, they had no idea, nor sense,
of levelling my litter, so as to keep me in a horizontal
position.   And what made it the more provoking was,
that my carriers having received instructions from the
chiefs to press all the hands they could on their way,
I was left lying in the heat of the sun during their
excursions to press hands to aid in conveying me
along.   Their indolence by this order was gratified, and
I had to endure the annoyance every mile or two of
pressing hands, and of changing my carriers.   By this
means my progress was greatly impeded; but I found,
after crossing the Ootoogale, that my wound kept
gradually healing, and that simple applications had
done it some good.   I now began to care less for my
conveyance, and actually gave it up, and in a few days
reached Toogooso.   As we passed on the road, the
warriors " bonkered," or offered thanks to me, every
one being surprised at the bravery of the white men;
and I was honoured with the designation of " Tombooser," or "the brave warrior who was wounded at
Ingoma;" and by this title I was ever after accosted
while in the country.

At Toogooso I had the pleasure of meeting my

friend, Lieutenant King, who had come expressly
to see me, and had only arrived a short time
before me.   We went towards the palace to pay
our respects, when Chaka, with a jocose manner,
and an artificial smile, said, " Yabosa Tombooser,"
and told me to point out the part where I was
wounded; I complied, when he observed, "that is
a cowardly sign; you must have had your back
turned to your enemy; and if you were my man, instead of King George's, I should have you killed."
I was silent, and thanked Heaven for having made
me a subject of the king of England, instead of
the king of the Zoolas. Chaka, however, seeing me
a little chagrined, gave me four milch cows, and said,
" that he was only jesting, and that he had heard of
the gallantry of our little party from the messengers."
After sitting a short time, discoursing on the operations at Ingoma, all of which pleased the exulting
monarch exceedingly, he directed us to retire to our
hut, which we did to regale ourselves after the dangers
and fatigues of our expedition. My friend King
and myself found no little gratification at meeting to
enjoy the pleasures which this release from all fear of
Chaka's resentment for the affair of the violated girl
afforded.   My wound now healed rapidly.

Before I proceed any further with my diary, I may
be permitted to digress a little, and to comment on the
following paragraphs from the " Travels and Re-

searches in Caffraria, by Stephen Kay *; because
the author, with great deference for his talents, and
with great respect for his missionary calling, has
rather overstepped those limits which a regard for
truth ought particularly to have prescribed to him.
In his work, page 401, he observes, speaking of the
Europeans then sojourning in Natal,—" And, incredible as it may appear, there are now in Caffraria,
also, Englishmen whose daily garb differs little from
the beast-hide covering of their neighbours; whose
proper colour can scarcely be identified for the filth
that covers them; and whose domestic circles, like
those of the native chieftains themselves, embrace
from eight to ten black wives or concubines !

" It is almost superfluous to add, that the life of a
black has, in the estimation of such degraded wretches,
become quite common; and that the hope of gain, or
the desire to procure the favour of chieftains, has not
unfrequently proved a sufficient incentive to deeds the
most base and sanguinary. Twenty or thirty of the
natives having one day fled from the presence of
Chaka, and taken refuge in the rocks, where his spear
was not able to reach them, the enraged savage, bent
upon making them the victims of his vengeance, called
in the aid of these fire-armed men, who, horrid to
relate, by means of their guns, speedily brought down
the poor creatures like birds from the tree ! The

* Published in 1833, by John Mason.

reader will not be surprised to learn, that some of this band soon afterwards fell by the hands of violence, and that others of the party also were soon afterwards called to the bar of the Almighty!" The author then proceeds to pay a well-deserved compliment to Lieutenant King, and in no measured language to characterise Mr. Farewell as having been insensible to the dying situation of that gallant young officer; and as having made no effort, nor evinced a disposition to perform even " the most common office of humanity " to the individual who had risked his life and his property in the cause of the man whose aid he sought in the evening of dissolution.   He goes on afterwards to wind up his illiberal and unjust censure, and observes, " Of all that went to settle at Natal, two or three only remain; and it is but too evident, that those, instead of promoting the work of civilisation, have, in a great measure, abandoned themselves to the habits and manners of savage life."

Mr. Stephen Kay, in his work, has told us that he is a " corresponding member of the South African Institution," or, in other words, that he is one of the missionaries appointed to disseminate Christianity among the heathen in Southern Africa.   In either character, I am willing to respect him; but as a censor, I am not disposed to submit to his reproofs, nor tamely yield to the sweeping and unqualified charges he has thought proper to allege against the European party located at Natal, of which I am one of the survivors. I do not presume to know the particular duty which devolves on him as a Christian missionary, nor is it possible I should for a moment conceive that the society, from which he sets out on his spiritual mission, can warrant, or in the least countenance, one of its teachers in disseminating that which the teacher himself must know, or apprehend, to be a deliberate calumny. The paragraphs I have cited, bear witness of a malignant spirit in the pious missionary, which but little accords with his sacred avocations, and manifest a hostile desire to hold up individuals to public condemnation, from the mere report of persons whom he ought to have known, before he became credulous enough to confide in their details.

This christian-like missionary, in the warmth of his zeal to diffuse the advantages which his society offer to the uncivilised African, has forgotten, I apprehend, that good old maxim, " De mortuis nil nisi verum," or he never would have had the boldness, or the effrontery, to have attempted to impose on the public confidence such a tissue of deliberate falsehoods as the paragraphs in question contain. And, in the next place, in the moments of his intemperate and malignant desire for reproving individuals upon the questionable testimony of natives, or on the more suspicious evidence of low and discarded Europeans, he would have thought of that precept which it is his duty, as a spiritual teacher, to inculcate,—" Thou shalt not bear false witness against thy neighbour."

This pious gentleman begins with charging the Europeans, at Natal, with having habiliments similar to those of the natives; wishing it to be inferred that this is from choice, and not from necessity. Does this captious reprover recollect, or is it one of the facts he did not elicit from his communicants, that the Europeans had no means of obtaining clothing in the first instance, and that it was only subsequently, and after the return of Lieutenant King with Mr. Farewell, that they could get a supply?

As much entitled to credit, also, is his charge of filth and concubinage; nor can the liberal and sensitive mind be brought to countenance an evident intention of a christian teacher to hold up the reputations of men, situated as we unhappily were, for the censorious world to reproach. It indicates too much of a morose and intolerant disposition in a man, who attempts to asperse the unfortunate (and to blast their hopes of being well thought of by their countrymen) by the dissemination of such equivocal charges, unsupported as they are by any testimony save the vehement reprover's own details. I challenge the pious author to prove his allegations of either filth or concubinage, that the public may be enabled to judge who is entitled to its confidence,—he who accuses, or he who repels.

To use the charitable gentleman's own language, " it is almost superfluous to add," that the next paragraph, in which the Europeans at Natal are charged with being

" degraded wretches," and of having been guilty of
" deeds most base and sanguinary," is, in point of
gross calumny, of a parallel with the preceding ones,
—a pure invention, I fancy, of the writer's own fruitful and visionary mind; or a compound of false-
hood and abuse, begotten in the brain of some malignant communicant, and which this spiritual author
subsequently nurtured and cherished.

The European party, on no occasion, for the sake
of gain, became willing instruments in the hands of
the Zoola monarch, to put to death natives who had
" taken refuge in the rocks," and had fled from the
wrath of the despot. The Europeans were under the
sentence of death themselves, for the conduct of the
two Hottentots who had violated the girl, as I have
detailed previously in this volume; and who had no
means of escape from the dreaded sentence, but by
engaging to go to war with the tribe at Ingoma, and
where our presence was the means of saving them
from annihilation, and not in contributing to it: the
terror of our arms saved the spilling of human blood,
and the horrible massacre that always accompanied
Chaka's wars. This is a fact to which Mr. Stephen
Kay's powers of invention will not be able to furnish
a contradiction. Instead of making these poor people
the victims of the savage monarch's vengeance, we
saved them from his implacable wrath, and from utter
extermination.

asserts fell by the hand of violence, I can only say,
that I know not who they are; they were not of my
party, I take leave to say, for both Lieutenànt King,
and Mr. Hatton, his chief officer, died from the effects
of disease incident to tropical climates. Mr. Fynn, a
gentleman above the reach of Mr. Kay's malignity, is now residing in Natal, highly respected
by the natives, who look up to him as a friend.
He evinces as much solicitude to spread civilization
and moral instruction amongst the unlettered and
ignorant Zoolas, as any zealous missionary from the
London Society. Mr. Fynn is a man of unimpeach-
able integrity, and of strict moral worth; abóve
all, he studies to do good, and not to propagate evil:
he is neither a slanderer, nor a dissimulator; but a
generous and a humane man.

The last paragraph of this liberal author—namely,
that the Europeans had, " in a great measure, abandoned themselves to the habits and manners of savage
life"—is another shallow invention of Mr. Kay, and
rests alone upon his single testimony, unsupported by
any corroborative circumstance whatever. The only
observation I shall make on this is, that I trust the
veracious author's pious avocations, and love of
African researches, may induce him to extend his
perambulations to Natal, where, probably, he will
find, instead of the savage native, without an idea
above the brute with which he once almost herded,
a body of people now becoming convinced of

the existence of that which they knew not until those Europeans, who Mr. Kay *so generously says* " have abandoned themselves to the habits and manners of savage life," had assured them—namely, the existence of a God who made them, and of a future state of rewards and punishments. I have done with Mr. Kay for the present; and only regret that his want of common charity, and his disregard of truth, should have occasioned me to have noticed his conduct with some warmth; I hope, however, in future, when he shall be disposed to speak of individuals in terms so illiberal and uncourteous, that he will not overstep the limits of truth; and that, before he vilifies the conduct of absent persons, he will give himself the trouble of correctly ascertaining if they deserve his reproach. Mr. Kay has never been in Natal; he has no knowledge of the country, nor of its people, but from the representations of natives who may chance to fall in his way. I should, therefore, suggest, before he attempts to sit in judgment on the actions of men who have resided there, that he will go and see what they have done for the good of the people; and, further, I say to him, " Go thou and do likewise."

March 18th. — To-day the white people arrived, and we marched in the order of Zoola warriors towards his majesty, who was seated with a party of select men. The king shook his finger repeatedly at us, as a mark of his satisfaction, and observed, " If I

had such men I should be as happy as King George."
A party of warriors arrived with a numerous herd of
cattle.   They had been absent about three months
on an expedition to the westward, not fighting any
particular tribe, but maintaining a kind of predatory
warfare, contending with all, and plundering as they
advanced.   In this expedition the Zoolas penetrated
N.W. of Delagoa Bay.   They arrived at an immense
river or lake, and travelled on its banks for a fortnight
in an easterly direction, with a river to cross, but
could not find anything like a fording-place.   They
met with some yellow people on horses, who compelled them to return.

The Armasootoos, a numerous race, who are
divided into several tribes, surprised one of the
Zoola regiments of young warriors (called Indar-
bencoola, or a large mountain, from their supposed
strength), who had taken a different route to their
comrades, and killed them without showing the least
quarter.   The Zoolas on these incursions come to no
general action, but merely confine their operations to
plunder, whenever they find they can accomplish it
with a chance of success.   They sustained several
losses of chiefs and men, but on the whole returned
with a considerable booty in cattle, the main object
for which the Zoolas go to war.

The king presented Lieutenant King with seventy-
eight head of cattle, and distributed the remainder of
the captured herd among his people.   Lieutenant

L 2

King returned to our home, but my wound being
nearly healed, and hearing that Mr. Farewell's party
were about to take a trip to the eastward, in search for
ivory, I remained, with the determination of accompanying them as far as the territories of Ens-vac-a-ler
(a king tributary to the Zoolas), for the purpose of
opening an intercourse with him.   We proceeded
along the sea-side, and visited several parties of sea-
cow or hippopotami hunters: I was rather fortunate,
and in ten days after leaving Toogooso, I reached
Ens-vac-a-ler, who received me with great kindness
and treated me most hospitably.   He was unwilling,
however, to trade, but much disposed to receive
presents: after some little reasoning and persuasion,
I obtained his ivory.

   I was the first white person who had visited this
chief, although both his people and himself had met
the European party at the residence of Chaka.   From
hence I proceeded to the mouth of the Umslatus,
and purchased a small quantity of ivory.   The different places at which I called on this tour were quite
unknown to Mr. Farewell's party; I therefore made
the necessary arrangements for a future trade, and
then returned home with the hope of having a pro-
fitable business with my newly-discovered hunters.
My wound being healed, I travelled fast, arrived
home on the 12th of April, and was much gratified
to find that our vessel was being planked, and that a
chance of soon leaving the country would be afforded
to us.

15th.—Yesterday our harmony at the dock-yard was interrupted by the extraordinary conduct of Mr. Hatton, and caused all our hopes of a speedy departure from Natal to vanish for a time. The cause for such extraordinary proceedings on the part of this man, who was supported by the seamen, was inexplicable, nor could we elicit from them any reason for their departure from the engagement into which they had entered for building the vessel.

Lieutenant King, finding these people persisted in refusing to work, and that persuasions were unavailing, declared he would burn the vessel on the stocks, and proceed to Delagoa Bay by land, there to obtain a passage from this country to the Cape of Good Hope. I could not help remarking how soon our most pleasing anticipations are blighted, and by what simple circumstances our strongest hopes are made to flit like a shadow before us. Two days before, I had exulted in the prospect of a speedy departure from Natal, when, by the conduct of an ill-disposed man, who had become malignant, and knew not why, my exultation changed into sorrow, and my moments of joy were obscured by a cloud of apprehensions. To get to Delagoa Bay I feared would be an undertaking of inconceivable hazard, and from thence to the Cape, one of doubt and difficulty. It was not very consolatory to find, after having escaped so many trials and contended with danger in every shape, that we had no alternative but to remain

in Natal, or force our way to the Portuguese
settlement.   These dismal forebodings, and not very
cheering prospects, however, made no deep impression
on me—I did not despair, for

> "Hope, the glad ray, glanced from eternal light,
>   That life enlivens, and exalts our powers
>   To views of fortune,"

buoyed me up, so that I did not sink under the weight
of accumulated disappointments, but set to work
cheerfully to secure our little ivory, and prepare for
the contemplated journey to Delagoa Bay.

After some little consideration, and finally arrang-
ing with Lieutenant King, I equipped myself and
proceeded to Toogooso to obtain from Chaka an
escort to Delagoa, and wait until my companion
arrived, when I should ascertain if it would be better
for me to proceed to Delagoa by myself and obtain
a vessel for the removal of our property and ourselves
from Natal, or pursue the plan first laid down.

While here, a messenger arrived to announce to
me that Lieutenant King and Mr. Hatton had arranged
matters amicably, and that the latter had amply apolo-
gised for his abrupt conduct to us all. I returned
home again by way of the Umlallas, and purchased
ivory on my way. I was most happy to find every
thing going on most harmoniously, and that our vessel
was fast being brought to a completion.

I now felt much inclined for a little rest, having
been constantly travelling for the last eight months,

and exposed to danger and toil in all its hideous shapes; and although we were in want of many things which we might obtain from Delagoa Bay, yet we seemed disinclined to make an effort to reach that place. At last, however, it was thought advisable that we should endeavour to get there, as, among other necessaries, we were greatly in want of medicines, —indispensable things in Natal; when John Ross Lieutenant King's apprentice, a lad of about fifteen years of age, acute, shrewd, and active, was appointed to go the journey. No European had been known to make the attempt, and succeed in reaching that place from Natal. A man named Powell, one of Mr. Farewell's party, set off to reach Delagoa; but he was never heard of after his departure. I seemed to have a great inclination to accompany Ross, but Lieutenant King dissented. The boy too, by going without any other European, would not be likely to excite the king's suspicion that we wanted to obtain a vessel for the purpose of leaving his country, as he had a great desire to have white people with him. Chaka afforded us every assistance in sending off the lad, by at once giving him an escort to protect him and to furnish him with food on the way. We were, however, apprehensive that the king would dispossess the boy of his several articles for us; we therefore had to adopt a preventive, and accordingly, after he had been gone about twenty days, I proceeded again to Toogooso, thence to Umboolalio, where

the king was residing, and who was glad to see me.
I remained several days, and the boy not returning,
I sent messengers to meet him on the way, and
returned. On my way home I fell in with Lieutenant King, who was proceeding to survey the
mouth of the river Umslatus. I was induced to go
with him, and on our journey we halted for the night
on the banks of the Ootoogale, where, to our great
surprise, the lad John joined us. He had not met
any messengers, but had taken the precaution to
avoid seeing the king, and from having heard that I
was at the river Umlallas shooting hippopotami, he
thought it advisable to take the route of that river, to
fall in with me*. We were much entertained by a
detail of his journey to and from Delagoa, and with
what resolution a lad of his years undertook a mission
pregnant with so much danger.

It appears, after having left the residence of Chaka
with his escort, he travelled moderately for eighteen
days, and arrived at the residence of king Mackasanny,
chief of the tribe called Amansluangers, by whom he
was well received, and with whom he remained a
day. He then obtained guides, and crossed the river
Mapoota in the native boats†, and arrived at the town

---

* The distance from Natal to Delagoa Bay is about 300 miles.

† These boats are made by burning trees until they are reduced to
planks; they are then sewn together with a cord made of rushes, and not
unlike hemp; and although the boatmen are obliged to be continually
baling them, yet they answer the purpose for crossing the rivers very well.

of Delagoa, on the banks of the English river, on the twentieth day. The river Mapoota * he described as being a formidable stream, over which the native boats find it difficult to convey passengers after the heavy rains, from the great rapidity of the current. His account of the country through which he passed is partly interesting ; though he states it as being low, level, and frequently marshy, and abounding with all descriptions of wild animals, particularly the rhinoceros and the zebra, both of which he saw a great many in every direction. The natives in the vicinity of Delagoa are a filthy, inhospitable, treacherous, and vicious race; but they treated him with civility and decency, not from courtesy, but fear; from the apprehension of the wrath of Chaka, which would have followed any insult offered to his escort, or his people generally. The Portuguese were exceedingly kind to him during his short stay of three days, but repeatedly said that they could not help suspecting him to be a spy sent by Chaka, as no Christian would think of sending a boy like him that distance. John, however, said that he produced his dollars to show the governor that he had arrived for the purpose of purchasing medicines and other necessaries, and that he was not a spy of Chaka's, but one of a party of Europeans who had been wrecked off the coast of Natal, and had located there until they should build a

* This river is called by the natives, La Zoota, and receives the waters of the rivers Ungovoomo and Pongolo.

vessel in which to leave the country for the Cape.
The governor told him that he might purchase at the
stores what he required. On his proceeding to
do so, he fell in with a Frenchman, commanding
a vessel in the slave trade, then taking a cargo, who,
not only took him to a store, but furnished him
with a great many useful articles gratis, so that
he returned, having only expended two dollars, and
yet had as many things, of various descriptions, as ten
of his people could carry. The cause, he said, of his
short stay in Delagoa, was the barbarous and inhuman
treatment to which the poor natives were subjected,
in being chained together, and treated with such great
severity and brutality, as made him apprehend similar
conduct towards his party; for they remarked what
fine boys he had, and spoke of their value, and what
they would fetch. This made him apprehend they
might be disposed to seize them all, and sell them;
he, therefore, deemed it a measure of wise precaution to leave without any delay.

John Ross is, doubtless, the first European who
ever accomplished a journey (by land) from Natal
to Delagoa Bay and back. When I look at his
youth and reflect on the country through which he
had to pass, and that he had to penetrate through
wild, inhospitable, and savage tracks, in which the
natives had never been blessed with the sweets of
civilization nor the light of reason, but were existing in a mere state of animal nature little exceed-

ing the instinct of the brute; when I look at this,
and also further reflect that the whole surface of the
country was infested with every species of wild and
ferocious animal, and every venomous creature, all
hostile to man, I cannot but conceive the journey of
this lad as one that must be held as exceedingly
bold, and wonderfully enterprising.

July 15th.—The morning being fine, we crossed
the Ootoogale (leaving John Ross to proceed to
Townshend), and pursued our former route to the river
Umlallas; after which, we shaped our course by the
sea side until we reached the Hunters' Kraal, where
we put up for the night. I have before given a
description of the country in this quarter, so that
to repeat it would only be fatiguing my readers
with that with which they are already conversant.
After passing the river Umlallas, whither we had
advanced, we travelled two days over a very fertile
district. The old adage of "variety being charming" was here happily realised, for nothing could
exceed the landscape presented to us. Travelling
on the summit of a continuity of high lands or
ridges, adorned with highly cultivated spots, and
interspersed with truly attracting hamlets or native
kraals, we knew not which most to admire, the ocean
on one side, all calm and serene; or the rich and
verdant savannahs on the other, bestrewed with
numerous herds, all indicating a richness of soil,
pleasing to the traveller, and gratifying to him as
being the works of a beneficent Creator.

. It is almost impossible to pourtray with accuracy the many varied scenes which the face of the country in this particular part exhibits; nay, the whole surface presents such ornamented features, that I have always regretted my own deficiency in not being able to particularly and nicely describe them. Whatever poets have in their fiction pourtrayed, may be found realised here; and the painter might enrich his store of objects for the exercise of his pencil, from the many interesting scenes with which this part of the African continent abounds. It is to be lamented also, that no enterprising individual has sought Natal as the field of his genius for exploration, because I am well convinced, had such an effort been made, my country might have benefited exceedingly by the information which an enlightened mind, in search after objects worthy of his intention, would have had an opportunity of conveying; and the commercial part of this community would have derived inconceivable advantages from these sources, for the exertion of enterprising men, which are to be found in this but little known portion of the African continent.

But the time is fast approaching when a more extended knowledge of this country will be disseminated, and when it will be sought as a vent for the manufactures of the United Kingdom, and for general commercial enterprise and speculation.

CHAPTER XIII.

WE had been admiring the scenery in the vicinity of the Umlallas, and were pleased at being now ready to proceed towards the coast where the river disembogues itself, for the purpose of surveying. We prepared for the following morning.

19th.—Accompanied by the sea-cow hunters, our guides led us through a morass, and afterwards over sands and into thickets said to be the track of these animals. We arrived at last at a delightful valley, or rather a ravine, near the side of the bay, where we discovered the banana-tree growing spontaneously and in a state of luxuriant vegetation. We sat down and enjoyed the sweets which this happy discovery afforded us. We afterwards proceeded to the mouth of the river, to take a survey of the spot. The bay presented many very interesting objects. It formed a circle, and was well sheltered by the land, which rose gently round the whole, and had a magnificent effect. The mouth of the river was narrow, but apparently of a convenient depth to admit small vessels. The sea in the bay was moderate, and a bank was seen about half a mile from the mouth; this appeared to be a dangerous shoal, as the swell of the sea broke over it moderately. The wind from the north-east blew rather fresh, and it was Lieutenant King's opinion that boats might land here with great facility. After spending two or three hours in viewing the variety of objects which attracted us, we returned to the kraal whence we started, and being much fatigued we retired to rest, satisfied with our day's enjoyment.

21st.—Took leave of the hunters (after renewing my former arrangements), and took an inland course to the residence of the king. We passed the territories of Ens-vac-a-ler; and the following day, at noon, reached his majesty's residence, who was pleased to see us, and ordered a bullock to be killed.

23d.—We accompanied the king to his kraal at Tipenschlangoo, whither he went with three thousand men to enlarge it. The great number of people employed conveying branches of shrubbery, each one having a branch held above his or her head, resembled a moveable forest of underwood. As they arrived, each party laid down his branch where it was intended for him to work.

These kraals are divided into four or more divisions, called iss-carbes, each division having a minor chief, subject to a principal, or Indoonah. It is expected that the respective parties attend to the building of the division to which they belong. After putting down their bush, they all stood up at regular distances, in order that the addition to the kraal should be formed. This being regulated by the king, they set to work entangling the thorn-bushes, then placing them on the ground to form the exterior fence. The inner fence, or cattle kraal, is generally built somewhat neater, and occasionally wattled, or framed with sticks crosswise, in an orderly manner. In the afternoon Mr. Fynn joined us, when we spent the day together agreeably.

24th.—It being a fine morning, I walked about the kraal; met several natives whom I knew; and ascertained from them that many of their companions, whom I had known when I was with them before, had been killed for having had a criminal intercourse with the royal females.

At noon Chaka sent for us. On entering the palace, and approaching the place where he was lying, he ordered every one away, and desired his interpreter to call Mr. Fynn. He then sent the boy some distance to get a bullock as the means, we understood, of getting rid of him for the present. The king then invited us into his apartment, a thing he never had before done. I could not help perceiving that there was a reserve, or a peculiarly grave manner in him, to which we had not been accustomed. He looked at us sternly, but with a wily air, as though he wished to communicate something, yet feared to do so; or rather as if, to judge from our looks, whether he might confide in us some matter of deep importance. At length, however, after having scanned us narrowly, and deliberated a little, he broke silence by thanking Lieutenant King for the medicines he had sent, which had been instrumental in restoring the lives of some of his people. He then gave us a basket of boiled beef and a pot of beer, and, after looking out at the door to see if any one was present, said, " that he should like to cross the water to see King George, but feared that he should not receive a welcome reception; he would therefore send a chief, under the charge of Lieutenant King, as soon as the vessel should be finished. He further said that he would send two elephant's teeth as a present to King George, to show that he desired to be on terms of amity with him."

He wished, also, that Lieutenant King would procure some more medicines for him, and particularly some stuff for turning white hairs black, as he had heard from Mr. Farewell that such stuff was to be got on the other side of the water, and he wanted it very much for his aged mother. He appeared to be more than ordinarily anxious to obtain this latter preparation, and promised to reward Lieutenant King with abundance of ivory and droves of cattle, provided he should return with it. He begged of us, in the most entreating manner, to keep this request a profound secret, and not betray the confidence he had reposed

in us. We assured him that his confidence should
not be forfeited, though we might not be able to
obtain the stuff he sought.

Lieutenant King also observed, that two elephant's
teeth would be but a poor return for the number of
presents he had sent to him, and tried to impress him
with the fact, that every thing brought for him cost
money; but as money was an article of which they
neither knew the value, nor the ingredient, he could
not be made to comprehend, but merely asked if it
were intended to eat. He, however, told Lieutenant
King that he was going to hunt the elephant, and all
the ivory he obtained should be sent to King George.
He said he had given Mr. Farewell a quantity, who
had kept it in his store, therefore King George
had no knowledge of his (Chaka's) liberality, otherwise he would send greater presents.

He then proposed that I should remain as a hostage
for the safe return of his chief, and said jocularly, "that
he would kill me if the chief did not return soon."
He gave us six head of cattle, with permission to
return home, and repeated the confidence he had in
us. Late in the afternoon we called on him to bid
him adieu, and then proceeded on our return (about
five miles), until we reached the kraal of one of the
king's mothers. The idea of a man having more than
one mother is somewhat novel and singular, and
wholly confined, I fancy, to the Zoolas. The fact is,
that the father of Chaka had, like Solomon, his wives

and concubines, and every wife is, therefore, designated mother by his heir, as a distinguishing mark,
and held in the same character as a step-mother by
a European.   The duty of these step-mothers is
an important one, namely, to select young females
for the imperial seraglios, to superintend them, and
prevent any improper intercourse. They are made
responsible for all under their charge; and equally
so, that all additions are pure virgins.

25th.—The day being warm, we travelled at our
leisure; but before quitting our hostess, who was
indisposed, she desired Lieutenant King to administer
to her some medicine, which he did. Imagination
acts powerfully with these natives, which was proved
in this instance; for he gave the sable dowager a
dose of pepper, which she took, and observed, " that
it was exceedingly good, and that it warmed her."
This was more efficacious than sacrificing bullocks to
appease the Spirit. She therefore gave the bullock
intended for immolation to us, as it is their custom to
pay their doctors, fearing that, by not doing so, future
illness will afflict them.

26th.—This day Lieutenant King separated from
me, he pursuing his course to his residence, and I into
the interior in search for ivory.

27th.—This morning I visited the sea-cow hunters,
and purchased ivory; afterwards went to the river,
and shot two of the animals; then proceeded to
Umptwaller's kraal, and halted for the night.

28th.—The day being fine, I made a tour to the river Umlallas, and visited the kraals with an intention of selecting a convenient spot at which to reside, while my boys hunted the sea-cows. I could not, however, find one more eligible than that in which I was stopping, being on the margin of the river, and the natives round it quite friendly.

29th.—Commenced earnestly shooting the hippopotami; from their not having been disturbed for some time, they were quite inactive and disregarded our approach. We consequently were very successful, having shot nine, which stimulated my boys, who were eager to continue the sport. These animals are not bad eating, but they soon putrify. The native tribe here are fond of their flesh, though the Zoolas will not touch it, from their warriors deeming everything but domestic animal food as unfit for their sustenance. Towards evening, I set out with two boys to the first Zoola tribe to buy corn, leaving the others to hunt the hippopotami. We crossed the river on the banks of which we were sojourning, and proceeded towards the sea-side; but night coming on, and the moon being somewhat obscured, we lost our path, and got into an elephant track, when we heard a tremendous cracking resembling the breaking of branches from trees, and which we found to be an elephant who, exasperated at our approach, was tearing up every tree within his reach. This terrified us, and we hesitated not, but took another course, and at midnight arrived at a kraal where we got shelter until morning.

31st.—Yesterday went in search of corn, purchased as much as the boys could carry, and returned with it. This day, after an indifferent night's rest, we travelled to the residence of Umcodookers, where, the boys being tired, we halted for the night. I was hungry, and obtained for myself (a bonne bouche with the natives, and generally preserved for the owner, or chief,) a dish of the small entrails of a cow, broiled, as they are held in some estimation. The liver of the animal, another delicacy, is usually appropriated to the females, who roast it, as being more congenial to their nice palates, and better suited to their feminine tastes.

August 1st.—The chief was anxious for me to remain and partake of some boiled beef with him, which he said was preparing and would be ready at sunset. As he importuned me a good deal, I consented. He had killed the cow as a sacrifice to the Spirit, that it might preserve his kraal from destruction; having seen a wild cat, or animal they call " Imparker," in a hut in the night, which is held as a dreadful omen that some evil spirit would destroy the kraal. They are exceedingly superstitious, and are alarmed at trifling objects.

The sun now setting, and the cattle returning instinctively to the kraal for security against the wild beasts, during the night the beef, being done

almost to a jelly, was served up in baskets, and the
people of the kraal congregated round. The chief's
principal servant displayed his skill in quickly carving
that part which was not boiled soft, and in serving it
out to the females and for absent people, according to
his chief's directions. After this, without further ceremony, all began dipping their hands into the basket and eating until the whole of the bullock was
consumed, except the bones and the brains, which
always fall to the lot of the boys, the men not being
allowed, by the customs of Zoolas, to pick the bones
or to eat the brains of an animal.

2nd.—I returned to the Umlallas, and found that
my boys had been very successful in shooting, but
were in want of powder. Sent a messenger home
for some; in the meantime I set to work and extracted
the teeth from the dead animals, and cut up their
hides into stripes for shambucks *. The hyenas were
so numerous, that during the night they frequently
ran off with one or more heads; we therefore put
them in the water to secure them; and found afterwards, from doing so, that we extracted their teeth
with greater facility. For several days we engaged
in pursuit of the hippopotami, which at last got shy,
when we prepared to return home.

11th.—Messengers arrived at this kraal to announce
the death of Umnanty, the king's own mother. Every

* Or sambuck, a whip.

native now prepared to proceed to the king's residence, as is customary, to mourn for the deceased. I being out of powder, proposed to return home; my boys objected, saying that the king would be angry at my not going to see him on such an occasion. I thought otherwise; and the next morning started towards home, and reached Mogarkie's kraal, where I met one of my boys with a supply of powder. Being now strong, I changed my course, and returned to Umptwaller's, Jack having joined me with two natives.

13th.—Hearing that my friend, Mr. Fynn, was at the imperial residence, I sent messengers to him to ascertain if there were any occasion for my proceeding thither. The sea-cows having now become shy and difficult to shoot in the water, I determined on trying what I could effect on land.

14th.—I got up before daybreak, and proceeded to the track of these animals to watch their going to the river. Saw one of a large size, and stationed ourselves on the border of the river amidst the reeds; when it got abreast of us fired eight shot, and killed it. Just after break of day, I was surprised to see the hunters' kraal on fire: my boys apprehended that it was a party come to destroy the people, this being the usual time of the year when they made their attacks. They advised me not to go out so early, as I might get injured. I was too much inclined to sate my curiosity, thinking too that if the conjecture of my boys should be realised, I might probably save

some one, and thus do a little service in the cause
of humanity.

I set off with two of my boys, leaving the remainder to eat up the animal we had shot.   We
soon arrived at the kraal, and time enough to be
witnesses of a most inhuman and savage exhibition—one that even exceeded the ferocious
exploits of Chaka.   The first object that immediately
struck me was, two huts nearly consumed.   Amidst
the burning embers were three women and two children of the master of the kraal, whom Sedunger's
people had sought to massacre, because he had not
gone to the king's residence to mourn for the queen
mother*.   It appears that a party, three times the
number of the people belonging to the kraal, came
in the night, and at the dawn of day surrounded the
chief's hut; he hearing the noise, and from experience knowing too well from what it proceeded, remained quiet, and prepared to defend himself with a
long spear.   His opponents were foiled—nay, they were
intimidated for the moment by his position, and feared
to return to the combat; they then had recourse
to stratagem, to decoy him from his hold, but
finding their efforts to induce him to leave his hut
unavailing, they set it on fire, and in their act of

* She had been repudiated by her husband Esenzenconyarna, and afterwards was guilty of great infidelity, by cohabiting with a commoner of her
father's tribe, by whom she had Umtwagarty, who will appear in these
pages hereafter.

doing so he sallied out, severely wounded one man
of the party (who was placed at the door to prevent his escape) and ran off, but finding himself too
quickly pursued to finally escape, he jumped into a
pit where his atrocious followers inhumanly mutilated
and killed him. The commoners of the kraal fled
to the thickets and jungles, the usual places of security;
his wives and children only remaining to be the
horrid victims of these wretches, who sacrificed them
in the flames of their own hut. Having completed
their savage commission, these ferocious agents of
a still more ferocious master sat down to exult in
their success, and indulge in the fruits of their
rapacity, whilst the miserable victims were consuming
in the flames around them.

Such a scene exceeds in horror all I had seen; I
shuddered at the sight, and almost forgot where I was :
I recovered myself, and thought that I felt more than
man, but forgot, in the moment of my roused indignation, that, with the exception of my two boys,
I was alone. But to whom is such an act of unexampled barbarity to be attributed, but to the insatiable
monster who ordered the attack, and on him ought
the vengeance of Heaven to fall for such a foul, such
a black and inhuman deed. Had his agents refused,
they would have forfeited their own lives for their
unwillingness. But this is no palliation, and though
they may be thought not equal to the savage monarch,
yet they cannot escape the imputation of having been

willing instruments, knowing that the confiscation of the property of the chief and his tribe would be the reward of their infamous labours.

The villain wounded by the chief who had defended himself with so much resolution, entreated that I would come to him. This I was not disposed to do, for I could render him no assistance, as his wound was mortal, the spear of the brave warrior having entered his breast and rendered respiration nearly impossible. I afterwards recollected that it was judicious to keep on friendly terms even with assassins, and that it might be even prudent to make some show of attempting to save the dying wretch; I therefore went to him and bound up his wound, and as they had some faith in gunpowder, thinking it an efficacious medicine in such cases, I gave him a little inwardly, and applied some, at their solicitation, externally; but the savage died, after having endured excruciating pain,—a just retribution for his having attempted to destroy the man by whose hands he had himself received his death wound.

I returned to my boys who were at Umptwaller's kraal, and in sad consternation from the number of people who had been killed for not having gone to the imperial residence to mourn for the queen; and not having heard from Mr. Fynn, I resolved to go to the king to pay him the usual compliment of condolence. I set off accordingly with my two boys, leaving Jack with my shooting party. On my

way I received a message from Mr. Fynn, to say that
he had returned towards home, and advised me to
do the same, as the chiefs and people were being
killed in every direction by command of Chaka, for not
presenting themselves to mourn; thus exciting his
suspicion of their having connived at his mother's
death.

This horrible and fiendish slaughter was continued
for a fortnight, to strike the people with terror, and
make them approach the insatiable monster with
awe. He had an impression also, that by a decree
so ferocious and bloody the people would live in fear
of his dying, when similar massacres would ensue;
and that to avoid them they would not encourage
the Umtwagarty, but would do all in their power
to preserve the life of their monarch. The day
being sultry, I halted until the cool of evening: in
the interim, some people arrived at Sedunger's to
inform him that the chief Umptwaller and his mother
were both sacrificed.

Sedunger wished to send my boy to the several
kraals to prevent the people leaving them, so that
he might succeed with his warriors in carrying the
bloody and savage decrees of his master into more
extensive execution; but I would not consent; on the
contrary, I sent them on to apprise the people of their
danger, which induced the latter all to fly to the forests
for shelter. He constrained me from going on such a
mission, when I showed a desire to do so, conceiving that

I should not fulfil his commands, and it gave me infinite delight when I found that my boys had executed my orders with so much precision and promptitude. The people having left the kraal, my party took possession of it, and while there a body of natives came for the purpose of destroying it; but on some of my men firing their muskets the murderous villains stopped, being intimidated by the very sound, and all finally decamped with great haste and consternation. Thus we not only succeeded in saving the people from destruction, but the kraal also.

15th.—This morning it rained heavily, and I could not proceed until mid-day. I arrived at the kraal already mentioned at night. I intended to have proceeded farther, as my boys had gone on. Jack remained to tell me what had occurred. The butchering party got into the kraal after my people had retired, and I found them killing a bullock for themselves to regale on. The wretches had cruelly tortured a poor female in order to extort from her a confession where the chief's property lay. I arrived too late to save her —she was nearly dead. The night was rainy and dismal; to have proceeded further would have been hardly practicable; and the great number of hyenas that were devouring the dead bodies made it dangerous to leave the hut; I therefore remained at the kraal for that night.

16th.—The morning was exceedingly damp, and not favourable for travelling, but being anxious to

M 2

come up with my party, I set off, taking with me two cows—not an unusual thing for a chief or person of note to do. I pushed on, until overtook Jack with the two boys and two girls who had chosen to join us, as their brother and guardian had been killed.

It rained heavily, but we still proceeded, rather than halt at any kraal, as the massacres were still going on; every place was in a state of alarm, and every native in indescribable consternation. In the afternoon it cleared up, when I ordered our fire-arms to be got ready, and loaded with ball cartridges, and afterwards marched forward until we arrived at Umdunger's kraal, where we put up for the night.

19th.—Yesterday passed Sedunger's kraal, where Jacob's people tried to persuade my young natives to leave me, but their efforts were unavailing ; and to-day we crossed the Umgani. On our way we saw many dead bodies, that seemed to have been recently killed, and stretched for wild animals to devour in the night. We arrived at Fort Farewell, about 3 P. M., and as it was high-water, I could not get to the Point to make a signal for the boat to come from Townshend, so we took up our abode for the night with faithful Rachel, the Hottentot woman, whose hut is always open for the stranger to enter. She is a good and hospitable creature, and deserves the protection of Europeans.

20th.—To-day crossed over to our dockyard, when Lieut. King rejoiced to see us safe returned, a thing he much apprehended, from the horrible state of the country through which we had passed. The following day we all proceeded to our new kraal, which we had designated Cin-ta-banto, from the number of people we had collected and saved from destruction during the frightful executions of the innocent natives by the decrees of the monster Chaka.

September 3rd.—During the last several days, I was preparing for, and had proceeded on, another journey to the king, with medicines, and nothing of note occurred until I arrived at the Loongoic mountains, where we met with parties of the natives passing in different directions, bewailing the queen's death. In another part of our way we met also a number of the king's girls, with brass collars round their necks. My boys ran some distance from our course to avoid them, which is the customary respect paid to these females by all the males who may meet them; but the white people being considered as the king's domestics and favourites, had the privilege of keeping the path, which I did, and they soon accosted me in the usual manner, that is, " I see you, give me a pinch of snuff." In a humorous way they asked me innumerable questions, and said one to another, " Look at his hands and feet, how pretty they are,— just like ours." They put up my shirt sleeves, to look at my arms, and uncovered my head to examine my hair, and many other things, which their extreme curiosity urged them to inspect minutely. I tried to get

away from them, but they pulled me back again, and
asked how many wives I had, and many other ridicu-
lous questions, until I got fatigued with their importunities. We managed, however, to get from them
finally, and by a little exertion to reach the king's
residence at sunset. He was in his palace, and glad
to see me, and invited me into the interior of his
residence, where he was amusing himself with his
ladies. I gave him the present of medicines, sat some
time conversing relative to events at Fort Farewell,
which he was ever eager to hear, and afterwards retired to seek for a hut. In the night he sent for me,
which is a common occurrence, for when he cannot
sleep he sends for the white people to amuse him.
He gave me a basket of boiled beef, I then talked
him to sleep, and quitted him.

4th.—This morning I wrote to Lieut. King, to inform him that the king was most anxious to see him.
The weather was cold, dreary, and dismal, and indicated rain; this, with the hideous howling of the
natives, singing their songs of mourning before the
king, in recollection of his departed mother, for whom,
in her life time, he displayed no filial affection, and
towards whom he was insensible and indifferent,
was extremely distressing. The king is a dissembler
and a most professed hypocrite.

5th.—The king rose early, and made an excursion
with his warriors; they returned in the afternoon, and
sang and danced until late in the evening. At night,

as usual, he disturbed me.   He could not sleep, and
asked me to procure him some medicines, " to make
him live until he was very old," as he had heard that
George III. had lived to an advanced age.

6th.—It was a rainy day. At noon, the women
began their mourning howl, enough to put one in a
state of trepidation. It gave me one of those insupportable visitations of ennui which are far from being
agreeable. The king's girls now issued from the
palace; their savage master was under the dominion
of a more powerful chief than himself—Morpheus;
at which time, these nymphs usually, if it be a wet
day, gambol like ducklings in the water, and exhibit
themselves in a variety of characters and attitudes.
They gathered round me, and began to examine me
with no little scrutiny, without perceiving my diffidence and displeasure, and heedless of the king, who,
if he had seen them, would have instantly put them
to death, and in all probability have done me the
honour of removing me from this " sublunary world,"
without consultation, or having my acquiescence.
They, however, on these occasions are pretty wary,
and know when they can take such liberties with
impunity.

7th.—The king went with the greater part of his
people to a distant forest, to perform the national ceremony of discarding their mourning dress (if it could be
called a dress, being nothing more than a few strips of
skin in front and behind, from hip to hip, descending

from the lower part of the waist to the knees), after
having duly mourned for the death of royalty. They
then proceeded to the river, to perform the customary
ablutions. Mourning, after this, was permitted to
cease throughout his dominions.

8th.—Henry Ogle, one of Mr. Farewell's party,
arrived to-day on a visit to Chaka. The king, whom
I went to see this morning, familiarly smiled, shook
his finger, gently touched my face, and observed,
he did not notice that I had manifested any symptoms of mourning for his mother. The interpreter,
however, said, that I had expressed great regret,
which in truth I had, for she had been a good woman.

The restless monarch then took a walk round his
premises, as if in deep contemplation, and on his
return sent for me; when, in conversation, he said
" I am like a wolf on a flat, that is at a loss for a
place to hide his head in;" the Zoolas had killed all
his principal people and his mother, and he said he
would now go to the other side of the water and see
King George."

There being now an end to the mourning, Chaka had
frequent consultations with his people on the subject
of a projected attack on the tribe of Armampontoes,
and such tribes as are to the westward of them, until
they should reach the possessions of the white people.
The warriors were all unanimous in favour of this design, as it bid fair to open a fine field for plunder,
which is the only object and stimulus for war that

the natives. have.   Spies were at once sent off to
obtain a complete knowledge of the country, the
passes to it, so as to arrive in its rear, and to find out
positions in which the enemy might be attacked with
impunity.   It is not the Zoolas' system of warfare
to meet their enemy openly, if they can avoid it :
they like to conquer by stratagem, and not by fighting; and to gain by a ruse what might be difficult for
them to achieve by the spear.

12th.—I took leave of the king to-day, and proceeded easterly to collect ivory.   I crossed the river
Umslatus on two trees fastened together as a raft, the
alligators and hippopotami making it quite dangerous
to cross by any other means.   I found a good deal of
ivory here, but the people from Delagoa had been
before me to try to obtain it, but had been unsuccessful.

13th.—I returned from this place to the Zoola
sovereign at the desire of my friend, Lieutenant
King, for the purpose of securing the ivory promised
by Chaka, particularly as Mr. Farewell was about to
proceed thither, where he might obtain it.   I arrived
at a time when he was making preparations for his in_
tended expedition against the western tribes; he was
glad to see me, and conversed freely on the subject of
his design, and wished to ascertain if they had fire-
arms like those we used, which he apprehended exceedingly; I told him that I was not certain, but
did not conceive the white men had penetrated so

M 3

far. After this, as he paused a little, I thought it a
favourable moment for speaking to him on the subject
of the ivory; when he assured me he had a considerable quantity, that his people were still hunting
the elephant, and he intended, in a short time, to
collect all his stock and forward it to Lieutenant
King; if he found there was not sufficient to load the
vessel, he should continue hunting until she was
ready to put to sea. His idea of the capacity of a
vessel was an extraordinary one, and remarkably
showed his ignorance of their capaciousness. He
conceived that one of his huts, filled with ivory or
elephants' teeth, would be a sufficient lading; and
that, from his numerous people, any deficiency might
be speedily supplied by his hunters. It proved, however, that he had never seen a vessel, nor had any
communication with one on the Natal coast. After a
lengthened conversation on this subject, he retired,
which was a signal also for us to repair to our huts.
For four days he objected to my returning home.

Several natives, who had been suspected of
cowardice in the last war, underwent the horrid and
savage punishment of impaling, and were then left for
the wolves and the vultures to consume, of which
(together with every species of wild animal, attracted
by the innumerable executions,) a greater number
were heard every night.

21st.—Having left the king in order to return to
Townshend, I had advanced on to Gormarnes' kraal,

where the people refused me refreshment; my followers, therefore, went into the hut of the queen, and
took two calabashes of thick milk. This is usual, and
according to the custom of the Zoolas, who compel
sustenance to be offered to the traveller. Towards
white people Chaka issued an especial order, that at
all times they should be amply supplied with food, as
it could not be expected they knew how to obtain it;
therefore, in any case when refused, they were to
have permission to plunder, and to use force to obtain
it; and those from whom it was taken were denied
redress. But the natives belonging to the establish-
ments of the Europeans' town, frequently abused this
privilege, and overstepped its limits; this they did in
the present instance, when a little persuasion might
have accomplished what they obtained by force and
plunder. It was nearly ending in bloodshed, before
I was aware of the circumstance, but, on being informed of it, and proceeding to the place, I found
they were contending, and the natives enraged with
my people. I tried to appease them, but nothing
that I could do had the least effect. Finding they
began to throw missiles, and that one struck me
on the leg, I loaded my musket with some Indian
corn for shot; on discharging it, the whole ran away,
and left us masters of the kraal. After expostulating
with these people, and making some show of returning to the king to complain of their having proceeded
to assail us, when they might have had satisfaction

from me for any misconduct of my people, their captain came forward, and entreated me not to return to
Chaka, as he knew the consequences would be fatal
to them; my boys, too, who evinced some little terror,
began to beseech me to proceed homewards, with
which I complied. The queen of the kraal expressed her sorrow for the interruption I had met
with, and said, if I could point out the individual
who struck me with the stone, he should be killed; she
then gave me a young bullock to " shlow-oo-ler," or
make peace; this I refused, being perfectly satisfied
in getting so well out of the fray.

October 26th.—Having been absent a few weeks, I
arrived at Townshend last night; on my way touched
at Fort Farewell, and saw Mrs. Farewell for the
first time since the disunion in our European settlement. I was also exceedingly pleased to perceive the
rapid progress made in the building of our little bark,
which was to transport us to the Cape of Good Hope.

Being now on the eve of setting off on another
interior journey, I was taken violently ill with inflam-
mation, which attacked me in the side below the ribs.
After three weeks' violent sufferings, I began to
recover, and felt somewhat flattered that I should be
able to get out again in a day or two, when I was
suddenly attacked with dysentery, which, from its
severity, reduced me to such an ebb of debility, as
rendered me quite incapable of any exertion. All
further efforts in travelling were now out of the ques-

tion; I could only notice the daily labours of our party at the dockyard, and the efforts they were making to bring their labours to a close. It was gratifying to see with what cheerfulness they wrought to accomplish so desirable an end; and it was no less pleasing to look forward with the hope of soon seeing the vessel on that element for which she was designed, wafting us to that happy port to which we were looking with fond hopes, and delightful anticipations.

CHAPTER XIV.

THE new year (1828) having commenced, though very inauspiciously for me, (not being yet recovered from the serious effects of my indisposition, but more or less subject to remittents,) I looked forward with great anxiety to the time when I should be enabled to leave this coast, and enjoy the change which another climate might afford, so as to recover my wonted energies, and be enabled to resume my avocations as a commercial man.

The launching of our vessel, now nearly completed, occupied my thoughts, and commanded all my attention. I looked wistfully at every effort of our builder (Mr. Hatton) and his assistants, and could not help admiring the zeal and perseverance which they manifested to accomplish the object of their labours. Some little squabbles now and then occurred, which for a time interrupted their progress; but they were of such a character only as frequently accrue between seamen, and arise more from the envy which authority generates, than any want of respect from

subordinates to their superior. There was some acri-
mony, it is true, at times, but it did not emanate from
men predisposed to render our stay on this coast more
miserable or more protracted. Such trivial disputes
arose as will accrue under all commands, where there
has been a little relaxation of discipline and order, and
these could not be avoided in our situation, where
the principal had lost the power of controuling the
dependant. For myself, these insignificant conten-
tions, although harmless, I admit, gave me a good deal
of concern, and much agitation and regret, not singular in a person visited as I was with daily indisposition,
and seeing that such petty broils only retarded the
completion of the vessel, by which alone I could have
a chance of relief. I had nothing to do with these
squabbles, not being personally engaged in them, nor
in any way responsible for the consequences that
might ensue from them. I made, it is true, some
efforts to appease, when I found they were growing
warm and violent, and often ran the risk of meeting
a severe rebuff for my pains. I therefore became
mute, left them to settle their differences as they
thought proper, and looked on with apparent un-
concern. At length their strife becoming fatiguing,
and discovering that they were contending for a
bauble, the parties mutually agreed to a cessation
of hostilities: preliminaries of peace having been
signed by Lieutenant King and Mr. Hatton, and
ratified by all the parties engaged, every thing re-

covered its wonted tranquillity and our work of building was brought rapidly to a close.   I began to look
forward to the hour of release from our abode, and
for the renovation of my health and strength, so
greatly impaired by a long and lingering indisposition.

During this period of disputation, however, Chaka
evinced more friendship towards Lieutenant King,
Mr. Fynn, and myself, than he had ever manifested
before, though we had received ample proofs of his
partiality on several previous occasions ; whilst, on
the other hand, he exhibited a cool indifference towards Mr. Farewell.   He sent us presents of two or
three bullocks at a time, and expressed a great wish
that Lieutenant King would take one or two chiefs
with him to negociate a friendly alliance with King
George, whom, he said, " he esteemed as a brother."
He also sent three fine bullocks to Lieutenant King,
which the messenger was commanded to say *were the
king's mouth ;* at the same time to intimate that it was
his wish Lieutenant King should kill Jacob (who
will be noticed hereafter), as he (Chaka) was afraid
that this person would incense the governor of the
Cape ; but to such a course Lieutenant King seriously
and immediately objected ; and thus Jacob's life,
placed in jeopardy by his own bad conduct, was spared.

At the beginning of the month of February, we
were agreeably surprised by the arrival of Mr. Mackay, master of the Buckbay packet, a small schooner,

of about thirty tons burthen. He had touched on a
trading voyage from the Cape to Delagoa Bay;
sold part of his cargo to advantage, taking ivory in
barter for it from Messrs. King and Farewell, and
afterwards proceeded to the before-named port. We
put some brass bangles and beads on board of his
vessel, to be sold by Mr. Mackay on our account,
upon his arrival at Delagoa.

We had now our schooner ready for launching, every
thing having been completed for that purpose, and after
naming her the Elizabeth and Susan, she glided gently
into the sea, floated on the bosom of the ocean, and
brought up her bows to the billows, as if evincing the
desire to take a longing farewell of the spot that had
given her birth. Thus, after encountering inconceivable difficulties, and contending with obstacles enough
to unnerve the stoutest heart; after having been in the
midst of the forest, encompassed by wild beasts, and
oftentimes by equally wild natives, seeking for, and
then cutting down, timbers, preparing them for our
purpose, and getting them to the dock-yard on the
coast; after encountering and overcoming these obstacles, our little bark was launched upon her destined
element, on the 10th of March, 1828, having been
built in the space of three years; a period of time,
which, under the extraordinary circumstances attending the builders' progress, may be considered a
labour equally creditable and astonishing.

Lieutenant King and his anxious crew now busied themselves in fitting out the new bark for our voyage, aided by Mr. Hatton her builder, to whose zeal and unabated labours we were all indebted for this happy consummation of our hopes. In consequence of my continued indisposition and debility, my worthy friend, Mr. Fynn, with his accustomed kindness, voluntarily undertook to proceed to the king to arrange the business of the intended mission, when Chaka appointed Sotobe to be his principal chief on the mission, conjointly with Lieutenant King; confiding in the latter, however, the whole of the executive duties, and every other matter connected with it. Another chief, Bosomboser, was to accompany them, but return on their arrival at the first port with tidings of their reception, of the friendship shown to them, and likewise the terms existing between the English and the frontier tribes with whom Chaka designed going to war; he had, however, promised to delay it until this chief returned with the Cape government's opinion of the step he was about to take.

Jacob was appointed interpreter, although he could not speak much English, and but little Dutch. It was agreed that Sotobe should take two wives, and Jacob one, and that Mr. King should furnish them with three of his native boys as servants. The object of the mission was particularly detailed to

Lieutenant King by Chaka himself, when he created him Chief of Toogooso, and promised him great advantages if he brought his people safely back.

I have before mentioned, that Chaka suggested I should remain with him as a hostage, but from my indisposition, Mr. Fynn consented to remain in that character as surety for the safe return of the chiefs. The business being thus arranged, Mr. Fynn returned to us, leaving the chiefs to prepare for their voyage and to follow him. They arrived in a few days, bringing with them four bullocks as a present for Lieutenant King, and one as a sacrifice to the Spirit, that their mission might be propitious, and their return insured.

The schooner was now ready for sea, and Mr. Farewell, with the native mission and myself, being all in waiting to proceed on board, preparations were made to do so. On the 30th of April we embarked, after taking leave of our friends, and receiving from the poor natives their howlings and their tears of regret at our departure.

Our vessel glided smoothly out of the bay, and we perceived the people looking at us sorrowfully until we could be scarcely discernible. The heavy swell caused the schooner to be uneasy, and next morning, the 1st of May, she was brought to, all hands being down from sea sickness, except Lieutenant King, the old chief, and the boy John Ross. We soon found, from the current setting strongly from

the westward, that we were off the river Umtugarty,
and about twenty-five miles to the eastward of the
port of Natal. We had the wind from the south-
east, and the weather being exceedingly clear and
pleasant, we commenced making all sail possible,
keeping along shore, within about ten miles distant,
so that we were favoured with an opportunity of
taking a view and of admiring the varied scenery
which the whole length of coast presented. The extensive track of country is all waste and uninhabited,
lying between Natal and the river St. John, in the
vicinity of which also wild animals of many species
amazingly abound, and the elephants are to be
found in droves. Near this river, and on its right
bank, the country seems inhabited, as we could discern cattle herding, and now and then native fires
interspersed along the shore.

Our passage was a short one, as we arrived safely
in Algoa Bay, and anchored on the 4th of May.
After coming to an anchor, the wind suddenly shifted
round to the north-west and gradually increased to
a gale, which, had it met us before we entered the
Bay, might have kept us at sea a month.

Mr. Frances, the Port Captain, and Surgeon Ware
came off to our vessel, and were glad to meet their
old friend Lieutenant King, as also Mr. Farewell.
They both expressed their astonishment at our
little schooner, and complimented Mr. Hatton, the
builder, for his skill, ingenuity, and zeal, to which

he was justly entitled. We were all, doubtless, very anxious to get on shore, and set our feet on a civilised coast once again. In the morning, Mr. Frances, who had returned the evening before, came off, and took Lieutenant King, Mrs. Farewell, and the Caffres on shore. Mr. Hatton and myself remaining until we could obtain some clothing to land in, our stock being exhausted; in fact I had only a pair of duck trowsers, and a frock of the same material, made up by myself into these garments, but which exhibited little of their original appearance: from having stood the pitiless storm, and the more severe service of constant wear, they began to

Let in new light through chinks that time had made.

My cap, composed of the skin of the civet cat, was the best piece about me; shoes I had none, I had discarded them two years ago, having been rendered useless, and could obtain no others.

In the afternoon a boat came off without any clothes, we therefore jumped into it, clad to the best of our means: when we landed, the people gazed at us, wondering what people we were. I hastened, on stepping on shore, to the shop of Mrs. Robinson, and obtained as decent a fit out as I possibly could for the moment, and afterwards sat down to a tolerable good dinner. Our hostess was kind, good-natured, entertaining, and apparently interested much at our return, anticipating that we had come with a good freight

of ivory, and that we should require an unusual supply
of necessaries. She was correct enough as to the
latter, for our necessaries were exhausted; but she was
egregiously mistaken in her estimate of the former,
for our cargo was small.

We were not long strangers, for the inhabitants
(being proverbially hospitable, particularly Mr.
Chabeaud, the commercial agent,) came to us, and
were exceedingly kind. Mr. Chabeaud and Mr. Edmund Francis, who were friends of Lieutenant King,
manifested much civility and liberality towards us.

We took up our abode at Mrs. Robinson's
" winkle *," the only one in the place in which
we could be accommodated. I wrote to apprise
my friends of my arrival, whilst Lieutenant King
did the same to the Colonial Government of the
Cape, announcing the arrival of the mission from the
Zoola monarch. He immediately received a reply,
directing him to have the chiefs entertained at the expense of the Colonial Government, until an opportunity
should occur for conveying them to Cape Town; at
the same time strict injunctions were given that they
should not be permitted to approach Graham's Town,
nor to view the frontiers.

We were now expecting daily to go to the Cape,
when one day, during the absence of Lieutenant
King, Major Clocte visited the Caffres. He told me
that he was directed by the governor to ascertain the

* A tavern.

object of the mission from the Zoola monarch; and as
the interpreter, Jacob, could not translate with sufficient explicitness, I put such questions to the principal
chief, Sotobe, as the Major requested me; not, however, that I thought he was authorised, although he
came with Captain Eratt and Mr. Vander Reit, the
principal individuals of the port, but merely from a
feeling of courtesy, to which I conceived them entitled, and because the chief wished me to be present.
The questions being rather of a singular character and
tendency, impressed the chiefs with the idea that they
were deemed spies, and that Lieutenant King would
meet with considerable trouble on their account; I had
therefore some difficulty to dissuade them from such
an erroneous conclusion.

They were soon very kindly treated by the inhabitants, and acquired some little experience in drinking
ardent spirits. These at times they took to excess,
which occasioned serious quarrels between Sotobe
and the interpreter, Jacob, giving me a great deal of
trouble in preserving order from one, and submission
from the other.

The repeated questions of Major Clocte, and the
reports of the king being near the colony, impressed
them strongly that they had no hopes of going to the
governor, or of the minor chief returning according to
the directions of Chaka; they therefore grew exceedingly impatient, and became so alarmed, that they
made several attempts to run off, and find their way

to their country by land. This rendered our situation somewhat serious, and highly responsible, when
also we reflected on the precarious and critical position
in which our friend Mr. Fynn was placed, and placed
too, from motives of great kindness and consideration
for my bodily health.

Lieutenant King felt a little incensed at Major
Clocte presuming to interrogate the chief Sotobe,
without his (Lieutenant King's) presence, to whom
was confided the whole executive duty of the mission,
and he did not forget to convey to that officer his displeasure at such a manifest want of courtesy.

It may not be uninteresting to particularise the
several questions put by the Major, and the answers
given by the chief, Sotobe.   I give them verbatim.

Question by Major Clocte.—" Can Chaka write,
or make any characters whereby to show that he sent
the chiefs on their mission, and to show his authority ? "

Answered by Sotobe.—" No.   He cannot write or
make characters. "

Q.—" How is Sotobe to be known as a chief, and
how is he distinguished as such ? "

A.—" By the bunch of red feathers ; and there is no
one allowed to wear them but the king, and two or
three of his principal chiefs."

Q.—" Did you come by your own free will and
consent ?"

A.—" We were sent by our king to show his

friendly disposition towards the governor and the white people; also to ask for medicines," &c.

Q. " What authority have you from your king to show that you are sent by him ? "

A. " We have nothing. We were sent with Lieutenant King."

Q. " Have you no sign, or token, or feather, or tiger's tail, or tooth, to show that you were sent by Chaka ? "

A. " We generally send cattle, but as the vessel could not take them, Chaka has sent an ivory tusk."

Q. " Will Sotobe go to Cape Town with me ? "

A. " No; we have been here so long, that we are quite tired, and we wish to go back to our king."

Q. " What was your motive for coming here, if you did not intend to see the governor ? "

A. " We have heard that our king is near the colony, and we want to return, as we understand that the governor will protect the neighbouring tribes, and our king was not aware of it before our leaving Natal. We also hear that Lieutenant King is going to meet Chaka, and we cannot leave him; we were sent with him, and we know no other person. We look upon him as our father and protector. Unbosom Boser ought to have returned long ago, and then I could have gone to see the governor, as my king wished me to do."

Q. " Provided Unbosom Boser returns from hence, will Sotobe go and see the governor ? "

A. " As Lieutenant King is absent, we cannot say anything about it; we will not leave him, as he is sent with us, and he is one of our mission."

Q. " How is it possible that Lieutenant King can go to Cape Town with you, and back to Chaka with Unbosom Boser ? "

A. " I do not care who goes back with Unbosom Boser, so long as Lieutenant King remains with me ;—I am particularly entrusted to his care."

Q. " Suppose there was no such person as Lieutenant King, what would you do then, or if Lieutenant King should not return to you ? "

Captain Evatt and Mr. Vander Reit here remarked " you had better not put that question, it may probably hurt their feelings, they might suppose that Lieutenant King was to be put out of the way."

Q. " What did you consider Lieutenant King to be ? did you consider him as a chief; a person authorised by government to act for them, or as agent for them ? "

A. " We look upon Lieutenant King as a subject of King George's, and a Chief, as he is our principal at Natal, and always had the command of the people."

Q. " If you were to return without seeing the governor, would you not be punished by Chaka ? "

A. " No. We have been here so long without getting any intelligence from the governor, that we now wish to go away on our return, and inform the king that we have heard the white people will protect the neighbouring tribes."

After this interview the major had frequent conversations with the natives on the mission, to which I was not a witness; I shall not therefore detail the nature of those conversations from their report to me. They told me, however, he made them very uneasy, and that they would consequently return home without seeing the governor; but not without Lieutenant King, from whom, on this occasion, they declared their determination not to be separated.

Another interview also took place between the chiefs and Major Clocte, at which Captain Morris of the ship Duke of Bedford, Mr. Edmund Francis, and myself were present.

Question by Major Clocte.—"You must now decide whether you will return with Unbosom Boser, when the vessel is ready, or go on with me to the governor? Mind Jacob, (addressing the interpreter,) I mean you to go with me."

A. "I have no objection to go with you, but I cannot leave Lieutenant King, he is sent with us on this mission; our king has put every confidence in him, and we consider ourselves under his particular care."

Q. "Ask him, if he expects that Lieutenant King will return with him to his country, after seeing the governor, and if he looks to Lieutenant King to send him back?"

A. "I cannot think of leaving Lieutenant King, but if you or any other person have a desire to accompany us, with him, we should not object to it, as our king would always be glad to see any white man in his country."

Q. "How is it that you differ so? yesterday you said you would all return; to-day you want to go on with Lieutenant King to the governor, and to return your wife with Unbosom Boser?"

A. "Yesterday I was very unhappy, and much depressed about my wife. She is very ill, I wish her to return with Unbosom Boser, but she will not. My reason for saying that we would all return was, because you told us yesterday that you had been near Guika's, and saw we could not get back by land, and that the vessel we came in could not go back from this place without a written order from the governor; and your repeated questions made me unhappy."

Q. "If you like you can all go back from hence with Lieutenant King, as you have refused to go to the governor with me?"

A. "We do not refuse to go with you to the governor; we say that we cannot go without Lieutenant King, as our king has made him a chief, and he is our principal on this mission; he knows the road, we do not, (meaning that Chaka, their king, had confided to Lieutenant King the whole charge of their mission) and cannot proceed without him."

Q. "Tell him Jacob, (the interpreter,) that I know the road, and that I am sent expressly to take him away."

A. " Your path is from the governor here, and our path with Lieutenant King is, from Chaka to the governor."

Q. " I am a chief under the governor, and when the governor heard that you were in his country, he sent me expressly to bring you to him; he knows nothing of Lieutenant King, he is not a chief, neither is he a person authorised by the governor to act for him; if you like to go to the governor with me alone, you can."

A. " Lieutenant King is a chief in our country, and sent by Chaka to communicate with the governor, and we cannot go with any other but him; if we were to leave him what would our king think ? "

Q. " What is it that makes you adhere so much to Lieutenant King, do you always expect him to be with you ? "

This question was put to them out of my hearing ; I afterwards called on them to answer it.

A. " Because our king has sent us with him, he is kind to us, and our king has given him every information respecting this mission, and trusts to him, as we are unacquainted with your ways."

Q. " If Sotobe will go on with me to the governor, I will find a large present to send on to his king by Unbosom Boser. If you will not go on with me, you can go back to your country when the vessel is ready, together with Unbosom Boser."

A. " How is it that you are constantly asking us

questions? we have told you all that we have to say, and that we wish to see the governor. You make us quite unhappy talking to us so repeatedly about one thing; and I now begin to think that you suspect us to be spies, and that we are a people come to steal your cattle, and will not allow us to go back again."

Here Major Clocte was going to reply, but at the instant Lieutenant King entered the room, when the major was quite silent; consequently the chiefs conceived him to be an intruder, and afraid to speak before Lieutenant King, when Sotobe spoke in an angry tone, which was not interrupted by the major, as he was engaged relating to my friend King the substance of the major's interrogations.

"Why do you come here alone," said the indignant chief when his coadjutor and leader had appeared, "why do you come here in the absence of Lieutenant King, who is our principal on this mission; he knows all about Chaka, and he is a white man and knows your ways, and you know we do not; it is to him you ought to apply for information respecting the object of our visit here, and he is competent to satisfy you."

It was in this manner that the chiefs were subjected to annoyance, and by an insignificant display of paltry authority and petty power, which commanded no respect, but rather excited feelings of no ordinary indignation. A species of perplexing interrogation

that might have been resorted to by an Old Bailey
pleader, but little becoming the dignity of a British
officer deputed by the governor of a high British
dependancy.   What could have called for such an
attempt to confound two or three unlettered people
on an especial mission from their king, and cajole
them to court the amity of the Commander of a
British Colony, I know not, nor can I divine, but I
have no hesitation in declaring unequivocally, that it
redounded but little to the credit of the officer who
was the governor's organ; and when the governor
himself shall have it recur to his memory, he will
find it accompanied by no pleasing associations.   To
what did these interrogations tend?   To elicit the
object of the mission alone, or to frighten the ignorant
and untutored chiefs into a confession of some
ulterior design?   If the first, the interrogator overstepped the limits of a just conference; if the
latter, I can only ascribe to him a want of that
penetration and nice discernment, by which an
innocent man on a fair mission may be distinguished
from the secret and designing negociator, warily elicit-
ing the information which he is deputed to acquire.
There was so much design, so much cunning, and
such an absence of that ingenuousness so peculiarly
characteristic of a British agent, that I feel for the
littleness of the representative of the British governor,
whilst I cannot but applaud the indignation of the

Zoola chief. Had Major Clocte, in the first instance, consulted Lieutenant King, and apprised that officer of his intention to interrogate the chiefs on the subject of their mission—had he declared that he was commanded to do so by the governor, something in the way of exculpation might be offered; but nothing of the kind was done; the moment sought for the interview was in the absence of Lieutenant King, to whom the common courtesy of making known the intention of government was never offered. The mission now prepared to return to Natal, and the chiefs were elated at the thought of reaching their native homes, having had quite enough of British colonial civility, and their desire of amity with the natives of Zoola.

We were detained in this port three months, and although this mission had not concluded so successfully as we anticipated, nevertheless it would be one thing for Chaka to understand, that were he to make any irruption on the tribes bordering on the British lines he would be checked;—thus far he would be able to govern himself accordingly.

From what I have stated on the subject of the mission, and from the chiefs expressing a wish to have me constantly with them, and manifesting a desire that I should return with them to Natal, my situation became very disagreeable. I had a wish to visit my friends whom I had not seen for three

years; but I also possessed a friend who, in the hour
of sickness, had generously stepped forward and
voluntarily given himself as a hostage for the safe
return of the chiefs ; I could not, therefore, be
guilty of the unwarrantable ingratitude of not seeing
that friend out of jeopardy, by cancelling the bond
which occasioned it.

CHAPTER XV.

AFTER it was ascertained that the mission was to return to Natal, we made preparations for the voyage. On the 2nd of August, to our surprise, H.M.S. Helicon arrived, for the purpose of taking the chiefs on board, and to proceed with them to Natal. By her a present was sent by the government at the Cape for the king, and another for the chiefs, who were now directed by Major Clocte to repair on board; they were much gratified with the hope of returning home, but they stoutly refused to go on board the Helicon unless Lieutenant King or myself would accompany them. Major Clocte did not lack persuasions to induce them to go under the care of the commander of the ship, but neither his eloquence nor his manner availed; nor were the government presents sufficiently attractive, for they peremptorily refused going unless we consented to accompany them. Lieutenant King agreed to go on board the ship, and return with them to Natal; the schooner was got ready, our little supplies and the horses we had agreed to take were shipped, when the chiefs were taken on board, conveyed over the bar, and embarked in the Helicon accompanied by Lieutenant King. It came on to blow hard, rendering it impossible to have every thing complete before the 9th, when the wind having moderated a little, and veered round favourably, we proceeded to sea. I took my departure in our schooner, which being small, and the sea running high, pitched heavily, and I became exceedingly sea-sick; two of our horses died, and the others were with difficulty preserved alive.

We kept along the coast, having it full in our view, and on the 17th found ourselves abreast of the river Umcomas: the wind became baffling, attended with a little rain, but we glided along shore, and, favoured at intervals with a breeze from off the land, hove to about four P. M. abreast of Natal Bay. We saw some Caffres on shore, and perceived Lieutenant King pull off from the Helicon towards the bar, but from the surf running heavily he returned. He came on board our schooner, however, the next morning, and appeared ill. It came on to blow hard, and finding that the vessel drifted in shore, we slipped our chain cable and made for the port. We lost forty fathom of chain cable and our best bower anchor. The tide was ebbing fast, and we struck several times on the bar, but got safely over, and in endeavouring to proceed up channel got aground on the bank. We saw three Europeans on the point, who cheered

us three times as we passed, and seemed glad at our
arrival. The notorious Hottentot Michael—whose
criminal conduct with the native girl put the lives of
all the Europeans in jeopardy, from which we had no
means of escape afforded us, but were obliged to go
to war and run the risk of being killed, and for which
we have been most undeservedly reproved and slan-
dered by a pious missionary—attempted to swim off to
the vessel, and was taken to sea by the ebbing tide.
Every one tried to prevail on him not to do it,
but he persisted, and compelled his Caffre, an expert
swimmer, to follow him, and who, seeing the danger,
threatened to leave his master, but was told by Michael
if he did not follow him he would kill him the moment
he returned to the shore; at this instant this execrable
wretch sank to rise no more, and thus paid the forfeit
due for a life of cruelty and vice of the blackest
description.

My friend Mr. Fynn came to us, whom I was
happy to see, and to release from his sacred obligation
to Chaka. I was also anxious to learn the events in
our absence on the mission. We stole a few minutes
to hear his detail, and to communicate with the officers
of the Helicon, who wished to know something of
Chaka's movements.

The king it appears had been to pay my young
friend Mr. Fynn a visit, at his kraal near the Umsin-
cooler, or Bloody River, and remained with him while
his forces proceeded to invade the tribes to the west-

ward. Chaka had apprehended that the Europeans at
Natal would object to go, or let their people proceed
to engage with the frontier tribes; therefore, immediately after we sailed in the schooner, a report was in
circulation that Umgarty, his brother, had run away
with a quantity of the king's cattle, who sent messengers to command the people belonging to the Europeans that could use muskets to go and retake them.
This command, although highly objectionable to
them, they dared not refuse. They therefore proceeded to join the Zoola forces, when they took an
inland route, accompanied by the king, to Mr. Fynn's
kraal at Bloody River, where his majesty remained,
reserving one regiment for his own protection, and
sending the remainder on the expedition, first placing
Mr. Farewell's party with one division and our
party with another, Ogle and the Hottentot accompanying them, whilst Messrs. Farewell and Fynn
sojourned with the king. The force proceeded to the
country of the Armanpootoes, when the inhabitants
fled to the forests; the Zoolas then passed through
without molesting this tribe, and proceeded on, until
they reached the Red Caffres, within two days
march of Hinson's. Meanwhile Mr. Fynn had
taken great pains to dissuade Chaka from his present
design of disturbing the neutral tribes on the frontier,
and of laying the country waste for the purpose of an
unrestricted intercourse with the white people. Chaka
had certainly given orders to his generals to sit on

their shields if they saw the white people, and if the
latter commenced hostilities to retreat, it being his
wish to continue on friendly terms with Europeans;
and at the rational suggestions of Mr. Fynn, he sent
messengers off to command his forces to return, and
wait the result of his mission, as he had before promised us, and which happened very opportunely and
fortunately for him, as the colonists had heard
that Chaka was approaching. The neighbouring
tribes, through fear and trepidation, and to excite
the commiseration of the European settlers on the
frontiers, spread exaggerated reports of the depredations committed by the Zoola monarch on his advance,
which induced the troops and the colonists to unite in
a body and march to repel the invaders whenever they
made their appearance; but by this time the Zoolas
had made a retrograde movement towards their own
lines, leaving the British frontier forces, who, from
error or from some cause which it would be difficult to
divine, attacked the inexperienced, harmless, and inof-
fensive tribe of Maduan (who had been subdued
some years before by the Zoolas), committed great
havoc and slaughter, dispossessed them of all their
cattle; and finally, in all the exultation which victory
excites, returned to their colony, inflated with the
triumph they had achieved.

Chaka's party returned exultingly also, but from a
different cause; they had avoided a collision with white
people, and the disaster that had befallen Maduan's

tribe; they had, on their return, subdued four other tribes, and dispossessed them of all their cattle; not even the Armanpootoes were permitted to escape from their predatory power. These poor and weak people had conceived themselves perfectly secure from molestation by the Zoolas. As these latter did not disturb them on their advance, the former had consequently returned to their homes; but these credulous and confiding people soon had a visit from the retreating forces, who took from them all the cattle they possessed.

The commando now returned to the king, with about 10,000 head of cattle, when his majesty ordered this force to proceed to the eastward (without permitting them to go to their kraals), to attack the tribe of Sochungurnes, who had possession of the country beyond Delagoa Bay, and whom the Zoolas had before conquered, and driven them to their present place of settlement.

Having now ascertained the whole of Chaka's movements and designs, I hastened, together with Mr. Hatton, to the point, for the purpose of communicating with the officers of H.M.S. Helicon, and to inform them of the state of affairs, when that vessel suddenly put to sea, apprehending, we presumed, from the breeze freshening, that they might drift too near the coast.

I now returned to the schooner, where I found my friend Lieutenant King infinitely worse, arising from anxiety and various perplexities, all tending to excite him, and thus increase indisposition. Accompanied by our friend Mr. Fynn he went to our residence at Townshend, whence, after remaining an hour or two, he was carried to his kraal, "Mount Pleasant."

I was engaged at our vessel (which had grounded) in landing the horse and stock, as from the illness of my friend the whole superintendence devolved on me. Towards sunset I proceeded to Mount Pleasant; the beach was lined with natives, all glad to see us. My friend Mr. Fynn met me, and we walked together to the kraal, when he told me that he conceived Lieut. King to be exceedingly ill, and that his complaint was either a disease of the liver, or a pleurisy; on my entering his hut, my gallant friend spoke to me in a low tone of voice; I then began to perceive that Mr. Fynn's opinion was too true: his face had become much changed, his bowels quite disordered, and he felt languid and uneasy. I sat with him until late, and then retired to repose. At about midnight, the native servant, at Lieutenant King's request, called Mr. Fynn and myself, we hastened to him, and were sorry to find him worse: after we had remained with him some time, he seemed to be dosing, and we returned to rest again.

August 19.—We again visited our gallant and afflicted companion early this morning, when he appeared a little revived. I went to the schooner to land the present for Chaka, and the property the chiefs had collected, then returned and opened the case (which was large and heavy), and took out its contents for its better conveyance to the king.

This present from the Colonial Government consisted of some sheets of copper, which were neither of value, nor of use to the Zoolas; a piece of scarlet broad-cloth, the only article of value; and some medicines; with a few knives and trinkets, or gewgaws, of neither worth nor attraction. We had them laid out to the best advantage, taking first the precaution of having Sotobe the chief, and Jacob the interpreter present, to see them taken from the case; when they gave it as their opinion that the present was a paltry one considering that it came from such a great nation as the English, and was intended for so powerful a monarch as Chaka. However as I thought that the king knew nothing of the value of medicines, I enhanced their worth as much as I could; and to add to the whole, Lieutenant King sent a valuable looking-glass which cost 120 rix-dollars, a quantity of beads, and a variety of little amusing trifles. In the evening Unbosom Boser and Funroy, a native boy, were despatched to announce our return.

23rd.—They had been absent three days, and came back bringing with them two bullocks to be sacrificed to the Spirit, for Lieutenant King's speedy recovery; and that his sickness might be transferred to Sotobe, for remaining at Mount Pleasant so long, instead of pro-

ceeding on to the king to communicate the result
of his mission.   His majesty also sent his commands
for Sotobe to proceed to him immediately, and bring
all that they had accumulated.   He was likewise
ordered to direct some one of Lieutenant King's
party to accompany them, as the Zoola monarch was
particularly anxious to hear what communications
they had brought from over the water.   In the
evening two of Chaka's servants arrived, and repeated the former message, saying that the sickness of
Lieut. King ought to have taken hold of Sotobe; they
also asked for medicines, which were given to them.

24th.—The messengers returned last evening, and
I prepared the present for conveyance to the king.
Lieutenant King, being a little better to-day, was
carried to Townshend, when I took leave of him, and
set off with the chiefs and our charge on our journey.
The horse we had brought from Algoa Bay had been
so bruised on board the vessel from the rough passage,
that I was compelled to take a pack-bullock and leave
him behind to recover.   We had not advanced more
than four miles, before we met one of the messengers,
who had gone on with medicines, returning.   I asked
him what news, but he made me no answer; when he
reached the chief, however, he began to display his
powers, both of tongue and action, as commanded by
the king; and said, that he was proceeding to Lieutenant King, to know the cause of Sotobe's detention,
that Chaka was in an unusual rage, and that he had

thrown the bottle of medicine on the ground, and broke it into a thousand pieces. He further stated, that Sotobe was to go on immediately, and not wait for the present, as the king would not accept of anything so paltry. He then set off on his way to Lieutenant King. I observed that Sotobe was about to send some one to the king, as they sat talking awhile, Sotobe appearing uneasy, and even distressed; he also said "that their lives were in danger as Chaka would surely kill them; that I, being a Malongo or white man, should escape, but that they would get punished for all who had displeased him."

At length they proceeded, confiding in the influence of the white people with Chaka. We arrived at Umsega's kraal at dusk. The natives all came out to congratulate me on my return, bringing a pot of thick sour milk, and some ground Caffre corn, from which I made a hearty meal and lay down to repose. I was soon disturbed by a loud confusion of voices, when my native boy, Nosapongo, who had been with us to Algoa Bay, came to my hut, and with some consternation, said, "I can't help feeling for you, as you have had an unpleasant time on the other side of the water, but from what I have been hearing this evening you will have a good deal more to put up with here." He told me to listen to the Zoolas, who were talking, but I could only catch a word occasionally, as their hut was some distance from mine. I therefore desired him to go and ascertain what they

were talking about. He soon returned and said, that
my Zoola party were rehearsing what they were to
say to Chaka, so that they might be perfect before
him; and that he could see they intended to forget
their own disputes, maintain the same opinions, and
misrepresent all that had occurred, so as to excite
the king's wrath against the white people, and put
me in a precarious situation.

This was not very encouraging to my further
advance with them or the presents under our charge,
but returning, I thought, would rather give a colour
to their villany, whereas, by proceeding, I might
be enabled to exhibit their deep plot against my
life.   Moreover anything unfavourable resulting
from my not going before Chaka, so as to induce
me to return without seeing him, might, in the precarious state of Lieutenant King's health, hasten his
dissolution; I therefore determined on going forward and submitting to the consequences.

25th.—From the resolution of last night, I rose
early this morning and set out with the chiefs, who
seemed unusually kind, and more than ordinarily good
natured and communicative. I eyed them as the lynx
would his prey; I watched every look, and studied
every feature of the chiefs and their interpreter, and
could discover that Nosapongo was right.   The principal, Sotobe, whom I accosted as we journeyed on,
seemed disposed to be familiar, when I asked him
what he intended to say to the king at his first inter-

view. He observed, that as Chaka was very angry, he should depend solely on the influence of the white people for forgiveness. I told him without hesitation that I should tell the king nothing but facts. We walked on and pretended to be amused at Sotobe's conversation, until we arrived at an etanger, or cattle kraal, where we put in to refresh, as we needed it, the day being excessively warm. Here the minor chief beat one of my boys, at which I expressed my indignation, and threatened to resent it; I, however, abstained from violent measures, but expostulating with him for the liberty he had taken, and admonishing him severely, he seemed exceedingly humbled, expressed his contrition for the offence, and finally besought me to take a pinch of snuff as a customary peace-offering.

Our party having now got up, we pressed forward collectively until sunset, when we reached the kraal of one of the king's domestics—a distance of about thirty miles from Natal. In consequence of the chief of it being absent in war, we could obtain nothing but thick milk, which, although I liked it, did not agree with me, from having been accustomed during my absence to Algoa to a different food. Moreover the acidity of the milk had disagreed with me so much as to render me extremely uncomfortable. In the evening I was visited by all the females of the place, who were very importunate for beads, and of whom

I saw no means of getting rid, without complying with their soft looks, and tender supplications.

26th.—The day opened most auspiciously, the sun began to peep over the mountains and to spread its enlivening influence. The chiefs soon overtook me, accompanied by the messengers who had gone to Lieutenant King. At noon, the day had become oppressively hot, and my pack-ox had manifested an indisposition to proceed. We halted under the umbrageous foliage of some magnificent trees, when some of Sotobe's girls came to us with several pots of beer, which afforded us a refreshing and reviving draught. We afterwards moved on until we arrived at the river Mufootic, from whence we sent off messengers to announce to the king our approach thus far. In the mean time we bathed and clad ourselves in our best habiliments, and arrived at Toogooso at sunset, where we saw his majesty sitting outside his kraal with about two hundred warriors. He seemed to look towards us with indifference, and viewed our presents as we set them before him with ineffable contempt. I saluted him and sat down, as I could not speak at the distance I was situated from him. I, therefore, waited until an opportune moment presented itself for conversing with him. Meanwhile Sotobe and his retinue stood up, and from having noticed Chaka's marked conduct towards me, the former

began to put his scheme into execution for exciting
the king's wrath against us, by addressing him in
the following words:—" You mountain, you lion,
you tiger, (very appropriate I admit,) you that
are black, (more appropriate still,) there is none
equal to you; you sent us to the other side of
the water; we have been, and who has crossed the
great waters but ourselves? Did our fathers know
anything of the white people? No. We know much
more than they did, and there's no king equal in
power to you. Has any other black king sent
people to cross the great waters as you have done?
We have been to a small town, and seen an officer
from government, who annoyed us by asking us
numerous questions, and we know not whether he
looked upon us as friends or foes. Our long absence
has been a scene of misery to us, and what is still
worse our king is angry with us, and why? because
we have delayed attending to the presents, and because
Lieutenant King is sick, whom we did not like to
leave in his present state."

After having concluded his long, and, so far as
concerned us, disrespectful speech, which Chaka did
not appear to notice, as he was the whole of the
time talking to his warriors around him, Sotobe and
his retinue sat down. Although I had placed the
present before Chaka, he asked me where it was, and
what had become of the large case which had been
sent by the governor. I told him that the case had

been opened for the convenience of transporting its contents. He asked the chief, Sotobe, if he had been present; the latter replied, that Mr. Fynn had desired him to sit outside the hut, when the contents were handed out for him to view.

Chaka now addressed himself to his people and said, " you see these rascals (meaning Sotobe and his retinue) have not attended to my interest; they have been deceiving me." Having heard all that his chiefs had to say, he tried to encourage me to speak against Sotobe by abusing him; he then said, " it is all that fellow Fynn's fault, for putting Lieutenant King up to opening the chest, he is like a monkey, he wants to peep into every thing." He after this requested me to point out among the presents, what came from the governor of the Cape, and what from Lieutenant King. On examining them, he observed, "that Lieutenant King's present was more valuable than that of the government. What a pity it is he is sick, I think they have been giving him poison on the other side of the water."

The looking-glass greatly attracted him, exciting his curiosity and admiration; he directed me to hand it to his people. For a time it afforded me a fund of amusement, and notwithstanding my troubles, I could not refrain from laughing at their attitudes and gestures. They all looked at it with astonishment; at the same time they held their mouths, and sought as if they thought to catch the figure by placing their hands behind it. Some put their hands before their eyes, occasionally glancing from the corner, to take a peep to see if it were imitating them. Chaka now perceiving that his warriors were in a consternation, wanted to assume the appearance of being bolder than his subjects; he, therefore, ordered me to place the glass at a little distance in front of him, when he looked with one eye on the object, while he nearly stared me out of countenance with the other; and with an expression of fear, he led me to understand, that he expected me not to play any tricks with him. I advanced it nearer to him gradually; and at last impressed him with the knowledge that it merely reflected his own figure, that there was nothing in it alarming—nothing the work of enchantment, but that it was simply a production of art, and used in the white man's country for the purposes of his dressing-room.

The natives were now astounded at the boldness of the king, and not less so at the glass itself—observing, that they were assuredly much older than their forefathers, who had never seen such a charm ; and they seemed to assume no little importance for having overcome that trepidation which the effect of the glass had primarily occasioned.

It had nearly become dark when Chaka, who at first treated the presents with contempt, became anxious, from the effects of the glass, to know what the others consisted of, and to ascertain if we had brought the

preparation that was to make white hair black, and
to prolong age, so that he might live as long as King
George the Third—whom he understood had lived to
a patriarchal age; for this purpose, therefore, he dismissed his warriors, desiring me to follow him into
his palace, and bring the presents: this gave me a
favourable opportunity of conversing with him on the
subject of the mission, and of the incidents which had
occurred during our late absence from Natal.

I told him that the present from the government
was to show the amity and goodwill of the English
towards him—and that it was the particular request
of the governor that he would not go to war with
the tribes under their protection. He interrupted
me, and said, the white people had no control over
the blacks, and knew not how to command them;
that those whom they assumed the right to take
under their shield, and to support when assailed, were
daily committing depredations on the tribes tributary to him, and taking off their cattle; he should,
therefore, go to war with them when he thought it
good policy to do so.

He now abruptly broke off the subject of war,
and immediately turned the conversation on matters
of a more pacific character. The first thing he
introduced was the present of the medicine chest,
in which all his hopes and interest seem to have
centred; and the oil, the great attraction—the charm
that was to promote longevity, and turn his white

hairs black; or to grind him, when old, into the prime of his physical strength, and the maturity of his passions.

At Chaka's desire I opened the chest; when he told me, with a sagacious look, and apprehensive of being seen or overheard, to observe if any one was coming. Finding all still, and that we were not perceived, he dexterously took out a case of lancets from the chest, and began to examine the black case, which was neatly ornamented with a gilt etching. This, I presume, he took to contain the miraculous, or sacred medicine, for which he so anxiously sought; for he ingeniously conveyed it under his mat on which he reposed, and in his opinion quite unobserved by me. He afterwards desired me to hand him every thing separately, and to explain to him the use of each article; he looking on with intense eagerness and anxiety. The first package was bark, which I told him was a specific in cases of fever, and of a strong and efficacious property in cases of debility; he replied, in a sulky tone—" I am strong enough: do you think we are such weak things as you are?" I then handed to him some ointment, the properties of which were healing, and were applied to sores or wounds; when on looking at it, he, with a sort of savage grin, observed—" do you think we are such scabby fellows as you are?" The next was spirits of lavender, which, when I explained to him, was to revive the spirits in cases of depression, he took it significantly; and asked " if I thought they ever wanted any thing to exhilirate them, or that they were ever dull ? " After having handed to him every article, and given to him a description of the application of each, and received his petulant replies, he, in a kind and gentle mood asked me for the " medicine he wanted," namely, the ointment for changing the colour of the hair; for, said he, " these are of no use to my subjects : they are not troubled with the disorders you mention ; the best medicine for them is beef—and when my people are not able to eat, they are of no use to me." After again repeating, " the medicine I want is the stuff for the hair;" and perceiving that I had not got it, he turned round on his mat on which he was reclining, and fell into a sound sleep. This relieved me for the present, and enabled me to retire to my hut and reflect on the wisest step to take in so critical a situation.

In the morning Chaka sent for me again, and renewed his inquiries respecting the hair oil—on which all his hopes seemed to hang, and for which he persisted with his usual pertinacity; observing, " that he thought Lieutenant King was to bring it himself." I detailed to him the particulars of the mission, which gave him no concern ; nor did he heed what I said, as the chief had been communing with him, making any thing I might say of no avail. He, however, indignantly observed, that he had heard Lieutenant King had been constantly with the ladies, and that I had attended to the business. The king abused him for neglecting his interest, and for deputing to me what he ought to have done himself. He protested strongly that he would kill me, as " I had been putting Lieutenant King up to roguery." Abuse towards me was now become common, and his repeated threats that he would kill me made me quite callous; I became so insensible either to his language or his gestures that I, at times, must have convinced him of my being heedless of his passion or power.

He said that he would send John Cane (who was present during this disagreeable interview) to the governor of the Cape, and find out if we had stolen any of the presents, and obtain what we had neglected—the hair oil. He then took Lieutenant King's native boy, Nasopongo, from me to send him with Unbosom Bober and Noma-Schlabe on the mission with Cane, giving them instructions to proceed to the Armampontoes and collect the ivory for the colonial government. Cane requested him to allow him a few people that he might take a little of his own ivory to purchase some articles for himself, and make a decent appearance before the authorities of the Cape ; when Chaka took one of the chief's old cloaks, that had been made to his taste, and ornamented with yellow ribands, and giving it to Cane, said, " there, if that is all you want to carry ivory for, you will not be in need of people now; you may make a decent appearance in that dress of your own making."

After this mission had been arranged, I called on

the chief Sotobe, and the interpreter Jacob, to be
confronted with me, and hear what I had to advance
in contradiction of their shameful misrepresentations
to the king, which had occasioned his becoming so
enraged with me; but I could obtain no redress: these
sagacious fellows finding that they had exculpated
themselves, by propagating innumerable charges
against Lieutenant King and myself, were not disposed to renew the subject, fearing that their villany
might be made apparent, and their lives put in
jeopardy.

CHAPTER XVI.

THE extraordinary violence of the king's rage with me was mainly occasioned by that absurd nostrum, the hair oil, with the notion of which Mr. Farewell had impressed him as being a specific for removing all indications of age. From the first moment of his having heard that such a preparation was attainable, he evinced a solicitude to procure it, and on every occasion never forgot to remind us of his anxiety respecting it; more especially on our departure on the mission his injunctions were particularly directed to this object. It will be seen that it is one of the barbarous customs of the Zoolas in their choice or election of their kings, that he must neither have wrinkles nor grey hairs, as they are both distinguishing marks of disqualification for becoming a monarch of a warlike people. It is also equally indispensable that their king should never exhibit those proofs of having become unfit and incompetent to reign; it is therefore important that they should conceal these indications so long as they possibly can. Chaka had become greatly apprehensive of the approach of grey hairs; which would at once be the signal for him to prepare to make his exit from this sublunary world, it being always followed by the death of the monarch. Having heard, therefore, that a medicine could be obtained which would prevent his hair from becoming white, he became solicitous to have it; and nothing could appease him when he found that his sanguine hopes could not be immediately gratified. At the Cape, or at Algoa, it was not likely that this nostrum ("Rowland's Macassar," or whatever other absurd preparation it might be,) could be got; but the savage could not be induced to believe this, as Mr. Farewell had, most injudiciously, told him of its being easily attainable. Our return without it, therefore, made the ferocious despot unrestrainable in his wrath against me; and I expected hourly that he would have consigned me to the forest as food for hyenas. His intemperate rage also was much encouraged by Sotobe and the villanous interpreter Jacob, who had made successful efforts to impress on him that the English had no king—that King George was the name of a mountain; and that we had mentioned him as a great man for the purpose of deceiving and terrifying other nations;—in fact, that the English were a people of no power or repute; and that he (Chaka) might subdue them with only one of his regiments.

. Inflamed by disappointment, and indignant from

conceiving that we were a people of a petty race, I
began to perceive that I stood on the brink of eternity, and that the next look of the savage might be a
signal for my death. In this state of horrible suspense
I remained three days, during which time I was incessantly abused, and often threatened with immediate
execution: I at last told the merciless savage, when
he assured me of death, that I was a single individual only, and could not contend with his power;
but that if he should kill me, my death would
meet an avenging hand, which would fall heavily
on him and his nation; for that violence to a British
subject was never allowed to escape the strictest investigation. Chaka laughed at this address; and said,
" the Maloonquan, or little white man, is a spirited
fellow, he fears not death." I replied to him, that
it was true, I did not fear death.

After this colloquy, I repeatedly applied for permission to return home, but he refused every time;
so I took the liberty of going without it, in spite of
his threats and his rage.

It was late in the afternoon when I left Toogooso,
and early the next day I reached Townshend, where
I found my friend Lieutenant King worse than when
I left him. His disorder had now arrived at a dangerous point, and seemed so firmly seated as to become irremediable. He was greatly reduced, and
so weak that he was confined to his bed. Both Mr.
Fynn and myself were constantly with him, and we

made his moments of pain as light as we could. We sought advice in Buchan's medical work; and administered to him agreeably to its directions, but without any good effect. I resolved, therefore, to visit Mr. Farewell, (who was the early friend of Lieutenant King, and deserved well from him,) for the purpose of getting his advice, or to prevail on him to call on his now dying friend. Nothing, however, could soften him into a compliance with the wishes of those who sought to alleviate the dying moments of a good and gallant young man. Disputes of a pecuniary nature, which redounded little to the credit of Mr. Farewell, had excited hat gentleman's malignity; and had created a division between two brother officers which no after manifestations on the part of my young companion of his desire that all should be forgotten, could soften or remove. As it was the dying wish of Lieutenant King to shake Mr. Farewell by the hand in token of departing in peace with him, I again applied to the latter, who addressed a note to me explanatory of his not being able to come—a poor, frivolous, unnatural, and ungrateful excuse, such a one as made Mr. Fynn and myself blush that we had been his associate.

This unfeeling note I received while sitting by the bed-side of my young friend; I read only part of it to him; as he was anxious, however, to see the whole he took it out of my hand and read it, let it fall carelessly, and, after a deep sigh, said; "he wished he had

not seen it:" and then remarked, " Oh Nat, what
a pity it is that you have not an opportunity of writing
to the colony. Cane has gone away to injure me,
that was the reason he did not call. Oh! what
will my friends think of me?" On this subject he
seemed to speak with great anguish, and at some
length, which agitated and weakened him; I tried
to appease him, and spoke on other subjects. In the
afternoon we thought he was revived a good deal, and
that he appeared easier; he begged of me not to
leave him, dosed a little, then spoke affectionately
of his mother and sister—and with a sigh, that would
have made any but the ungrateful man sympathise,
said "that he only wished to live for their sake."
He desired me, if it pleased the Almighty to take
him from this world of misery and strife, to burn all
his family letters. He then complained of his feet
being cold, when Mr. Fynn and myself bathed them
in warm water, and wrapped them up. Two of the
fingers of his right hand became immediately insensible and discoloured. He wished me again not to
leave him; and requested Mr. Hatton to sleep at
Townshend instead of at the kraal. At about dusk,
Mr. Hatton entered the dining room, and our dying
friend desired me to call him: at this moment both
Messrs. Hatton, Fynn, and myself, perceived a great
change. The symptoms of dissolution had come over
him; a cold and deathlike perspiration succeeded—
when in a soft but singing voice he said, " Hatton

take hold of my hand." Mr. Hatton took his left
hand; he said, "no Hatton, take my starboard hand;"
and then desired us to do the same. Thus shaking us
each by the hand, he said softly, "do the same for the
last time, I feel myself going very fast, and every
one ought to be present on this occasion; as to you
Hatton, we shall meet again shortly, give me a hearty
shake of the hand. I know I have all your good
wishes, and I hope we shall meet again in the realms
of bliss. I wish you all every happiness that heaven
can bestow. Remember me to my boy Jack (John
Ross who had been sent to the king's), and let my
funeral be as decent and respectable as possible."

After this he seemed as if engaged in prayer, and
expressed a wish for us to join in prayer with him.
In his appeals, he frequently mentioned his mother
and sister. He then turned to me and bade me give
him sixty drops of laudanum. I told him I feared that
quantity would be too much for him; but he said,
"never mind, give it to me; it is my last request?" I
handed him fifteen in a few drops of water; he
looked at me sternly, and said, "you have been my
companion a long time, and can you now with confidence tell me, here are sixty drops of laudanum?"
I was so affected by this appeal to me, that I could
not abstain from manifesting my inward grief. I
said to him that I thought there was as much
as would do him good: but while holding it by his
bedside, his voice failed, he articulated something,

as if a prayer—then laid himself straight, and with one heavy breath departed this life, in confidence of peace in that world to which his spirit had flown. It was about nine o'clock in the evening of the seventh of September 1828—a day which the survivors of our shipwrecked party who witnessed the afflicting scene will well remember, as having bereft them of a most estimable companion, and a sincere and gallant friend.

I had occasion greatly to lament the decease of Lieutenant King, to whom I had become associated in the latter scenes of his life; with whom I had been a partner in difficulties, and on occasions of no ordinary trials and perplexities; whose friendship was warm, whose mind soared above the littleness of paltry prejudice, and never descended to caprice or inconsistency. There was a sincerity in every expression, and an ingenuousness in all his actions, that demonstrated his love of truth, and his dislike of everything that was dissembling and insincere. He was generous to his friends and liberal to his enemies;

> Large was his bounty, and his soul sincere;

and those who had the pleasure of his intimate acquaintance never sought to break the bonds by which his friendship was linked to theirs; he had the happy facility of making himself esteemed, and his society courted. His friends admired him, his officers esteemed him, and his sailors loved him; and—save

an occasional dissension, which our peculiar situation, doubtless, generated—we lived in Natal, in a
bond of goodwill towards each other, of which he
set the first and the brightest example. Poor King!
his memory will live in our recollections to the latest
time.

His unhappy crew did the last offices for their
deceased master, whose death they so much lamented.
They washed and dressed his corpse, and prepared
it for its last abode; his faithful natives, whose
attachment for their kind chief was manifested by
tears and howlings during the night, rendered the
whole scene very affecting. By the demonstrations
of sorrow which pervaded their unhappy countenances,
they greatly elicited our sympathy, and assurances
of protection.

The day of interment having arrived, the whole of
the vicinity was crowded by natives from the surrounding districts, all lamenting the death of our
friend. Their lamentations were sincere, their tears
were genuine drops of sorrow, that fell involuntary from
their streaming eyes: they were not artificial; nor
were their exhibitions of grief constrained as at the
death of a native chief, to save themselves from being
massacred by their savage and ferocious king; they
were real, emanating from their hearts and evinced
by their looks.

A lasting tribute to the memory of my gallant
friend has been paid by Mr. Kay; and it does him

credit, as well as softens in a degree the asperity which his condemnation of the European party at Natal had excited. That gentleman says* : " Much benevolent attention was paid to the Natal settlement at its commencement by a gentleman of the name of King, formerly a midshipman in the navy. His vessel, the Salisbury, in which the party visited Natal in 1823, is said to have been the first that ever entered that port during the lifetime of the oldest inhabitant; and was shortly after lost. But having obtained another, and hearing that Lieut. Farewell and his companions were greatly in want, he again visited them a year or two subsequently, for the purpose of taking supplies, and was cast ashore at the entrance of the harbour. This led him to resolve on remaining there; and, assisted by his crew, he succeeded in building a completely new vessel out of the wreck. His days, however, after that occurrence were few and full of adversity. Disappointment seems to have awaited him at every step, and he at length sunk under the ravages of grief and dysentery : a disease which frequently prevails on that part of the coast. This took place in 1828, and under circumstances of the most melancholy character. When languishing in a native hut, almost alone, he repeatedly sent for Mr. F., who resided at no great distance, requesting his friendly aid and company; but, to the everlasting disgrace

* Kay's Caffrarian Researches, Part 2, chap. 16, page 401.

both of the name and memory of the latter, although this unfortunate young man had risked both life and property in his behalf, he never so much as went near to perform for him, in his dying moments, any the most common office of humanity."

Mr. Kay has, not only in this, paid a well deserved compliment to the memory of Lieutenant King, but he has also handed down the conduct of Lieut. F. for the reproach of posterity; and were it not from feelings of respect for the friends of that individual, who afterwards met an untimely end, I should have added to the censure of the pious author, what my own personal knowledge would have enabled me to state on the melancholy occasion of Lieutenant King's decease.

Every thing having been arranged for the interment of our deceased friend, and in the most becoming manner which our limited means would permit, the whole of the European party assembled at Townshend to perform the only remaining respect to their lamented companion. The procession moved on towards Mount Pleasant at 10 A.M. The corpse was borne by his seamen, who were sorely affected, but sought the duty as their last service to a kind and a benevolent master. The Europeans followed, the whole body of natives being in the rear, whose lamentations were enough to " melt the heart to pity." On arriving at Mount Pleasant, and at the grave, which was dug near to his residence, Mr. Fynn read the funeral service with great feeling and solemnity, when the corpse was interred, and secured against the attacks of the wolves and hyenas, which might otherwise disturb the remains of our late friend during their nocturnal prowlings. After this had been completed we returned to Townshend, to pass the day in contemplating our loss, and in mournful dejection for the chasm which had been made in our little society. The next day Mr. Fynn, Mr. Hatton, and myself, proceeded to Mount Pleasant, to endeavour to soothe the grief of the poor natives, whose lamentations were really affecting : we did all we could, though that was but little, and we were necessitated to indulge them, under the impression that our presence rather increased their sorrow than diminished their grief. Thus was Lieutenant King esteemed by all, and by the natives looked up to as something more than a father.   Is it possible that one could have died with a better name ?   Let us then

> No further seek his merits to disclose,
>   Or draw his frailties from their dread abode—
>   (There they alike in trembling hope repose)
>   The bosom of his Father and his God.

In the evening of the 10th September, John Ross, the apprentice of the late Lieutenant King, who had been despatched to Chaka to announce the death of his master, returned, and informed me that the king expressed great sorrow for the loss of one whom he so highly valued. I was also informed by him that in future Tombooser (meaning me) would be looked to,

by his majesty, for every thing relative to our conduct in Natal; and, as he knew I was entrusted with
Lieutenant King's concerns, he told Ross that he
should now confide in me. Before the death of my
friend, however, he had expressed a somewhat different
feeling, and told John that he would give his master
thirty elephants' teeth to kill me, or have me thrown
overboard at sea. When the boy had taken leave
of him, he said, in a sorrowful tone, " go, and desire
that Messrs. Farewell, Fynn, and Isaacs will come to
me immediately, and give me an account of the death
of Lieutenant King, and the causes that led to it, as
also of his property; but before I have an interview
with them, they must send something that I may wash
myself from grief, and that the disorder may not take
hold of me." Having consulted with my friends, I
began to prepare for the journey.

CHAPTER XVII.

Having prepared ourselves to proceed to the imperial residence, and the day being somewhat inviting (13th of September), Messrs. Fynn, Hatton, and myself, with two of the seamen, went to Mount Pleasant, to remain for the night, and console the poor natives, who still lamented the death of their master and protector. On our way thither we passed a drove of hippopotami, grazing on the bank. We also met Mr. Farewell on the beach. We walked together to his house, as he had attended the funeral of Lieutenant King, and indicated a wish that any differences which had existed should be buried in oblivion. However indignantly we had previously felt, we could not refuse the *amende honorable*, but consented to take up our abode at his place for the night, and proceed from thence in the morning.

14th.—The morning being favourable, and feeling myself much recovered from my depression and other indisposition, we set off for Chaka's residence.

Mr. Farewell accompanied us as far as the Umgani, and then returned, with a promise that he would follow the next day. We proceeded in our usual manner, without any remarkable incidents on our march. The weather was occasionally unpropitious; heavy rains fell, accompanied by awful thunder and lightning, which compelled us to seek shelter in some of the hamlets on our route; and on the 15th we reached the kraal of Sedunger. The chief, an old friend of mine, was at war, but the girls were glad to see us, and saluted us on each cheek with a kiss, an unusual compliment to a white man, though a common custom among themselves. From hence we proceeded to Magie's kraal, when the chiefs sent us a cow to kill, but expected a present of beads of equal value; and here we were detained again by a prodigious fall of rain and tempestuous weather.

16th.—We were prepared for commencing our journey, but every thing was unfavourable; the ground was wet, and my pack-ox had got loose. My companions, however, set off, while I waited for my beast, which at last came; I proceeded and overtook my company at Gibbabanya, the station of one o₁ Chaka's regiments. The queen here welcomed us with a large calabash of thick milk, with which we refreshed ourselves, hurried on, and shortly reached the river Mafootie. We sent messengers from hence to announce our approach, halted to bathe and prepare to meet the king, then we continued to move

forward until we arrived at Toogooso, at about
four P. M. We found his sable majesty asleep, and
saw Jacob, who appeared to regret the death of Lieutenant King, and was much hurt (or apparently so)
when he found that we came to take our leave of his
sovereign. We saw the warriors running up the kraal,
which was an indication of the king being awake.
We went towards the palace, and saw Chaka outside
the kraal, where we found him with about two
hundred people, forming a half circle, with a few
chiefs sitting near him, trying six prisoners for steal-
ing corn. We had scarcely been seated a few moments when the despot ordered the prisoners for
immediate execution. Two of them, stout able fellows, tried to make their escape by leaping over
us with great agility, and making good use of
their speed: but the warriors finally secured them,
and stoned them to death. Chaka's servant (a fine
looking lad, a criminal also), thinking that his savage
master had forgiven him, sat quietly; but no sooner
had the warriors returned from the execution of the
other five, and taken their seats, than the sign
was given to remove the other unfortunate lad.
After this, which was merely done to terrify us, we
were permitted to converse with the Zoola monarch;
we told him that we had arrived at his request,
and came to explain the nature of Lieutenant
King's decease, which we did; but nothing could
remove the impression that some black person, either

here or at Algoa Bay, had administered poison to him.
He then said that he had mourned the death of his
friend, and regretted exceedingly having spoken
warmly to him and abused him; but that he was
irritated at not receiving the medicine, and the mission not having succeeded to his wishes.

After this he assured us that he had sent to
recal John Cane, and was now collecting all his
ivory for the purpose of presenting to us; that
he should send us to the Cape to negociate a
friendly alliance with the governor, and obtain for
him such articles as he wanted. To this, however,
we objected (although we were much in want of ivory
to pay us for our past services), as the chief Sotobe
and his suite had not yet been confronted with us on
the subject of the last mission,—their account of which
having been a gross exaggeration.

After much talk on various subjects, he said, " I
cannot give you any thing to eat, as you have neglected to conform to the laws of the Zoolas, by not
bringing a calf, that I might wash myself from grief
for my deceased friend." He then desired Gomany,
his minister, to give us a calf in the morning, that we
might perform the ceremony at the accustomed hour.

17th.—This morning the calf was brought, and
when the king arose and went to the cattle kraal to
bathe, at the hour of ten A. M., our servant cut the calf
between the middle ribs, took the caul from the liver,
then let the poor wounded animal run, to be devoured by

the wild beasts in the neighbourhood or by the vultures in the rocks. We went towards the king, Mr. Fynn carrying the caul. He desired us to pass it to each other, and sprinkle it round the king and my companions in succession; after which a pot of roots was handed for the same ceremony, and so soon as that had been performed, a stick was presented, on which Chaka spit, and said, " I look upon the deceased as one of my family, and had he been a brother of my own mother I could not have felt the loss more: I must, therefore, forbid you to moan again, as it will affect me seriously. I wish all his people well, and I will be a friend to his black people, of whom I know he was very fond."

We now left the Zoola monarch, and went in search of something to eat. We met Gomany in the kraal: he told us to wait a little. Presently two bullocks were sent to us to be killed by the king's desire, one as a sacrifice to the Spirit and rest for Lieutenant King's body, the other for our own use. Chaka in a short time sent for us again, and entered on the subject of another mission to the Cape when the vessel would be ready for sea. He offered me a kraal of cattle to conduct it, and promised to send his warriors to hunt elephants for me. As a remuneration for the presents he had received from me, as well as for my attention to his people on the last mission, and for the wound I had received in the war in Ingoma, he created me chief of Natal, and granted to me the tract of country lying

from the river Umslutee to the river Umlass, a space
of twenty-five miles of sea-coast and one hundred
miles inland, including the bay, islands, and forests
near the point, and the exclusive right of trading with
his people. After he had made his mark, as his signa-
ture to the grant, the interpreter made his, which
happening to be larger than that of the king, the
latter asked, in a stern manner, how it was possible
that a common man's name could be greater than a
king's? Insisting on having the pen and grant
again, he scribbled and made marks all over the
blank part, and said, " there," pointing to his signa-
ture, " any one can see that is a king's name, because
it is a great one. King George will also see that
this is King Chaka's name."

After this he requested we would go home, and he
would send for us shortly, as he had a good deal
to communicate to us, but was at present so much
depressed, " that his heart would not let his tongue
speak as he could wish, so recently after the death of
one he so highly esteemed." At our departure he
observed, " If you Maloongoes all return to your
native land, I have one consolation, that a white man,
and a chief too, lived a long time in my country without molestation from myself or from my people, and
that he died a natural death—that will ever be a source
of much satisfaction to me."

We now prepared to return home, and on the 18th
set off early; the weather as we advanced was

very unfavourable, and attended with thunder, lightning, and heavy falls of rain, making our first night most dismal and dreary.

19th.—We arose this morning, after having been disturbed much during the night, and prepared for moving on, but the weather was still unfavourable for travelling. The pass on the sea-side along which we had to go was very fatiguing, from the rains having softened it so much. On our way we picked up a cocoa-nut, which we concluded must have been thrown from some vessel at sea, as none are to be found growing in this country.

In the evening we reached the residence of Mr. Farewell, where we dined and slept.

24th.—I arose early this morning, finding myself much better after my indisposition. With Messrs. Farewell and Fynn I took a walk in our garden, to view its productiveness, and see what could be done for its future improvement. It being before breakfast, when the sun had not yet reached a sufficient altitude to be very powerful, I felt it cheering and renovating, and anticipated making a hearty meal, such a one as would render me capable of making some exertion afterwards, and, I was not disappointed. After our morning repast, however, and as we were starting for the river Umsegas, Mataban came from Toogoosa, nearly exhausted from exertion, and, with a countenance betokening something of mighty import having been done, told us tremulously that Chaka

was dead!   We were not so much astonished as
anxious to ascertain the cause, and importuned
him to tell us as soon as he could, when he said,
" that there was a long tale to relate."   After
recovering himself from the effects of his great
exertion, having left Toogoosa only the evening
previously, he informed us, that while Chaka was
sitting the night before, with two or three of his
principal chiefs, admiring the immense droves of
cattle returning to the kraal, and probably contemplating the deaths of innocent people, he was surprised
at the boldness and presumption of his principal
domestic, Boper, who approached him with a spear
with which they usually kill bullocks, and, in a
voice of authority, asked the old chiefs, who were
humiliating themselves in the presence of the despot,
" what they meant by always pestering the king with
falsehoods and accusations ?"   The audacity of Boper,
who had been always an humble suppliant, excited
Chaka's surprise, nor were the exasperated chiefs
without their apprehensions, and made an effort to
secure Boper, but they were foiled; for, at that
moment, Umslumgani and Dingān, the two eldest
brothers of the king, stole unperceived behind him
and stabbed him in the back.   Chaka had a blanket
wrapped round him which he instantly threw off,
and made an ineffectual attempt to escape that
death to which, by his blood-thirsty decrees, he
had consigned many of his innocent and unoffending

subjects. He was overtaken in his flight by his
pursuers, when the domestic Boper pierced him
through the body with his weapon; he fell at their
feet, and in the most supplicating manner besought
them to let him live that he might be their servant.
To this, however, no heed was given, they soon
speared him to death, and then left him to execute
a similar deed on the chiefs who were with him, and
who had attempted to escape, but were arrested in their
flight, and put to death in the same manner as their ferocious master. One of them was an old grey-headed
man who had, but a short time before, put to death
his seven wives with their children, for not having
mourned for the death of Chaka's mother. The
assassins now returned to the dead body of Chaka
and danced round it, as much elated as though they
were rejoicing at the death of a tiger, an animal they
greatly dread.

The people of the kraal fled in great consternation,
except the chief Sotobe, and one or two others, who
seized their spears as if designing to attack the
assassins; but they were deterred by their opponents'
menacing attitude, and by their address. " Don't
you know it is the sons of Essenzingercona who
have killed Chaka for his base and barbarous conduct, and to preserve the nation of the Zoolas,
the sons of our fathers, that you may live in peace
and enjoy your homes and your families; to put an
end to the long and endless wars, and mourning for

that old woman Umnante, for whom so many have
been put to a cruel death:" thus saying, they
went to the palace, where they dared not enter
an hour before; and Sotobe went to his kraal. It
appears that the death of Chaka had been long pre-
meditated by the brothers, by whose hands he fell;
and that the late savage massacres had hastened a
resolution, which might, otherwise, have been stayed
for a time.

The Europeans now began to apprehend that the
death of the inhuman Chaka would create a civil war
in his dominions, and their situation be consequently
pregnant with danger. Under this impression, Mr.
Farewell came over to Townshend, where we were,
in some measure, able to make a good defence, should
the Zoolas manifest a disposition to disturb our settlement. Near our premises was a thick bush, almost
impenetrable, which entirely protected us against
any alarm from the rear. Our vessel was on the
beach, caulking, but as we could easily get her
afloat in case of necessity, she would be a convenient resource to fly to in the event of our being
assailed by too powerful a mass of natives.

25th.—We got all the late Lieutenant King's
effects on board in readiness for the worst, and in
the evening two messengers arrived from Jacob the
interpreter, to announce that Chaka had been killed
by his brothers, and that there was no fear to be
apprehended, as the nation would go on well as soon

as the exultation for his death should be over. For
several days, however, we were more or less in a
state of unpleasant suspense and alarm, on account
of the little confidence we had in any communications or assurances from the interpreter.

28th.—To-day, the morning being favourable, and
the sun shining with unusual splendour, I had determined on taking a ride to Issiburmene, a kraal of
Mr. Fynn's; passing some bush, on my way thither,
my horse became suddenly alarmed, and on looking round I observed a body of armed Caffres
making their way towards the kraal : I gallopped up
to them, when they ran into the thicket, but their
chief, whom I perceived to be Umsega Tobaler,
came out to me and said they were a few warriors
sent by Dingān and Umslumgani to collect cattle
taken during the last war; the sight of the horse
and the present state of affairs struck them with a
momentary terror, and caused them to fly to the
thicket. We proceeded on to Issiburmene, where
we sat down and talked about the death of Chaka,
and the present state of the nation. We ascertained that Dingān's proceedings were quite acceptable to the people, and that there was little doubt
of his being pronounced king on the arrival of the
commando. I desired them to call at my place on
their return, that I might send a message to the
princes; after which I rode to Mount Pleasant, where
I found two of Jacob's men, who had been sent by

Dingān to announce to the white people, that his brother Chaka had been killed for his inhuman conduct, having become no longer supportable to his subjects. The nation had too long groaned under his tyranny, and had submitted to his atrocities until they could not find safety from his savage and insatiable decrees; they had, therefore, in order to put an end to so much spilling of innocent blood, accomplished the destruction of the man who had occasioned it, and indulged in its barbarities. Dingān expressed his hope that the white people would not be displeased, but make themselves comfortable, and confide in the assurance of friendship and protection which he offered them, and not mourn for the death of a tyrant, whose design was to have killed them all on the return of his force from its predatory expedition.

We directed the messengers to return, and thank Dingān for his information; and to tell him that the proceedings of the nation were agreeable to us; that we conceived the death of Chaka a just retribution for his innumerable atrocities, his unexampled vices, and for his barbarous executions of his unoffending people. We gave them some tobacco for themselves, and a bottle of brandy for Jacob, when they set off on their way, well satisfied with their present.

The assurances of protection from Dingān were very satisfactory to us, and appeased the alarm under which we had laboured for several days.   It was no less pleasing to us to find that the death of Chaka had given so general a satisfaction throughout his dominions: that it was likely to give to the natives a period of repose from the vexations and casualties of war, and from the terror which the savage decrees of the late king constantly created. The poor wretches had no moments of tranquillity, no repose from apprehension, nothing like domestic comfort, being assailed by barbarous innovations, and atrocious cruelties. They lived in perpetual alarm lest the finger of the despot should be held up as a signal of death or of devastation.

CHAPTER XVIII.

HAVING in the last chapter mentioned the death of Chaka, and that his successor Dingán had sent to the Europeans at Natal his warmest assurances of protection, and his wishes that a friendly intercourse should exist between them and his people, it is now my intention to advert somewhat in detail to the history of the extraordinary individual who has been noticed prominently in the preceding pages, and whose vices and atrocities seem nearly without a parallel—history furnishing no instance of a more inhuman despot.

The family of Chaka appears to have been a remarkable one for its conquests, cruelties, and ambition; and to have emerged from a tribe who originally inhabited a district about Delagoa Bay. As we have no records of its origin, and as tradition does not furnish any remote information respecting it, all I can advance is, that Chaka himself descended from Zoola, king of the before-named tribe, through a line of chiefs, all of whom appear to have inherited the vices as well as the power and possessions of their progenitor.

Chaka's father appears to have been named Essenzingercona, and to have made his way from the primitive location of his ancestors to the Umfeeroche Umslopie, or White River, (a branch of the river St Lucie), and to have there settled or colonised within about sixty miles of the coast. Here he built a kraal, to which he gave the name of Nobamper or Graspat, and is said to have kept the neighbouring tribes around him in great terror and subjection. He had thirty wives, and his concubines were almost innumerable, so that his race was not likely soon to become extinct; every week producing something illustrative of his right to the proud title of being considered the parent of many generations yet to come.

By one of his wives was presented to him the afterwards formidable and cruel Chaka, whose birth was conceived by his people to have been prodigious and miraculous; he was therefore held to be something superhuman. His mother (Umnante), it has been stated, becoming suddenly indisposed, as most ladies at times are " who love their lords," sought the aid of her female attendants on the occasion. The natives who had been apprised of the nature of her complaint that she was *enceinte*, could not conceive it possible, as her husband had not undergone a certain ceremony (circumcision), without which he was not thought capable of propagating his species. This

preposterous idea is still prevalent among the eastern
tribes. Such being the fact, the accouchement of
Umnante became a wonder, and her child was considered a prodigy; and as it was conceived in the first
instance, that her indisposition was the Chekery, or
dysentery, so the child was commanded to be named
in allusion to their puerperal blunder. Mr. Kay in
his researches[*], says, of the family and origin of
Chaka, " that his grandfather was called Zoolu, which
signifies ' heaven,' or figuratively ' high': from him
the nation is now called Amazoolu, that is, people of
heaven, or high people; they are often termed Zoolas
in English, which is, however, a corruption of the
proper name. The son of Zoolu was Menzi, which
signifies ' maker or worker.' Chaka was the son of
Menzi, and his name, in the Sichuana language at
least, means ' battle-axe.' The name also of his brother and successor, is Dingān, which is nearly equivalent to ' I of myself,' or ' I am.' "

As Chaka advanced towards manhood, he gave
evident symptoms of realising the opinions of the
Zoolas, that he was more than an earthly being. His
strength appeared herculean; his disposition turbulent; his heart iron; his mind a warring element;
and his ambition knew no bounds.

It was not long before Chaka attracted the notice
and ultimately the jealousy of his father, who resolved

* Kay's Researches in Caffraria, Part 2, chap. 16, page 403.

that he should die, and began to plot his death ; this he desired to effect the more from another motive ; he well knew from the fate of his progenitors, that the children when they came of age were allowed by the Zoolas to dethrone their grey-headed fathers, because they conceived that a young king is more capable of commanding a nation than an old one ; that while the physical powers of the one render him unfit for feats of war, those of the other are about to ripen into all their maturity, and fit him to set an example for his subjects to imitate.

Chaka's precocity, shrewdness, and cunning soon enabled him to learn the intention of his father ; and he fled, accompanied by his younger brother Umgartie, to a neighbouring tribe, called the Umtatwas. Here he was well received and protected by the chief, Tin-giswaa, who placed him under the care of his dictator, Gormarnie, where he soon distinguished himself among the warriors; he was also held in great esteem by them as a songster and a punster, both of which are considered accomplishments rarely inherited, and are in fact the only amusements in which they indulge, with the exception of dancing. At the death of his father, a younger brother took possession of the Zoola crown ; Chaka at once resolved to dethrone him, and place himself at the head of the nation.

After several attempts the king succeeded in driving him (Chaka) away to a distant and formidable chief, called Zovcedie, who was then at war with the

Umtatwas; this induced Tingiswaa to assist Chaka
in obtaining possession of the Zoola kingdom.

Meeting, however, with many obstacles in the
way, he formed a sure plan of destroying the young
king, which was very soon carried into execution.
Umgartie, his younger brother, and companion in
exile, repaired to the residence of the young monarch
with a story, that Tingiswaa had killed Chaka, that
he was obliged to fly for his life, and throw himself
at his brother's feet for protection. This important and
wished-for information was readily believed, and Umgartie was soon installed in the office of chief domestic;
being now constantly about the king's person, he
took an early opportunity to effect his bloody mission.

It was his province to attend him every morning
while bathing. On a chosen occasion he sent two of
his friends to conceal themselves in the long grass by
the river-side, and at a signal given, while the king
was in the act of plunging into the water, they rushed
forward and speared him to death ; the news soon
reached Chaka, who marched at the head of the
Umtatwas, and took possession of the throne.

The first act that marked his bloody reign, was his
putting to death all the principal people of his brother's government; those who were suspected to be
inimical to his becoming king, were also speared.
He then, after the death of Tingiswaa, went to war
with the Umtatwas, the tribe that had sheltered and
protected him while in exile; and after destroying

the major part, compelled the rest to join him. The Quarbees, another powerful tribe, were the next whom he annihilated. This African Mars ultimately depopulated the whole line of coast from the Amapoota River to the Ootogale.

Equal success attended his incursions among the interior tribes, towards whom he usually exhibited the most sanguinary conduct, pursuing them without mercy, and annihilating them with a ferocity too shocking to detail—too harrowing to be narrated; I must therefore pass over this more than inhuman part of his savage life, lest it tend to darken, rather than illumine the inscrutable justice of Providence.

This ferocious despot had now arrived at the zenith of his pride and ambition; and having, for the present, sated himself with the blood of the neighbouring tribes, he directed his thoughts towards his own government. This was imperative, as from his numerous victories, he felt himself at the head of an overgrowing and gigantic nation.

At the onset, he commenced by disciplining his forces, which were numerous and elated with victory, attributable to the dauntless and irresistible spirit of their chief, who set them an example in the field, by a display of his physical powers for combat; and by a bold and martial indifference for his enemy, however formidable they appeared. His intrepidity made him a terror to his opponents, and his ferocity kept his people in awe. When he entered on a war with a

power, his whole mind and soul were irrevocably
bent on annihilation; he had no redeeming qualities;
mercy was never for a moment an inmate of his
bosom; he had indulged in the sacrifice of human
blood, and nothing could sate his monstrous appetite.

His soldiers, (his warriors, as they are designated,)
without any inherent courage, were ever and anon
eager for battle, and shouted for war from the love
of plunder; they knew full well that their renown
was enough to make their enemies crouch before
them, and they gained more by the terror of their
name, than they achieved by their prowess in arms.
They have this alternative in the field, either to
return triumphant and participate in the spoils, or to
be deemed cowards and suffer an immediate and
cruel death.   In the troops of Chaka there was
no moral courage; they fought to avoid being massacred, and triumphed more from the trepidation of
their opponents, than from the use of their spears.
But cowards are said to be cruel, and the troops
of this despot are an illustration. The war at Ingoma,
in which I was engaged, convinced me that those
whom we conquered were equal in capacity to the
troops of Chaka, and that the latter possessed no
innate courage.

The numerical force of the Zoola monarch was great
at this time, and he took especial care to make his
armies as effective as possible; for this purpose they
were inured to every species of unnatural abstinence.

They were prohibited from marrying, and forbade all sexual intercourse, under the idea that it deprived man of his physical strength and his relish for war ; and that in the field his thoughts were apt to be directed towards home, instead of towards his enemy. In this, however, Chaka certainly set the example. He had no queen, although he had at each of his palaces from 300 to 500 girls, who were denominated servants or sisters. If any of these became pregnant, they were immediately taken away, and some imaginary crime alleged for putting them to death. The warring propensities of the despot, his habitual ferocity, and insatiable thirst for the blood of his subjects, often induced him to single out the aged and decrepid to be put to the spear, observing with savage pleasure " that they were in the way—that they could not fight ; that they only consumed the food which would make the young warriors strong, and therefore it was a charitable act to put them out of the way." This order being carried into execution, he built a kraal between the Umlallas and the Umslatus rivers, to which he gave the appellation of Gibbeklack, " or pick out the old men," in commemoration of this base and barbarous deed.

It has been remarked by an ancient historian, that in peace children bury their parents, and in war parents bury their children ; it appeared otherwise in the dominions of Chaka ; there, Death reigned without a rival, and without control ; there, whether

in the time of peace or war, he gloried not only in
the extent of his conquests, but in the richness of
his spoils.

The unexampled cruelties he practised, and the
plausible reasons urged for perpetrating them, were
a sure means, not only of governing the terrified and
wondering Zoolas, but of confirming the universal
belief among them, that he dealt in charms and
witchcraft, and held nightly converse with the spirit
of his forefathers which appeared to him,

And told the secrets of the world unknown.

After having established a strong force of nearly
one hundred thousand men, about fifty thousand of
which were warriors in constant readiness for battle *,
and forming his whole force into regiments, he began
to elect rulers, to abolish the old laws, and enact
new ones.   He also thought proper to drop his
primitive appellation of Checker, and assume that of
Chaka, by which name I have distinguished him as
being that by which he was most generally known.

He finally succeeded in establishing a sort of *Zoo-
lacratical* form of government (if I may so term
it, for I do not know anything resembling it in
either ancient or modern history), a form that
defies description or detail; that can neither be

* Vide Kay's Researches, page 403.

comprehended nor digested, and such a one as gives
protection to no living creature; that puts the subject
at the mercy of a despotic king, whose nod may consign him to death, innocent or guilty, and compel
the father to murder his innocent and unoffending
child; force brother to execute brother; and the
husband to impale his wife. After a form of government had been established recognising all these bar-
barites, a calm ensued, not unlike that which intervenes
between the first and last shocks of an earthquake,
when all are in consternation, fearing that the next
moment they may be swallowed during the devastating
convulsion. This pause from war and sanguinary
executions, was usually occupied in the superstitious
ceremony of appeasing the spirits of the departed, and
in endeavouring to soften the pangs of the living, by
sacrifices of bullocks, and by distributing the property
of the murdered people amongst their executioners.
Several months have been occupied in killing bullocks—the spoils of his successful and inhuman
carnage—for the purpose of fattening and diverting
his people, as well as for occupying their minds
in manufacturing shields from the hides of the
slaughtered animals. He would likewise try to
divert them a little by amusements, in which they
could have no relish, but were necessitated to attend,
not with the view of pleasure, but from the fear of
death.

He next proceeded to introduce a new system of warfare. It had hitherto been the practice to carry several iron spears, and throw them at the enemy, besides the assegai or common spear (bows and other implements of war are not known to them), which he forbade under penalty of death.

For the purpose of proving his superiority and consummate judgment in military tactics, he determined that a sham fight between his regiments should take place in the presence of his whole nation. Reeds were accordingly substituted for spears; one regiment was to pursue the accustomed manner of throwing, and the other, who were allowed but one reed, were permitted to charge. The latter, covering themselves with their immense shields (six feet long and of an oval form), soon beat off their adversaries, and thus decided that Chaka's new regulation was the best. All the superfluous spears were then ordered to be destroyed, stout ones made in their stead, and each warrior was supplied with one: if he lost it in battle he was to suffer death. Thus his warriors had no alternative; their fate was inevitable; the fear of a horrid end by impalement made them fight, when otherwise they would have saved themselves by retreating in the event of being overpowered. The poor wretches were therefore doomed to conquer or die.

The king also determined that when an army was sent to attack a distant tribe it should be supplied with barely a sufficient number of cattle to suffice for its support until its arrival at the place of action, observing " that they must either conquer or perish."

In ordering any of his subjects to be killed, Chaka never gave his reason for consigning them to death until it was too late to recal the sentence of execution. A sign, given by the pointing of his finger, or by the terrible declination of his head, was promptly obeyed, and as promptly executed, by any one present. Thus a father did not hesitate to be the executioner of his own child; the ties of consanguinity availed nothing with the tyrant, his decrees must be carried into operation, and that unhesitatingly; and if after perpetrating the revolting deed the feelings of nature should predominate, and manifest themselves to the inhuman savage, the party was instantly ordered to be despatched, with the atrocious remark, " Take the Umtugarty away: let me see if loving his child better than his king will do him any good. See if your clubs are not harder than his head." The executioner was then permitted to repair to the kraal of the poor dead and mutilated creature, and there destroy every one who might be connected with it, to take the implements of war as his booty, and drive the cattle to the king, who orders its distribution among his warriors then present.

In delineating the character of Chaka, I have introduced the horrible deeds he perpetrated (to many of which I was an eye-witness), for the purpose

of allowing my readers to draw their own conclusions;
for my own part, I can only say, I am not aware
that history, either ancient or modern, can produce so
horrible and detestable a savage. He has deluged his
country with innocent blood; he has forgotten the
most sacred ties of affection, and, by a double murder
as it were, compelled the agonising father to be the
executioner of his own son, and the son to become an
inhuman mutilator of his own mother. The recital of
this monster's deeds would only be setting in array
against him the passions of my readers, and might ill
prepare them to encourage any favourable symptom
of such a man having betrayed remorse for his sanguinary conduct.

I have spared my reader the pang which many
agonising scenes would have occasioned, by not detailing their enormities; scenes that I have personally
witnessed, the recital of which would only increase
the horror already sufficiently excited; but if his pa-
tience will now allow him to bear with me but for a
short time, I hope I shall be able to lead him to an oasis
in this moral wilderness that shall be as refreshing to
his taste as water in the Arabian desert is to the parched
palate of the wandering Arab.

When a writer treads on new ground he possesses,
in my opinion, few advantages, but many and great
difficulties meet him in his progress. The assertion
of Solomon, in his time, " that there is nothing new
under the sun," justifies me in this opinion, although

I am not ignorant of the fact that many modern and learned authors have thought the contrary. Little heretofore has been known respecting Natal; the prolixity of my journal, therefore, perhaps may be overlooked. It was this want of information that made me think of recording my observations, and however uninteresting the details, " they are the truth, and nothing but the truth."

. For the purpose of employing the rising generation, Chaka gave orders that a number of new kraals should be built, for the residence of the cattle taken in the different wars, so as to secure them from the attacks of wild animals. Boys were allowed the privilege of milking them for their support, and occasionally a few head were given them to kill. These boys were called Umpuggarties or warriors; their duty was to beat and molest the Umcoondas, or those that had not joined the etangers or cattle kraals; they were commanded to do so (whenever they might find them) by Chaka's decrees; so that nearly all the boys were harassed until they joined these young tyrants. In all warlike excursions these youths were compelled to accompany the old warriors in the capacity of servants, and when they arrived at an age capable of wielding the assegai, they were supplied with shields and spears and formed into regiments.

Cambyses asserted that " anticipation was the greatest of all pleasures;" Chaka had been enjoying

this feeling for a considerable time, that is, between
the cessation of one war and the commencement of
another.   During this repose from hostile attacks on
his neighbouring tribes, he indulged in projecting new
movements and planning other predatory incursions
against those unoffending tribes whose forces were
weak and whose stocks of cattle were extensive.   He
looked forward at these periods with a sort of pro-
phetic spirit for the day to arrive when all his anticipations should be realised.   The new laws which he
had established, and the novel system of warfare so
successfully introduced, led him to conclude that his
warriors would be found invincible, and he issued his
terrific order " that they should turn out to conquer
or die."

The success of his operations soon verified his pre-
dictions, and the fame of his troops spread over all
the country.   Every tribe they met with became an
easy conquest, for to avoid being put to the spear they
ran into the forests, leaving their villages and cattle to
the mercy and rapacity of their insatiable invaders.
In this manner did Chaka lay waste and spread
devastation through the whole country, from the
Mapoota to the Omzinvoobo, or St. John's river.
Tribe after tribe were invaded, routed, and put to
death, either by firing their huts or by the spear.
Numbers of the poor terrified hunted wretches were
driven to seek shelter in the midst of the forests, and

there to become the victims of wild animals or the
sport of the wandering Zoolas in their pursuit of
other prey, who showed them no mercy.

He had now subdued all the tribes within the limits
of Delagoa Bay and Port Natal, the most powerful
of which, Enconyana, having been the last to fall
within his grasp, and had begun to contemplate an
attack on some of the frontier tribes ; but he manifested
an apprehension of coming into collision with the white
people, whose hostility he was avowedly afraid to
excite. This alone restrained him from attacking those
minor tribes who had thrown themselves under the
protection of the government of the Cape.   His
death stopped his merciless and ambitious career : he
fell as he deserved, by the hands of those whom he
had enraged by his savage propensities, and not one
it is said mourned his death.

The late Lieutenant King in his notes says of
Chaka, " he is a most cruel, savage, and despotic
king, one who has laid waste the country some hundreds of miles, namely, from the Amapondoes, about
two hundred miles south-west of Natal, to the southern
and most of the western parts of Delagoa.   Within
these limits there are many kings whom he has subdued, and are now tributary to him, submitting to
the most abject of vassalage.   The only powerful
enemy with whom he has now to contend are
Enconyana and Zueedee, who inhabit a district
north-west of the Mapoota ; these two kings having

collected their forces with the idea of disputing the palm with Chaka, and of at once putting a stop to his predatory incursions near their territories. They have made several advances, but have been severally and jointly repulsed. He is now in his turn preparing to advance on them; and although their united forces exceed by thousands the amount of his invading army, yet such is the discipline of his men, and so well arranged are his modes of attack, that nothing in the system of his opponents can possibly make any impression *." ·

Chaka seems to have inherited no redeeming quality; in war he was an insatiable and exterminating savage, in peace an unrelenting and a ferocious despot, who kept his subjects in awe by his monstrous executions, and who was unrestrained in his bloody designs, because his people were ignorant and knew not that they had power. He was also a base dissembler; he could smile in the midst of the execution of his atrocious decrees, and stand unmoved while he witnessed the spilling of the blood of his innocent subjects; and, as if nothing like an act of barbarity had been committed, he would appear mild, placid, generous, and courteous to all, assuming the expression of deep sorrow for the necessity which had called him to issue his bloody decree. The world has heard of monsters—Rome had her Nero,

* Since these notes of Lieutenant King, my readers will perceive that Chaka defeated these chiefs.

the Huns their Attila, and Syracuse her Dionysius; the East has likewise produced her tyrants; but for ferocity, Chaka has exceeded them all; he has outstripped in sanguinary executions all who have gone before him, and in any country.

It is too evident, had not this monster fallen by the hands of his injured people, that the unfortunate Europeans who were sojourning in his country, and who had received assurances of protection from him, in which they could not but confide, would have been doomed to destruction on the return of his forces from their predatory expedition. He thus at once exhibited the dissimulation of the despot, and realised what has been often affirmed, that " there is always danger when a villain smiles."

As I have said before, Chaka ruled his people by perpetually keeping them in a state of terror, and his command over them was also greatly facilitated by his continually impressing them with the power of charms, witchcraft or necromancy, which he practised, with inconceivable effect, on his poor, abject, deluded, and oppressed subjects. This he carried to such an extent as to excite a belief in their minds, that he had the power of knowing all their thoughts, and of seeing all their most secret actions. He pretended that he inherited this power from the spirit of his forefathers, who had deputed it to him. An instance of the extraordinary effect of his cunning in imposing on his people, by persuading them that he

was endowed with a sort of supernatural agency, I
shall relate; and as I had it from himself, I think it not
improbable, because I have had ocular demonstration
of his exhibitions in this way. He arose one morning
unusually early, and ordered a great number of his
favourite bullocks (black and white ones) to be killed;
they were accordingly instantly slaughtered. The
circumstance naturally excited the curiosity and surprise of his warriors, who became impressed with an
idea that something important was about to take place.
Their wonder was increased by his ordering the
inyangers to collect roots to prevent his people fret-
ting. He then called all his warriors together and
ordered them to dance until a late hour of the night,
when he told them " that Umbeah * had appeared to
him the preceding night and had communicated to him
that his father Esenzengercona was very angry with
the Zoolas for losing their fame, and not being
' schlanger-nee-pee-lie,' that is ' more shrewd and
cunning,' and superior to their neighbours;—that
the nation was getting too large and required constant
employment;—that there were plenty of enemies
yet to conquer before they could ' booser' (make
merry) and enjoy themselves: that Umbeah had also
told him he was living very comfortably under ground
where all the people who had died, were innocently
' boosering;'—that they had plenty of cattle and fine

* A noted chief in the reign of Chaka's father.

girls;—that there was no enemy to fight, and they therefore enjoyed the society of their girls."

This important dream was honoured with the slaughtering of cattle at all the king's kraals. All the descendants of Umbeah were created great men, and of course dreamt in turn something to corroborate the dream of their cunning and wily master. This astounding dream became the topic of conversation among the people for some months, little thinking the despot's aim was deadly. Umbeah's name, therefore, resounded through the whole of the kraals, to the great consternation of the ignorant and proscribed inhabitants; all the good deeds he did in his days were recounted and talked of, to the great joy of those who were conversant with the king's imposition.

During the days of the working of this superstitious ceremony of the savage monarch, an elderly man belonging to the tribe of the Cales (a tribe tributary to Chaka) was missing: no one could give any intelligence of him but his wife, who said, "that their hut had been entered in the night by an 'inconyarmer, or lion,' and that it took her husband from her side." The lion's spur or foot-marks were traced to its den, but no blood could be found, nor any vestige of the man discovered. This report was made to Chaka in the presence of his warriors; created a momentary surprise, but the wily monarch appeared unconcerned about it. Several months had elapsed, and the man, together with the circumstance was forgotten. At length he appeared amongst the warriors in the presence of Chaka. He exhibited a singular exterior: his hair was long, and worn differently from any other of the people: his dress was also dissimilar to that worn by the warriors. It consisted of a piece of bullock's hide, covering his hind part from hip to hip, and fastened in front with pieces of cord reaching to the joints of his knees, and thickly studded with brass balls. He appeared among them something in their estimation unearthly. He was afterwards, however, discovered to be the man taken away by the lion, and an investigation took place to ascertain how he came among them, and from whence he had arrived.

The man immediately rose, and said, in a stentorian voice, saluting Chaka, "that he had been to the Issetuter, with whom he had stayed three moons and was then desired to go and tell the 'Inquose incoola, or great king,' that they were 'boosering' (making merry), and would soon pick out all the Umtugarties (wizards) that the Zoolas might also 'booser.'" He then observed, "I am the son of Feteschloo, of the Cales, Umfunda-adgua-zooloo (tributary to the Zoolas) who was taken away by the lion, dragged to his den, sunk deep into it, and swallowed up by the earth. The lion went with me, and treated me as a mother would her child, until I came to some red earth, where the lion left me, and

in wandering about I walked upon earth that trembled
and gave way, when I fell into a deeper abyss
below, I became insensible from the fall, but, recovering, found myself in a fine country inhabited by
Issetuters (spirits). I saw all the old people who
had been killed in war, and those who had died at
home. They were much smaller than we are; they
have plenty of cattle, but all very small; the girls
are handsome, and live very comfortably. Umbeah
was Inquose incoola and boosered Carcoola (he was
a great king and enjoyed himself very much) and he
was also a great inyanger. In the night time he
strolled about, and no one knew whither he went, but
he always said he went to see his 'Umschlobo'
(friends)."

The people were not more amazed at his address
than they were at his harangue. Chaka made it appear that he was equally astounded at the audacity
of the man in appearing before him, and asserting
such a mass of gross nonsense and falsehoods. He
said that the fellow was an "Umtugartie" (wizard).
The people knew not what to think, for they had the
king's dream in their recollection. The "inyangers"
(prophets), however, were called to "nooker" (smell)
if the man was really a messenger from Umbeah, or
an Umtugartie, when they decided that the issetutor
had seen that some of the Zoolas did not believe the
king's dreams, and had, therefore, sent the lion to

take a man from this land that he might corroborate
them.

The messenger who performed this part escaped
the death for which Chaka intended him; he ever
after remained in the kraal about the king's person,
and wore the dress described to distinguish him from
the rest of the people. He had also the appellation
of prophet. A considerable time after, however, this
individual, who so miraculously escaped from the
lion, was carried off by a leopard, and was never
heard of more.

The whole of this ceremony was nothing but an
imposition to elate the people with a spirit for war.
It was designed by Chaka, and the individual who did
the executive part was instructed in the character.
It was by these means that the monster sought to
appease the pangs of his people, inspire them with
something like awe, and strike terror into them (by
his seeming unearthly character and hidden power),
that should check any disposition to revolt among
them for his inhuman massacres.

Chaka was, doubtless, ever on the *qui vive* for some
invention, or some scheme for amusing his people.
In the summer-time dancing was resorted to, and
new songs were composed, as it was considered dis-
graceful to sing the songs of the previous year. On
these occasions the regiments sing before the king,
particularly at the harvest season, when those who

excel receive the applause of the monarch, and not unfrequently get cattle, which affords the warriors a subject for conversation and amusement, until the harvest is all gleaned; they then immediately prepare for war. A winter scarcely came on without Chaka sending his warriors on some marauding expedition; every season brought upon the weak and tributary tribes visits of plunder; and his own peaceable people felt the usual scourge of the monster for some pretended offence to majesty, which no one had discovered, it being an invention of his own savage and brutal mind. He always discoursed of war and talked of conquering his enemies three months before he prepared for the attack. Previously to the time fixed on for his troops moving, he generally had a muster, when all who, on any previous occasion, had not done what was conceived to be his duty, or were suspected of being cowards, which were held to be synonimous offences, were selected and subjected to the customary punishment of impaling. In short, every thing which ferocity and barbarity could devise was usually resorted to, for the purpose of inspiring his men with a spirit for war. He used also on these occasions to promise them that when they had made themselves masters of the earth on this side of the water, that they should "booser" (enjoy themselves) with their women, and marry as many wives as they might think proper.

Thus the eve of going to war was always the

period of brutal and inhuman murders, in which he seemed to indulge with as much savage delight as the tiger with his prey. When he once had determined on a sanguinary display of his power, nothing could restrain his ferocity; his eyes evinced his pleasure, his iron heart exulted, his whole frame seemed as if it felt a joyous impulse at seeing the blood of inno- cent creatures flowing at his feet; his hands grasped, his herculean and muscular limbs exhibiting by their motion a desire to aid in the execution of the victims of his vengeance : in short, he seemed a being in a human form, with more than the physical capa- bilities of a man ; a giant without reason, a monster created with more than ordinary power and disposition for doing mischief, and from whom we recoil as we would at the serpent's hiss or the lion's growl.

It was an invariable rule of war with him never to give his troops more cattle or provisions than would barely suffice to support them till they arrived in the country of their enemy. They had strict injunctions to fight or die, to quarter on their enemy, and not return but as victors, bringing with them the fruits of their triumph.

He was exceedingly wary, and used great precau- tion in concealing even from his generals or chiefs, the power or tribe with whom he designed combat- ing; nor until the eve of marching did he make known to them the object of their expedition. By this he evinced some discretion, and precluded the possibility of his enemy being apprised of his intentions. In this particular, Chaka showed a judgment not common with the native chiefs, and peculiarly his own.

When all was ready for entering upon their march, he confided to one general his design, and to him he entrusted the command, should he not head his army in person. He, however, never confided in one man but on one occasion; upon no occasion whatever did he repeat such confidence. He made it an invariable rule always to address his warriors at their departure, and his language was generally studied to raise their expectations, and excite them in the hour of battle. He particularly detailed to them the road his spies had pointed out, inducing them to believe that they were going to attack any party but the one actually designed, and known only to the general-in-chief. This was judicious, because it kept his real object from being known, and, at the same time, prevented any treacherous communication to his enemy, who might get early intimation of his intended attack.

Chaka always kept up a system of espionnage, by which he knew at all times the condition and strength of every tribe around him, both independent and tributary; and these persons were always directed to make such observations on the passes to and from the country to which they were sent, as might be useful in leading the troops to the scene of action with the surest chance of arriving at their position, without being discovered on the one hand, or surprised on the other.

At the return of his warriors from an expedition, he was usually generous to them, it must be admitted, but that only occurred in the case of their having achieved a triumph over his enemies; in such cases he gave the captured spoils liberally amongst them, as an encouragement for future exertions and enterprise: but to return without having accomplished what he had anticipated, was a signal for a scene of woe and lamentation—a massacre of no measured description.

After an expedition his troops were permitted to retire to their respective kraals for a short period, to recover from their fatigue, whence in a short time, the chiefs were called to collect the people and hear the details of those operations in which the warriors had been engaged; at which time all who had evinced cowardice were selected, brought forth, received the fiat of their ferocious master, and were led off immediately to be impaled, as an atonement for their offence, and as an example to others who should feel disposed to pursue a similar conduct. Such warriors who distinguished themselves in battle were honoured with a *nom de guerre*, by which they were afterwards accosted.

The king also distinguished his regiments by giving them shields differently coloured. The great warriors have white shields with one or two black spots; the

young warriors have all black shields; the middle
warriors, or those that have wives, form distinct
regiments, and are called Umfaudas (inferiors), have
red shields.

All the regiments form three armies, and have a
portion of each of three distinctions in each army.
The first army is called " Umbalabale, or invincibles;"
the second " Umboolalio, or the slaughterers;" and
the third " Toogooso, or the hide-aways." The principal chief of each regiment is a member of the
" Ebarnschlo, or senate," of their own army. The
king, at his pleasure, calls on them, or any part
of them, to give their opinion on state affairs. In
such cases they are exceedingly cautious not to decide
against the wish of the king, who always submits the
matter for their consideration, first making known to
them his own opinion: should, however, they decide
against his wish, he can call another Ebarnschlo, and
if their determination accord with his views the latter
then become his favourites, while the former will be
necessitated to " schlowoola" (make peace-offerings)
for offending the king.

He can hold secret councils, and have any member
killed, not excepting even the principal chief, if he
fancy him opposed to his schemes. He is generally
at variance with one half his chiefs, who are members
of this military tribunal, and prevents their meeting
by having his regiments in opposite directions and
at positions at some distance apart. Although meet-

ings are not publicly prohibited, it is well known they create Chaka's wrath and suspicion, and that they terminate with death to such as assemble without his knowledge.   All meetings of this military council are held at the gateway of the king's kraal, or in the cattle-pound, which is their council-room, unless the king be present, when they meet in the palace.

Chaka had an extreme aversion to any thing like commercial traffic, and forbade it among his people. Towards the Europeans he always expressed himself decidedly opposed to any intercourse, having for its object the establishment of a mercantile connection with his subjects.   His whole soul was engrossed by war, and he conceived that any thing like commerce would enervate his people and unfit them for their military duties.

His eagerness for elephant-hunting, and to collect ivory from his tributary tribes, arose, not for purposes of commerce, but that he might appropriate it in presents, and occasionally exchange it for something ornamental which the Europeans might possess.

Chaka to his savage propensities added many extraordinary caprices and singular whims. He lay on his belly to eat, and compelled his chiefs to do the same, to show their dignity. They never took a meal without washing their hands: this custom, however, is confined to the king and his chiefs.

His servants always présent him with any thing he may require on the palm of the hand, having their arm extended horizontally; but this is not permitted to any other person.

. He used to bathe every morning at the head of his kraal; first he anointed his body with bruised beef made up into a paste with ground corn, then rubbed it off again, and threw the water over himself. After indulging in bathing a short time, when dry he a second time anointed himself with sheep's-tail fat or native butter. When we introduced soap he thought it a wonderful discovery, and afterwards used it in preference to his own method of cleansing himself. We presented him with a razor, and showed him how to apply it; and no sooner had he became acquainted with the mode of using it, than he threw away his own instruments for shaving, used those we presented to him, and seemed greatly delighted with them.

Chaka, when we first held a conversation with him on the subject of the existence of a Supreme Being, at once evinced he had no idea of a deity, and that his people were equally ignorant on this subject. On one occasion, as I have before related, when we communicated to him our opinions on the existence of God, who made the world, and of a future state, and told him that by a knowledge of letters all our confidence of being immortal beings had arisen, he expressed surprise, and wished much that the " doctors or missionaries" would come to him and teach him to acquire this knowledge. But he had no idea of religion, no symbol by which any thing like a knowledge of a Supreme Being could be conveyed. The grossest state of ignorance on this sublime subject pervaded him; but I have ever been impressed forcibly, from the desire he manifested to have among his people missionaries, whom he said he would protect and reward, that he might have been brought to some sense of reason on this important point, so necessary for the promoting of civilisation. I am proud to say of his successor that a ray of light has been seen in him. He is greatly advancing into that state of mental improvement which only now requires the more enlightened aid of missionaries, to ripen into perfection, when the unhappy people over whom the inhuman Chaka ruled with brutal and savage sway, may be enabled to enjoy those comforts which a country so congenial, and so abounding with the gifts of nature, is capable of producing.

Chaka, take him altogether, was a savage in the truest sense of the word, though not a cannibal. He had an insatiable thirst for the blood of his subjects, and indulged in it with inhuman joy; nothing within the power of man could restrain him from his propensities. He was a monster, a compound of vice and ferocity, without one virtue to redeem his name from that infamy to which history will consign it: I must, however, by way of conclusion, state that if Chaka ever had one redeeming quality, it was this, that the European strangers at Natal received his protection, and were shielded by him against the impositions of his chiefs.

CHAPTER XIX.

THE death of Chaka following that of my friend Lieutenant King, quite disarranged all the contemplated plans of the latter and myself to effect some sort of permanent establishment for the design of an interior commercial intercourse with the king and his people, the former of whom we thought might be brought to some acquiescence, and give us that permission and protection we sought. We were sanguine, had not the indisposition, and, finally, the death of my friend (whom I cannot but think Chaka held in great friendship, if it were possible such a feeling could have a seat in his savage breast), rendered abortive all our designs of effecting such an arrangement with him as should have realised our anticipations, and have discovered another of those vents for commercial operations that tend so highly to promote the prosperity of Great Britain.

The death of the two principals, therefore, having quite disconcerted me, and being young and inexperienced, I began to direct my attention towards returning to the Cape with the vessel and the effects of Lieutenant King, which I felt extremely solicitous to secure, in conformity with his dying request. For this purpose I began to consult with the officers and crew on the propriety of my carrying such an intention into execution.

I had now to contend with Mr. Hatton, the chief officer of the schooner, respecting my future wishes, whose conduct on the occasion was any thing but gentlemanly and just. To put an end, however, to all farther dispute, Mr. Fynn was consulted on the subject, and the seamen subsequently appealed to, who were to decide as to their future commander in so far as regarded the direction or destination of the vessel. This was done, and their choice fell on me; but I had inconceivable labour to go through, and great abuse to contend with from my opponent, who manifested a stubborn and malignant disposition, so unlike his former conduct.

October 5th.—The native boy, Nasapongo, who belonged to Lieutenant King, and had proceeded to the Cape with John Cane, at the command of Chaka, returned to-day, and informed me that the two chiefs who accompanied them had arrived at the Armanpootooes, and that Cane had proceeded on to the king. The boy said they had seen several white men at Farkoos, who were coming here. I proceeded to Mr. Fynn's residence, to stay until everything was ready for my departure.

6th.—The messengers whom I had sent to the residence of Dingān to congratulate him on his elevation, returned with three head of cattle as a present from the princes, with a promise of more on the arrival of the commando. They sent also to say, that they would be glad to see us, but recommended our stopping at home for the present, as everything had the appearance of a commotion, and indicated very strongly the approach of civil war, respecting the succession to the throne, as Umgaarty, a brother by the mother's side (this being singular, as Caffre kings always espouse virgins) seemed disposed to dispute the right to the throne. The tie of consanguinity in this case does not approximate near enough to stay opposition between these individuals. Umnanty, the mother of Chaka, was a daughter of the king of Amlanganes, who gave her in marriage to the father of Chaka, Esenzengercona; she was said to have been a masculine and savage woman, ever quarrelling with, and so enraging her husband that he was compelled to exercise some salutary authority, and reprimand her for the impropriety of her con-- duct: finally, her husband ordered her to be driven away, when she returned to the tribe of her father, and afterwards cohabited with one of the common natives, by whom she became pregnant, and had a son, whom she named Umgaarty; this person has become an individual of means and power, and evinced a desire to dispute the right of Dingān to the crown.

8th.—To-day, Ogle and Mr. Shaw, from Graham's Town, arrived at Fort Farewell, the latter in a two-fold capacity—that of trading, and on a mission from Colonel Somerset to Chaka. The object of this mission we could not divine; it set conjecture afloat, and we were on the *qui vive* to ascertain its object. The death of Chaka, however, rendered it abortive.

19th.—The chief officer of the schooner, Mr. Hatton, was reported sick; I went, notwithstanding the impropriety of his conduct, to see him. I found him exceedingly ill, and prescribed for him.

21st.—To-day Mr. Fynn returned from Toogooso, whither he had gone to see the princes; he said every thing looked well, that the princes had behaved exceedingly kind to him, and expressed a wish for the white people to remain in the country. They sent me two elephants' teeth as a present, and requested me to remain with Mr. Fynn.

Dingān had already abolished most of Chaka's ferocious customs, and abrogated all his unnatural laws. He permitted the warriors to marry, a measure before prohibited; and any violation of it would have been punished with instant death. This and other salutary measures had been adopted, which had made Dingān already exceedingly popular, and as he evinced an anxious desire to render his subjects comfortable, this popularity increased daily.

November 2nd.—Had information by messengers from Umbulalio, to announce that Umgaarty, in his attempt to dispossess Dingān, had been defeated and killed. Umgaarty had proceeded with his forces to mourn for the death of Chaka, when Dingān collected all his scattered troops, placed them under the command of Boper, and sent them off with instructions to proceed with a drove of cattle to meet the commando; the former was returning unsuccessfully, but the king privately directed Boper to make a forced march and fall in with Umgaarty. They proceeded on their march two days, so shaping their course as to enter on the rear of the enemy's position, and, at the dawn of day, having arrived in the night unperceived, they attacked it on all sides. Umgaarty's force fought desperately, and repelled Boper several times; but a body of young warriors having come up, who scaled the fences and got into the palace, they killed all the females, and having surrounded the chief, he fell by their hands; not, however, before he made great havoc in his defence, and killed eight of his opponents with his own weapons.

This event placed Dingān in quiet possession of his throne, and he set about establishing such regulations for the future government of his people as seemed best calculated to render them happy, and likely to raise his country to a high state of prosperity, which the conduct of his predecessor could never have effected.

I began now to contemplate an early departure from Natal, and having arranged with Mr. Farewell to take him off with me, I had the vessel got ready with all the despatch possible; in the interim, Mr.

Hatton died, which gave me less trouble in accomplishing this work, although I had to deal with some refractory men, who having been too long accustomed to range uncontrolled, began to manifest symptoms of insubordination, which required some resolution, as well as prompt and vigorous efforts to check and ultimately to subdue.

Having accomplished this, and made all my arrangements for embarking, everything being on board and only waiting for a favourable breeze to carry us over the bar, I rested from the fatigues to which I had been subjected, until the 1st of December, when the wind having veered to the north-west, we got under weigh, and glided out of the bay, striking, however, the edge of the bar on our way, without doing us any manifest injury. Thus we took our departure from Natal a second time, having during my last abode within its wilds lost my most valued companion and esteemed friend, and endured such fatigues as have not often fallen to the lot of an individual young and inexperienced like myself. But confidence and hope bore me up in the hour of depression; they encouraged me in the moment of grief, and bade me never despair.

END OF THE FIRST VOLUME.

LONDON:
BRADBURY AND EVANS, PRINTERS, WHITEFRIARS.

Lightning Source UK Ltd.
Milton Keynes UK
UKHW022316060223
416579UK00001B/444